Northern Folk

people who shaped the history of our region

by

Bernard McCormick

Business Education Publishers Limited

© Bernard McCormick

ISBN 1 901888 49 5
ISBN 978 1 901888 49 2

First Published 2005

Cover Design by Murphy Creative Ltd

Published in Great Britain by
Business Education Publishers Limited
The Teleport
Doxford International
Sunderland
SR3 3XD

Tel: 0191 5252410
Fax: 0191 5201815

British Cataloguing-in-Publications Data
A catalogue record for this book is available from the British Library

Printed in Great Britain by The Alden Group Oxford.

for Eileen, my wife and best friend

Content

Preface

Born in Coxhoe, the birthplace of Elizabeth Barrett Browning and currently living in Newton Aycliffe, I have had a life-long interest in local history and its pioneers. The achievements of people such as George and Robert Stephenson, Charles Parsons, and William Armstrong have fascinated me since I was a child.

However, it was not until my later years and retirement that I could afford the time to explore their lives and others like them and to fully understand the contribution they have made to the region and the impact their achievements have had on history and the country.

This book is a humble attempt to celebrate the lives of only some of the many men and women that are *Northern Folk*.

Bernard McCormick

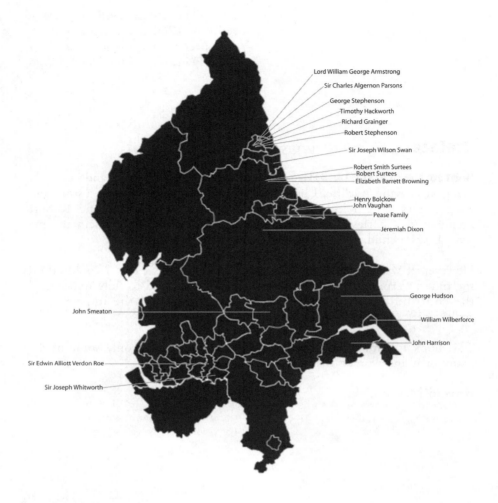

Lord William George Armstrong

Sir Charles Algernon Parsons

George Stephenson

Timothy Hackworth

Richard Grainger

Robert Stephenson

Sir Joseph Wilson Swan

Robert Smith Surtees
Robert Surtees
Elizabeth Barrett Browning

Henry Bolckow
John Vaughan
Pease Family

Jeremiah Dixon

George Hudson

William Wilberforce

John Harrison

John Smeaton

Sir Edwin Alliott Verdon Roe

Sir Joseph Whitworth

Northern Folk.

The Pease Family Dynasty
Early years from 1665

Joseph Pease was born in 1665, descended from a family of Essex landowners, one of which settled at Sikehouse, South Yorkshire in the reign of Henry VIII. By the end of the seventeenth-century, Joseph Pease was himself well established as a land owner at Pease Hall, Shafton Green, Felkirk, in the West Riding. In 1706, he married Ann Caldwell, heiress to her brother's business, a wool combers and merchants. Joseph and Ann had three sons and two daughters. It is the second son, Edward, who will progress this story, as he is of the most interest to Darlington and the North of England.

Edward's father, Joseph, died when he was eight years of age in 1719, leaving behind him his strong Quaker traditions; Joseph's mother was also of strong Quaker stock. In 1735, Edward married Elizabeth Coates also a Quaker from Caselee and Langley Ford, in County Durham. The marriage took place at Raby Meeting House, near Darlington. Edward's status was very vague. His elder brother, Joseph, had inherited the family property at Felkirk, and Edward entered the wool business, in Darlington, with his uncle, Thomas Caldwell, who would retire in 1760, allowing Edward to take over. So the foundations of the Pease Dynasty – of the North East of England – were sown.

It was halfway through the eighteenth-century that Darlington began establishing itself as a prominent market town, only second to Durham, in importance. Darlington district was rich in farming communities, especially in the vale of the Tees. In the early years, its population was approximately 3,300 inhabitants, who were more or less dependent on manufacturing created by agriculture, the woollen and worsted industries, the manufacture of linen and the tanning industry. In 1790 the Pease family were one of the biggest producers of linen; supplying yarns for manufacturers in Durham, Yorkshire and Cumberland. As wool grew in importance, just prior to the start of the industrial revolution, they became Britain's most important manufacturer of wool.

Pease's Mill, Priestgate founded 1752.

From the time Edward took over the company from his uncle, in 1760, there was a marked improvement in all aspects of the wool trade, especially in weaving and dyeing. The mill was situated at Priestgate, in Darlington, near the River Skerne; they also had a smaller mill at Leadyard, also Darlington. The mills generated years of uninterrupted work even into the present century; at one time employing 700 workers, buying wool from farmers, sorting it, and giving it to the cottages to be combed; the wool was then spun and sold. The money made from this industry enabled the Peases to come through many difficult periods, of which, without the revenue from the wool they would not have survived.

Statue of Joseph Pease.

Edward died in 1785, leaving a will, which was made shortly before his death, his estate left messuages, tenements, dwelling houses, shops, warehouses, and workhouses, to be equally divided between his five sons and two daughters; the silver plate collection was shared between all of his children equally. Each son was also to receive the contents of one room, while the daughters shared the Delftware and the china. The value of these legacies was £3900 each, but the main benefactor was Joseph, for he was the main successor to the woollen business. Prior to his death, Edward Pease had also branched off into banking; this was known as Pease Partners Bank. In the years between 1765-1799 the bank held 109 accounts paying an interest rate of 4.5% annually. Some accounts were mainly held for the Pease family, but the majority of the accounts were held for people scattered in villages, throughout North Yorkshire and South West Durham.

Backhouse Bank, High Row Darlington 1815-1864.

Joseph as benefactor rose to his position well. He was able to manipulate, for the banks benefit, both customers for wool, advancing them credit, and at the same time accepting funds on behalf of suppliers. So no matter what stage the wool trade, the bank made money and he easily expanded the woollen side of the business. At the same time (1774), his youngest sister married Jonathan Backhouse, founder of the banking firm J. J. Backhouse. Earlier in 1759 Backhouse had acquired the agency of the Royal Exchange Assurance Company. This alliance between the Pease's and the Backhouse's would prove very important in the years ahead. Also, both families were members of 'The Society of Friends', Quakers, which operated not unlike the 'Monopoly of Credit' established in the Lancashire cotton mills around 1780. The only difference with the Pease's, circle of business friends was that it was world wide, stretching as far afield as North America. Not all of 'The Society of Friends' were capitalists and profiteers, there were quite a number of ordinary farmers, shopkeepers, craftsmen and manufacturers, all under the protective umbrella of Joseph Pease and his associates; they were as loyal to these people as they were to the very rich. At the end of the day it was a fantastic structure of commercial enterprise, when members in difficulties, could and were, helped out by numerous strong business friends.

Society of Friends Hall, Skinnergate, Darlington.

Edward Pease: The Father of the Railways

Joseph Pease died in 1808 and at this time, although the woollen trade was very profitable, the Pease family still had a long way to go before they could compare themselves with the Lloyds, Barclays, Bevans, and Gurneys of the time. In 1796 the family began spinning worsted yarn and banking was still progressing on a small scale, with their trading spreading to Scotland, and the West of England. However, one of the main concerns in the North East of England, at this time, was the conveyance of inland coal to a navigable point on the river Tees and the man to resolve this problem was Edward, Joseph's eldest son.

Edward was very much involved in the furtherance of the coal industry, and the development of the railways. Born in 1767, Edward attended schools in Darlington, and at the age of 11 he was sent to the Quaker boarding school of Joseph and Sarah Tatham, in Leeds. On his return to Darlington at the age of 14, he was a typical product of eighteenth-century schooling: well educated in English, fair knowledge of Latin, proficient in French and able to paint and draw a little. He was extremely numerate, as later ledgers showed, and by the time he was 18 he was very acquainted with business; he would travel from place to place, buying and selling.

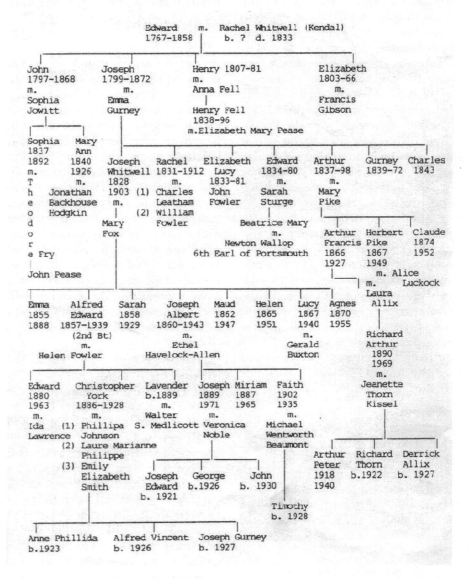

Pease Family History.

Edward Pease Father of the Railways (1767-1858).

Edward was said to be the 'Father of the Railways' and writers of the time such as Samuel Smiles, went even further, saying he was a man who could see a hundred years ahead. But this was not always so, for close examination of his diaries, shows that although he was a good supporter of the railways, his foresight did not go far beyond this; it would be his son Joseph who would push the Pease Dynasty truly into the Railway and Coal Industry.

At the start of the eighteenth-century, coal was the most important national product, and mines were being sunk, as fast as sinkers could be found to sink them. William Coulson, the celebrated master sinker of the times, had sunk about 100 shafts up to 1865. All landowners, lived in the hope of finding, coal, iron, copper, or lead on their land.

In 1767, the river Tees was found inadequate as a navigable river, and so a group of 153 promoters, among them the Peases and Backhouses, agreed to fund a survey for a canal. It was carried out by Robert Whitworth. The route proposed being Stockton by Darlington to a point on the north bank of the Tees at Winston and within easy reach of the South Durham Mines. Total length of the canal was to be 33 miles, at a cost of £63,722. The project was very adventurous and unfortunately, was abandoned, due to the lack of public interest. However in 1790, there was renewed interest, then again in 1810, when a channel did shorten the distance from the mouth of the Tees to Stockton by two miles. This was called the Mandale scheme; a dinner was held at Stockton to celebrate. Leonard Raisbeck the recorder of Stockton used the occasion to inaugurate a project for the construction of a canal or a railroad for the transportation of coals and other minerals. The Pease family was very interested. The original Winston scheme was put forward by John Rennie but was again abandoned in 1815, due to many bank failures in County Durham.

Later, Christopher Tennant, a leading merchant in Stockton, put forward a very revolutionary scheme and funded his own survey. The scheme was for a canal route to the Auckland coalfield via Rushyford, well to the north of Darlington. There were many anomalies to such a project; one being it would require 50 locks and the engineering problems were immense. However, it was known to be a sound commercial proposition; it came further North than Darlington and was indeed a shorter route to the coalfields. Tennant also hoped to get further coal trade from the coastal areas. The construction cost of the scheme was £205,283 and was endorsed at a public meeting held in Stockton in July 1818. Tennant led a deputation to London hoping to raise the money; four/fifths was required for the construction after which the parliamentary authorisation would be forthcoming.

Darlingtons Arch Bridge 1767.

The Yarm/Darlington supporters were livid and immediately put forward a rival scheme, this time including Piercebridge, as well as Croft and Yarm, with a tramway or railroad, to the colliery. George Coverton, a Welsh engineer, who had considerable experience of laying rail in Wales, also a relative of a Yarm promoter, was engaged as surveyor. His report was put forward on 18 September 1818, resulting in strong support of a continuous line of railway of 27 miles at a cost of £124,000, rejecting the canal schemes. This would prove the most economical and most efficient scheme, vindicating the views of Edward Pease.

Cauldron waggon used for transport of coal before railways 1786.

At a meeting held on Friday, 13 November 1818, at Darlington Town Hall, to consider Overton's report, Backhouse made a strong and effective speech in favour of the railroad project and demolished any further backing for the Tennant scheme for the canal via Rushyford. Backhouse went on to promise a return of 25% on £125,000. Backhouse appeared over enthusiastic and it was left to Edward Pease to install a little common sense back into the proceedings. He dashed calculations on the present railway figures saying that a railroad was assured a positive 5% return. He went on further to say that 5% profit was the minimum return on outlay and it was very probable that up to 12% could be made, but Edward said that he would be quite content with his 5%; anything over and above was sheer good fortune.

The meeting concluded: a 40 strong management committee was appointed, being made up primarily of those prepared to subscribe £500 to the project. The prospectus was devised by Joseph Pease, who was then only 19 years of age. It was issued on 15 November 1818, and within one week £25,000 had been easily raised. The subscription list had to be closed on 26 December 1818, and of the

1,209 shares of £100 each, the majority was local, with a list of the shares as follows:

Backhouse Family, £20,000
Pease Family, £6,200
Quaker Benjamin Flounders of Yarm, £5,000
Colonel William Chaytor, of Croft, £5,000
Thomas Meynell of Yarm, £3,000
Leonard Raisbeck (one of a few from Stockton) £1,000

There was also a great deal of outside money, mainly from the Society of Friends: The Gurney family, of Norwich, and London, subscribed, £20,000 and Thomas Richardson, of London, £10,000. Even if Tennant had managed to get his plan off the ground it would have been a non-starter, competing against these people, who had such close ties, kinship, and trust.

With the founders, Pease and Backhouse, the necessary legislation was settled in Parliament, but the schemes main problem was the landowners, and where the railroad would run. The two most influential landowners were the Earl of Darlington (later first Duke of Cleveland) and the Earl of Eldon, at that time Lord Chancellor in Lord Liverpool's administration. Both of these powerful people were against the project. It was thought that Lord Eldon was bought off; Lord Darlington stood his ground saying it was unfair and oppressive to the country, but it was generally thought that the main reason for his obsessive objection was that it would inflict damage to fox coverts. The first

Stockton and Darlington Railway Bill was defeated on 5 April 1819, by 106 votes to 93. The promoters were not dismayed by the narrow defeat, and they worked harder to get the Bill through; the Pease family lobbied strongly for extra backing in the House of Commons. A further survey was carried out, avoiding Lord Darlington's Estate; Lord Darlington tried every way to stop the railroad and even attempted to bankrupt the Backhouse Bank.

The promoters once again renewed the application to Parliament. This was after the death of George III in January, 1820. The lobbying was even more intense, and the Bill was very nearly lost again, by not complying with the rules of Parliament in that four/fifths of a public company should be available, before it could pass to Committee stage; £7,000 was the shortfall. Leonard Raisbeck in Stockton was contacted and was able to raise the money from Edward Pease, with only days to spare. Colonel Chaytor, who was the chairman of the committee, resigned from his position in protest to the growing dominance of Pease and Backhouse, prior to the opening of the railway in September 1825.

Right, Francis Mewburn: left, Jonathan Backhouse, early pioneers of the Stockton and Darlington Railway.

STOCKTON & DARLINGTON
RAILWAY
COACHES.

The SUMMER ARRANGEMENTS will cease on the 30th instant, and the Trains run the same as last season until further notice: viz.—

Winter Arrangements, commencing October 1st, 1840.

ST. HELEN'S AUCKLAND TO DARLINGTON.			DARLINGTON TO ST. HELEN'S AUCKLAND.		
First Trip		at half-past Eight o'Clock.	First Trip		at half-past Eight o'Clock.
Second Trip		at One	Second Trip		at One
Third Trip		at Five	Third Trip		at Five

DARLINGTON TO STOCKTON.			STOCKTON TO DARLINGTON.		
Merchandise Train		at half-past Six o'Clock.	First Class Train		at 10 min. bef. Eight o'Clock.
First Class Train		at half-past Nine	Merchandise Train		at 10 min. bef. Nine
Merchandise Train		at Eleven	First Class Train		at 20 min. past Twelve
First Class Train		at Two	Merchandise Train		at 20 min. past Two
Merchandise Train		at Four	First Class Train		at 20 min. past Four
First Class Train		at Six	Merchandise Train		at 20 min. past Six

STOCKTON TO MIDDLESBRO'.			MIDDLESBRO' TO STOCKTON		
First	Trip	at Eight o'Clock.	*First	Trip	at half-past Seven o'Clock.
Second	do	at Nine	Second	do	at half-past Eight
*Third	do	at Ten	Third	do	at half-past Nine
Fourth	do	at Eleven	Fourth	do	at half-past Ten
Fifth	do	at half-past Twelve	*Fifth	do	at Twelve
Sixth	do	at half-past One	Sixth	do	at One
*Seventh	do	at half-past Two	Seventh	do	at Two
Eighth	do	at half-past Three	Eighth	do	at Three
Ninth	do	at half-past Four	*Ninth	do	at Four
Tenth	do	at half-past Five	Tenth	do	at Five
*Eleventh	do	at a quarter bef. Seven	Eleventh	do	at Six

* Are in connexion with the first class Trains to and from Darlington.

Tickets must be taken at least Five Minutes before the Trains start.

NO SMOKING ALLOWED IN ANY OF THE COMPANY'S COACHES.

MARKET COACHES.

A Coach and Cattle Carriage will leave St. Helen's Auckland, on Mondays, at half-past Six o'Clock; and Shildon, at Seven in the Morning.

HORSES, CATTLE, AND CARRIAGES, CAREFULLY CONVEYED BETWEEN STOCKTON AND DARLINGTON, BY THE MERCHANDIZE TRAINS:—

Horse, 3s.—Gig, 2s. or Horse and Gig, 3s.—Four-wheeled Carriage, 3s. or with Two Horses, 4s.—Horned Cattle, 1s. 6d. each.—Sheep, 4d. each, or 3s. per Score.—Dogs, 1s. each:

If by the FIRST CLASS Train, Horse 3s.—Gig, 3s.—Horse and Gig, 4s.—Four-wheeled Carriage, 3s. or with Two Horses, 5s.

Railway Office, Darlington, September 25th, 1840.

COATES AND FARMER, PRINTERS, HIGH ROW, DARLINGTON.

Stockton and Darlington Railway 1840.

Edward Pease's influence and guidance would be greatly appreciated in these early days. There was a historical meeting between Edward and George Stephenson and Stephenson proved to be a great help as an engineer and guiding influence to the Pease's Scheme. Thomas Meynell became Chairman of the Company, he was a Londoner and his status fitted the post. Edward convinced himself of the practicality of the locomotive engine. He devoted his life and fortune to its adoption, and perfection. On 23 May 1823, the first rail was laid. He introduced George Stephenson to the world, and he also backed him. The original deed of partnership is owned by Joseph Pease and is endorsed by Edward Pease, Robert Stephenson, Michael Longridge, and George Stephenson.

The Stockton and Darlington Railway line paved the way for an even larger project: the Liverpool and Manchester Railway, with George Stephenson appointed chief engineer. When Stephensons Forth Street Works was born for the production of mainly steam engines, for the railway systems, it was Edward Pease's confidence in him that got it off the ground. Edward supplied the capital, for the venture, and so started a very successful business. Edward often referred to Forth Street investments. However, he declined to accept any profit from war steamers supplied to the King of Sardinia on religious grounds.

When the Stockton and Darlington Railway Company, first opened it was certainly not without problems. There was a lack of public confidence, resulting in bankers withdrawing further credit facilities. Edward, then Joseph took on the role of treasurer to guide the company trough the hard periods. A shareholder report on 9 September 1825, only three weeks prior to the official opening, raised doubts about its ability to pay the 5% dividend demanded by the main promoter. The project had mounting debts, even before coal drops and engine sheds had been constructed.

Further advancements had to be made: £40,000 from the Gurneys and £20,000 from Thomas Richardson, all guaranteed on promissory notes. This helped to meet the cost of the land purchase – at £25,000 this exceeded the initial estimate by some £7,000. There was also an amount of £32,000, which had been spent on successfully opposing a rival Tees and Wear project in 1824. The scheme even owed Jonathan Backhouse its treasurer £9,442 for acquiring land on behalf of the company.

Once again Edward Pease came to the rescue of the Stockton and Darlington Railway Company, when he agreed to meet the company's wage bill until new loans could be arranged. Gradually, though, the railway started to make money. In the first year 2½% return was made on revenue of £9,194, and there after it went from strength to strength. The second year (1826-1827) making £18,304, with £14,455 being accounted for by the carriage of coal. The equivalent figures in 1829-1830 were £23,727 and £20,951, and sufficient to pay a dividend of 5%. In 1826-1827, 80,446 tons of coal had been carried on the line and in the year 1829-30, 147,570 tons was transported. These figures were far in excess of the original estimate of Edward Pease and his associates. It was an amazing fact that between 1825-1830, the average price of a ton of coal at Stockton fell from 18s 0d to 8s 6d; this was brought about by a reduction of transport costs— brought about by the rail transportation of coal.

In 1827, the market price for shares in the Stockton and Darlington Railway Company was £160. Edward Pease had seen his project become extremely successful, and he now stepped down, saying he would not enter a railway meeting again. From then on, Edward the 'Father of the Railways', would devote the remainder of his life to the affairs of the Society of Friends; regularly attending meetings in London and visiting his many friends and relations. He remained in his residence at 73 Northgate, Darlington, where he looked after his greenhouse, his plums, apples and apricots. He was a lover of port and fine wine and often entertained guests with Lisbon, Madeira and Bucelas wines; he was nicknamed 'Neddy Pease' by his many friends. He was in deep mourning for years after the death of his wife in 1833. He was a 'flexible Quaker', and in business was a kind and considerate man. Edward Pease died in 1858 after a long life, fully earning his title as 'The Father of The Railways'.

Edward Pease (1767-1858) simple gravestone at the 'Friends' graveyard behind the meeting hall in Skinnergate, Darlington.

Joseph Pease

Joseph was Edward's, second son born on 22 June, 1799. Joseph married Emma Gurney, coheiress of Joseph Gurney, a wealthy banker and a Quaker. Their marriage led to the resignation of the then present Stockton and Darlington Railway Company chairman, Thomas Meynell, because of the Quaker monopoly of the company affairs. Joseph was educated in much the same way as his father at Tathams in Leeds, completing his education at a London Quaker school. As mentioned earlier, Joseph at 19 drew up the prospectus for the Stockton and Darlington Railway Company. His father had left him a massive financial stake in the railroad and like his father, Joseph was not affected in any way by this accumulation of wealth.

Joseph Pease 1799-1872.

Joseph Pease knew the importance of coal and in 1827 was in negotiation with Sir Thomas Claverine of Durham, regarding interests near Chester-le-Street, (Chester-le-Street fell in line with the proposed expansion of the Stockton and Darlington Railway). It was apparent that Stockton was not capable of maximum exportation of coal, the river could only take small craft, and for this reason Middlesbrough was seen as the obvious transportation dock. Joseph also saw Middlesbrough as being the new shipping port for south west Durham coal. Quakers from the south of England financed the necessary land for the project, along with, Thomas Richardson, Joseph Gurney, Henry Birkbeck, Simon Martin and Francis Gibson. Joseph's contribution to the fund of £35,000 included £7,000 loaned by his father-in-law, at an interest rate of 4%.

Port Darlington 1830.

The proposed site for development was a 520 acre estate, which would be developed into a busy seaport, which in time would become a thriving iron industry port as well as coal. It was through Joseph Pease's influence that the scheme acquired the finance and extra capital to erect the wharfs at Middlesbrough. From 1821-1830, 110,211 tons of coal was shipped from the port; from 1831-1840 it increased to 8,293,984, then the following decade a figure of 17,019,714, this was a significant rise in the amount of coal shipped from the Tees. At the time there was opposition to the industry from the House of Lords, and mainly from Lord Londonderry and Lord Durham. The reason for this was supposedly caused by a conflict of interest concerning their own coal industry. Norfolk Peers, Lord Dacks and Sheffield as well as Lord Faversham helped to get the Bill carried; the Stockton people respected these Lords for this reason.

At the same time, there was an attempt to tap the Stockton and Darlington Railway at Simpasture near Shildon, in the attempt to divert coal traffic to Port Clarence. This was fully endorsed by Parliament. Later, the same procedures were used, when the docks were erected at Hartlepool.

To prove that rail transport was a winner Joseph purchased two collieries, initially St. Helens, then, Adelaide. Other mine owners realised their mistake in not backing this mode of transport, but forever after were loyal to the Stockton and Darlington Railway. A tunnel was constructed 1,300 yards west of Shildon called

Brussleton Bank, to transport coal from the area. The same line was extended to Crook, then further on to the valley of Derwent at Consett. At the time Crook was almost virgin coal. The Wear Valley Railway terminated at Frosterly, but later continued to Stanhope, and through the extra efforts of Joseph, continued on to Wearhead, this was promoted to supply limestone to Cleveland for the making of iron ore.

Windlestone Colliery 1876.

In 1833 Joseph Pease replaced Jonathan Backhouse, as treasurer of the Stockton and Darlington Railway Company, quickly followed by his appointment to Chairman of the management committee. The success of the Stockton and Darlington Railway Company projects had a negative effect on the Clarence Railroad Scheme, which developed the north side of the Tees at Port Clarence. The Clarence Railroad Scheme was fronted by Christopher Tennant (who had previously backed the Rushyford-Auckland canal scheme). It was dogged by problems and was deeply in debt to the loan board, who eventually requested the appointment of a new board of directors. Joseph and the Stockton and Darlington Railway Company was blamed for 'ruining their closest competitor', when in fact the problem was internal and managerial. The Clarence Railway scheme, proposed a re-routing of their lines, giving two different routes, but they were unsuccessful with both, and it was ironic that Joseph Pease, as the representative for South Durham in Parliament, would be a member of the House of Commons Committee that was to reject both schemes. This showed how ruthless in business Joseph Pease could be.

J. S. Jeans in his biography, *A History of the Stockton and Darlington Railway* (1875) made the following comments about Joseph Pease:

> ...he was a speculator, doubtless, but he speculated wisely, and well. There was no gambling on his speculations, they were not determined on mere chance, or a fortuitous, chain of events, although there was a certain rise in attending them, which he never shrank from undertaking, need we dwell on the splendour of his conceptions, and the still more splendid execution? The enterprise he led, their results, and their rationale, the eminently practical character, and tendency of his genius. The impetus, which he gave to the railroad system, these and many other achievements, of his useful life, will find a permanent place in the history of his native town and country. As for his bounty, if not like that of Juliet, 'As boundless as the sea', it was measured only by his means, and

opportunities, he was an indiscriminative giver but, yet there was no really good object that appealed to him in vain.

Between the years 1831-1835, the annual dividend for the Stockton and Darlington Railway Company was 6-8%; from 1835-1841 the dividend was 15%. Improvements were needed in 1854 to the channel of the river Tees. A joint stock company was unable to find the finance for these improvements, so, the Admiralty nominated Joseph Pease as chairman. The new commissioners, Messrs Pease, father and son, Messrs Bolckow, Vaughan, Richardson, and Hopkins, overcame the early difficulties; the river had three feet of water, at low tide, and 15 feet rise at high tide. Ships with 7,000 tons of salt, and iron, on board, could leave the port for India, and Japan. The discovery of salt aided the port, and added to the general, trade available by deeper water.

The value of the Stockton and Darlington Railway Company shares, which were originally, £100, were valued now at £260. By 1840 the largest shareholder was Thomas Richardson, having 141 shares, but by 1842 Joseph Pease was the largest shareholder, holding 239 shares. In a period spanning 20 years, the Pease family owned 25% of the shares, and their original investment of £13,000 rose to a value of £60,000. Edward Pease had been exactly right when he made his speech on Friday 13 November 1818, at Darlington Town Hall, when he estimated that 5% would be a minimum return on capital and that there was a high

probability, of far more than this figure. The success pointed to sound management; Friday 13 was a very lucky day for the Pease family. At a census in 1841, in Middlesbrough, the population – 154 in 1831 – was then 5,463, the rise due primarily to the extra work the railway brought; there were docks, warehouses, foundries, and churches, all down to the extra work created by the railway.

However, in 1846 the price of Scottish pig iron, had risen from £2 a ton in 1842 to £6 a ton, affecting manufacturers in a big way. The Stockton and Darlington Railway Company had to ship iron ore from Whitby for the final stages of manufacture. The Clarence Railway started to use Hartlepool as a shipping port, resulting in the Stockton and Darlington Railway Company having to pay a penalty payment of £3,000, which they just could not afford. The period 1847-1851 was a severe crisis time for Pease and the Stockton and Darlington Railway Company; the Pease family were under serious financial strain. Edward, as early as 1846, noted in his diary that, from their collieries and woollen mills and also railways, there was no income forthcoming at all. Both Joseph and his younger brother Henry received financial help from their brother-in-laws, Francis Gibson, and Henry Birkbeck. Following the failure of the Union Bank, in Newcastle in October 1847, Edward reluctantly agreed to sustain Joseph's credit as treasurer, to the Stockton and Darlington Railway Company, by giving him an unlimited guarantee. At the end of 1849 Edward's shares were de-valued by less than £30,000 or even £40,000, and shares once valued at £360, were now selling at only £30; property once worth £60,000 now being worth £3,000. In 1847, with the threat of bankruptcy, Joseph's health deteriorated; he suffered insomnia and with it depression. In the early months of 1849, the first symptoms of glaucoma, affected him, this would lead to total blindness later in his life. However, at this time, there were two turns of events that would lift his spirit. Firstly, in 1846 he had joined his father in Robert Stephenson & Co. and his share of the profits was £7,000, this was set on prices prior to the recession. Secondly, the demand for coke had risen and at his collieries in the Auckland coalfields, up to 500 coke ovens continued to work happily away.

In June 1850 John Vaughan and Bolckow discovered major ironstone deposits at Eston, on the North facing side of the Cleveland Hills, near Middlesbrough. They had discovered the main seam, at its thickest point. Bolckow and Vaughan sent, in 1850, 4,000 tons of ironstone to their Witton Park furnaces. The following year 188,000 tons was produced by the partnership. The effect made on the Stockton and Darlington Railway Company was amazing. By the end of 1851 it was able to pay the guaranteed rents to the Middlesbrough and Redcar and Wear Valley railways, and also discharge all of its arrears.

The Cleveland ore contained a high amount of silica and needed high amounts of limestone for fluxing, this also generated extra work. The Stockton and Darlington Railway Company had good cause to be optimistic; their rail system touched the very edge of the ironstone find, and a further 50 miles on the same line, the main iron works. The sum of £10,000 a year was added to the pockets of the company. Gladstone visited Middlesbrough in 1861 saying that Middlesbrough was 'the youngest child of England's enterprise. It is an infant, but an infant Hercules'. In the year of Gladstone's visit, 500,000 tons of pig iron was produced on Teesside, by 1867, 1 million tons, in 1873, 2 million tons and a third of the total British output. In 1873 it produced 5.5 million tons, it also had 90 blast furnaces. Pease and Co. awoke a sleeping giant.

A proposal for a rail link between Darlington and Barnard Castle was now possible. Joseph Pease had authorised surveys for a possible line as early as 1833, but it did not get off the ground until 1844, when the carpet and shoe manufacturers of Barnard Castle, joined forces with the Stockton and Darlington Railway Company. There was an objector to the scheme and he was Henry Vane, the second Duke of Cleveland, who, like his father before him, was very protective to his way of life. In a public interview with Joseph Pease, he had spoke of the excellence of the Turnpike road, even when it was known that it was not satisfactory for transport. Joseph Pease remarked to the meeting 'you see the man you have to deal with; beyond his own interests he has no feeling'.

All discussions were in vain, at this time, but the committee and Joseph Pease, thinking that the Duke's opposition to the Bill may have mellowed, again revived it in 1852. New proposals were put on the table in that maintenance would only be charged at half the cost and this would also be the case with haulage, until the profit or dividend reached 4%. Joseph also agreed that the Stockton and Darlington Railway Company would meet the subscription of the project, which amounted to £22,000. A Bill of incorporation was drawn up and considered by the House of Commons in May 1853, the Duke of Cleveland again opposed the Bill saying that it was the device of a scheming artful individual, trying to deceive the people of Barnard Castle for his own benefit, since it would reduce the cost of the transportation of coal and other goods, along the Tees Valley, from the Pease's Collieries. Joseph Pease even suggested an alternative scheme showing that this was not the case, but to no avail and it was rejected in June that year. Again a renewed application for an alternative route was put forward, in the autumn of 1853, by two solicitors, with a representative of West Hartlepool, led by Ralph Ward Jackson, said that it was the aim of Joseph Pease to control the entire district.

Joseph had a good reputation for being very sincere and of having purity of motive. However, by the autumn of 1853 the Duke of Cleveland was openly attacking the Pease family and their expansion motives, which intensified when the Darlington and Barnard Castle line was approved in May 1854; strongly supported by the people of Barnard Castle. The line opened in July, 1856 with the Duke of Cleveland attending the opening ceremony; he expressed his hope that differences with the Pease Family would be forgotten. Cynics however, noted that he was permitted to nominate a director of the Stockton and Darlington Railway Company, later the North Eastern Railway Company, for life.

From 1841 to 1865, Joseph Pease devoted himself to educational and social reforms. In 1865 he became completely blind, but continued works of humanity as best he could. This was not confined to England; he declined an honour from Spain, of 'Grand Cross of Charles II,' for his efforts in supporting the moral advancement of the Spanish people.

In 1850 three separate companies were established, due to the extra mining activity: Joseph Pease and Partner was concerned with the colliery side of the business, together with coke ovens, and fire bricks. This included, Adelaide, St. Helens (near Bishop Auckland), Tindale, Sunniside, Pease's West, Bowden Close, Stanley and Wooley (near Crook), Esh-Winning, Waterhouses, Ushaw Moor, Brandon, Windlestone Colliery, Chilton (near Ferryhill). In 1870 the company's total output was more than 1 million tons of coal, one/third of which was converted to coke for smelting purposes. J. W. Pease and Company was one of the largest producers of ironstone in Cleveland, with an output of approximately 1 million ton, annually. Total

Cleveland production in 1872 was 6.3 million tons, the wage bill alone was £100,000 a year. J & J. W. Pease was a successor to the Pease's Bank, The Banking section was re-established in the time of Joseph Whitwell Pease, and was basically the counting house of the Pease companies, including the Stockton and Darlington Railway Company. After 1863 it became local banker to the North Eastern Railway Company (NER), and the Consett Iron Company.

Sinkers at Wooley Colliery 1864.

Joseph Pease died in 1872, a very wealthy man; an outside estimate of his estate at the time of his death being £320,000, three times more than the typical Victorian business man. This was primarily due to his hard and relentless work. His funeral was on 19 February, 1872. All commercial premises closed in Darlington, flags flew at half-mast at all NER stations. It was hard to describe in words such an amazing businessman as Joseph Pease. Reverend Henry Kendall described him as well as anyone could, he said:

> Joseph was one who's substance was mines and merchandise, and roads and horses of iron and very extensive possessions, so that this man

was the greatest of all men of the North East of England.

Joseph had high hopes for his eldest son, Joseph Whitwell, whom he hoped would carry on the family dynasty. Like Edward before him, his grandfather, Joseph Whitwell had to start from the bottom and at the age of 17 he entered into the family counting house as a clerk, to learn book keeping. After the merger of 1863, as a member of Stockton and Darlington Railway Company, he joined the board of the NER on behalf of the family. The future of the Pease dynasty was in his hands.

Sir Joseph Whitwell Pease

Joseph's eldest son was born in 1828, and became his fathers right hand. As his father's strength failed after 1850, he took on the ever-growing responsibility he would eventually inherit. One of eight brothers, most of these dying prematurely, Joseph was left relatively on his own to carry the burden of the whole of the family's public and private business. In 1852 Joseph Whitwell Pease became director of Barnard Castle Railway, his father also became a director, then they became joint treasurers — the railway after this went from strength to strength. In 1852-1853 a private company was formed, to develop the newly found iron ore deposits, and extend the railway to Guisborough. Joseph and his son acted as guarantors. The railway was subject to a fierce attack in Parliament. In one session alone it was in committee stage for 23 days in the House of Commons.

*Joseph Whitwell Pease (1828-1903)
with his family.*

were great difficulties with the liquidation of the old company, Joseph Pease and Company received substantial aid from the old Gurney connection, and also from the Bankers, Messrs Drewett and Fowler.

There were also financial troubles at Middlesbrough, the Peases being responsible for establishing the iron ore business there. At the works of Bolckow and Vaughan, bankers had placed the Sheriffs Officer's bailiffs in their works. The Peases came to their rescue. Joseph Whitwell Pease went to their bankers, and had the bailiffs removed. Securities were raised and deposited with the Peases, until the iron ore made their works profitable again. Many years later Joseph again came to their rescue, preventing another catastrophe.

The Peases, from approximately 1846, helped develop the Middlesbrough railway system; they constructed the dock area, saved the iron industry and opened the West Durham Coalfield. They turned Middlesbrough into a credible port and brought in other industries such as potteries, (managed by Isaac Wilson). Until this time, no railways existed between Darlington and York, the four horse coach was still in regular use. To develop the railway, finance had to be arranged privately, and the Peases again with their Southern relatives from Norfolk and London, arranged this. At one of their financial meetings Mr Samuel Gurney said to Joseph, 'Joseph, that railway of thine will Beggar Thee'. 'That entirely depends on the kindness of my friends', Joseph replied. The Darlington York Railway was completed on time (1845).

The Barnard Castle Railway was extended to Torbay and Penrith, with the backing of the Peases; and credit to Henry Pease, who secured the final link between the east and west coast. The last remaining section was Saltburn-on-Sea, which also owes the Pease family and Joseph in particular, for its existence. The extension to Torbay opened up the market for Durham Coke to the west coast where it was badly needed for smelting the rich haematite ore of the western mines of Cumberland and Westmoreland.

In 1857 there was great panic in the North East of England. The Coside (Consett) Iron Company were large debtors of the Stockton and Darlington Railway Company, and also of the Northumberland and Durham Bank. Joseph Whitwell Pease took the company in hand, a new company was formed, and there

The year 1854 saw the great amalgamation of all the companies as the North Eastern Railway Company (NER). In 1863 The Stockton and Darlington Railway Company, joined this alliance, and four members were placed on its board, Messrs Joseph Whitwell Pease, Henry Pease, Alfred Kitching, and Colonel Stobart. In 1865 the Newcastle, Carlisle and Hartlepool Company, added to the union. Sir J. Lothian Bell became Chairman, of the Locomotive Committee, and later, Deputy Chairman of the board. Sir Joseph W. Pease, became Chairman, of the Traffic Company, and later, Chairman of the board. Sir David Dale became Chairman, of the Works Committee. Henry Tennant, who had been accountant, to the Great Northern Company, then to the United Company, became, General Manager and later Director of North Eastern Railway Company (NER).

Marriage of Cousins: Henry Fell and Elizabeth Pease

In 1862, the marriage celebrations of Henry Fell and Elizabeth Pease, was a very lavish affair. Thirty Carriages left the bride's home, North Lodge, for the Meeting House, and on their return the guests were treated to a magnificent, déjeuner of asparagus soup, oyster soup a la reine, soup a la julienne, turkeys, raised ham and veal pies, pigeon pies, boars head, and racks of lamb; spring chickens, and boiled fowls, lobster salads, pressed beef and guinea fouls, aspic of eels, of salmon and shrimps, prawns and sweets, including six kinds of creams, five sorts of jellies, pastries, meringues, hedgehog, hen's nest, cakes fruit and ices, with non-alcoholic drinks, including temperance champagne.

The couple visited France on their honeymoon, they went to Paris, Bordeaux, Bayonne, and Biarritz, afterwards returning to their newly built mansion at Brinkburn, built by Joseph Pease, and Partners, with buff coloured brick, backing onto large grounds, near, Pierremont, the home of the groom's father. On the day of the wedding 700 workers at Henry Pease & Co's mills, enjoyed a railway excursion to Redcar where they were entertained by a band, which went with them.

Hutton Hall 1867.

The Pease's also had a home in Guisborough, called Hutton Hall; Joseph Whitwell Senior took his family there for a monthly holiday every year. Joseph Whitwell also had the shooting rights for the surrounding area. Alfred pleasantly remembered the summer evenings, at the house. In 1862, Joseph bought an estate at Pinchinthorpe, two miles, to the west of Guisborough, Hutton Hall, and this estate, totalled 2,700 acres. Home, however, was still very much Woodland at Darlington. Joseph Pease's London home was Princess Gardens, later he bought a house at 24, Kensington Palace Gardens. Joseph spent time here relaxing after a hard day, in Parliament, especially when lobbying for new rail projects. For some time Joseph had intended moving his whole family to Hutton Hall, he quite enjoyed the country life, and he could indulge in country pursuits, free from business pressures and politics.

Alfred Pease, Joseph's son, had very definite views about his families involvement in industry, saying, 'I disliked from childhood, the spoiling industrial hand, of my family, who thought they were always doing good work, in providing more and more, employment for people, I could see as a boy, that the more that they did this the more families of boys would be produced for whom more and more, mines and pits, and factories, would have to be made, till our lovely world would be ash heaps, chimneys, and hideous houses under smoke clouds'.

In 1882 Joseph Whitwell Pease, was offered a Baronetcy by the Prime Minister of the time, Gladstone, which after consultation with the rest of the family, was accepted, acknowledging that it gave public recognition for past members of the family and their achievements.

Hutton Old Hall

The Hall was the charm of antiquity, old gardens, in a sweet corner of the Cleveland Hills. The gardens were old world, the nursery door, and window opened on to a rose garden, York, Lancaster, Gloria Mundi, old fashioned roses, interspersed, with little box edged beds, of Verbena, Blue Salvia, and such things. The side of the house was half covered by an enormous, Jargonelle Pear Tree, the leaves of which flopped against, the window of the bedroom, in which Joseph Whitwell Pease and his brother Jack slept.

When Joseph Whitwell bought the Hall, he made sweeping changes, to the building. By 1867, the old cornfields, and Whiney pastures, were laid into a park, the old, hedge-rows, disappeared, and fine roads took the place of old lanes, and brindle paths; bridges replaced fords and stepping stones.

The refurbished Hall was built in Domestic Gothic style, with brick dressed in stone. It had two halls, a billiard room, five reception rooms, five bathrooms, a conservatory, a winter garden 91 feet in length, containing a central tiled walk, with fernery. Its cellars were reached by three staircases, housing Turkish baths, with tiled and marbled walls, and floors; cooling room, weighing room, furnace room, wine and beer cellars. The grounds and gardens were laid out, with weeping elm and cedar of Lebanon, clumps of rhododendrons, and other, flowering shrubs, and had a broad terraced walk, which led to the Italian Garden. It had stabling for 24 horses, a Booth's House, a Head Gardener's house, a Coachman's House, thirteen greenhouses, seven of which were free standing. These later housed grapes, melons, oranges, bananas, pineapples, figs, apricots, peaches, nectarines, plums, and pears. A miniature lake called 'the pond', was stocked with trout, and complemented by a boathouse, with a tearoom above it. All this was cleverly installed into 54 acres of private grounds; 20 gardeners were employed, and just as many house servants.

Joseph had arranged for the railway station to be built at the end of the drive. The railway was handy in many ways for the Whitwell Peases, who lived off the fat of the land. Sausages were imported from Cornwall, fish came by train from York, fruit came from wherever it was available, nectarines, peaches, apricots, melons, grapes, and York hams were all specially bought and were included on daily menus. Regular trips for the children, during their holidays to Falmouth where they had their steam yacht 'Rosemary' birthed. This was all due to accumulated wealth, over the years, and quite contrary to Quaker beliefs.

The Pease family, from minerals alone, supplied the North Eastern Railway Company (NER) with revenue of approximately £1,000 a day. Since Sir Joseph Whitwell Pease's death, 23 June 1903, one of his companies, Pease and Partners, had paid the North Eastern Railway Company (NER) alone, £9,000,000 in Railway, dues. In 1865-1903, the Peases provided many amenities for the people of Durham County, among which were schools, hospitals, mechanics and miners institutes, convalescence homes, libraries,

assembly rooms. The family have also done much for their home town of Darlington with Joseph Whitwell Pease's grandfather, Edward, providing Darlington municipal buildings, a market place, a free library and North Road cemetery, along with many other gifts.

Public Library in Crown Street, left to the Darlington People by the Peases.

The Pease's were a very remarkable Darlington Family, who not only funded the railways, but persisted through one major problem, after another, until, the railways were fully established, not only Stockton and Darlington and Middlesbrough, but the entire North of England.

John Harrison

1693-1776

John Harrison was born at Foulby village, near Pontefract, Yorkshire, in 1693. Harrison was a mechanical genius; inventing an accurate means of telling the correct time with a mechanical clock. Modern shipping, overland transport and flight, could not have been achieved without completely accurate timekeeping; one second out in calculating a course by sea, land or air could result in being miles off course.

John Harrison had a very humble beginning. His father, Henry Harrison, was a carpenter who worked for the local landowner, Sir Roland Winn, of Nostel Priory. Education in the late seventeenth-century was rare for children like John, who did at least manage to learn the basics of reading and writing. However, this lack of education did cause him problems in later life; he was never able to express himself easily, and explaining his ideas was always a problem.

As a child, John was fascinated by any machinery with wheels or cogs, which included windmills and waterwheels – they simply amazed him. Clocks in such a small village as Foulby, except possibly at Sir Roland Winn's house, were extremely rare. Indeed, it actually was at Nostel Priory that John first saw a clock. The slowly swinging pendulum fascinated him and he listened to the striking of the hours and half-hours. Then his gaze shifted to the movement of the toothed wheels inside the case. The whole movement of this clock fascinated him so much that he would watch it all day.

John Harrison's house Barrow 1700.

When John was seven years old, his family moved from Foulby to Barrow-upon-Humber; where Sir Rowland Winn had a second estate. The journey, a distance of some 50 miles, had to be covered on foot, carrying what few goods they had on a packhorse loaned from Sir Roland Winn. Most children of this age never ventured far from their village, and now John was travelling 50 miles! He was very excited about the journey. Early one morning the family set out to travel to their new home at Barrow. The tracks were rough and deeply rooted and for most of the journey, extremely muddy.

John found his new village far more interesting than Foulby; a short distance from it was the river Humber.

The port of Kingston-on-Hull stood on the opposite bank. John and James, his younger brother, spent many hours watching the coming and going of large ships into and out of the port. Little did John realise then, just how important his future invention would be to the navigation of these same ships.

A portrait of John Harrison 1759.

In Barrow, the village parson befriended John and helped develop his reading and writing. He only possessed one book, on philosophy, by a priest called Nicholas Sanders. Philosophy did not interest John one bit, but it was a book nevertheless, and a basis for furthering his reading and writing skills. He copied down every word in the book together with every diagram. He did this over and over again until he could memorise the words. He kept copies of this throughout his life, as evidence of his reading and writing capabilities.

John Harrison became a carpenter, following his father into this trade. He also made money surveying and measuring land which suggests that the parson perhaps tutored him in mathematics. He certainly knew how to calculate, as the timepieces that he went on to make, proved. His father taught him the art of wood turning and carving and he became a very capable carpenter. Over the next few years (1713) he studied the movements of clocks in other people's homes and memorised these. John would soon produce a clock of his own design out of wood using the techniques his father had taught him. However, one problem he encountered on the way was friction. Light lubricants were just not available in 1713, resulting in even a small amount of friction upsetting the fine and delicate mechanism he was developing. Harrison deduced that wood rather than metal would be prone to less friction; he was also aware that some woods were naturally self-lubricated.

The amount of work needed to construct his first clock was immense. Each of the toothed wheels were made in four segments and these were put together by two circular layers of wood, one on each side, which were smaller in size so they did not overlap the teeth; oak was used because of its hardness. One can imagine the extreme accuracy needed to cut the teeth on the circumference of each wheel; they had to correspond exactly. The face of the clock was made out of metal, and the figures and the divisions were scribed very finely on its service. John and his brother, James, made a number of these long case clocks, which had wooden wheels. Indeed one of the early long case clocks resides now in London, at the Worshipful Company of Clockmakers' Collection in Guildhall.

John Harrison certainly wasn't going to be satisfied with his first clock. He knew that although his initial clock was good, there were many improvements that could be made. His aim was to produce a clock with accurate time. What he had to consider was temperature change; a good timekeeper in winter would lose in summertime. The metal on the pendulum expanded in the heat and contracted in cold weather. The longer a pendulum is, the slower it swings, and though the difference in length is slight, the inaccuracy in time is considerable.

It took an ingenious person like Harrison to solve this problem. No two metals expand equally with heat. Harrison carefully considered brass and steel; brass expands in heat nearly half as much again as steel. Harrison made his pendulum in the form of a gridiron. When assembled, the downward expansion of steel exactly compensated for the upward expansion of brass rods and thus the pendulum remained at a constant length. Gridiron pendulums can still be seen on older clocks. John came up with other solutions to clock manufacturing: the *grasshopper escapement,* which shifts the power from the slowly falling weights to the pendulum and *going ratchet* which enables the clock top to keep going when being wound.

The real challenge came to Harrison in 1714 when the British Government passed an Act of Parliament offering rewards of £10,000 and £20,000 to anyone who could find an accurate method of calculating longitude onboard ships at sea, to within half a degree (two minutes of time). The methods would be tested on a ship sailing 'over the ocean, from Great Britain to any such port in the West Indies as those Commissioners choose…without losing their Longitude beyond the limits before mentioned', and should prove to be 'tried and found practicable and useful at sea'. A body known as the Board of Longitude was set up to administer and judge the longitude prize. This was a huge sum of money and the government did not offer this without good reason. The matter of determining longitude at sea had not even been considered until ships began to travel long distances. Before the sixteenth-century, ships did not venture far at all, possibly a few hundred miles from shore. When they began to get more adventurous and sailed over a thousand miles across the Atlantic, *then* longitude became very important.

The King of Spain was thought to be the first to offer a large reward for calculating longitude. Ships were being lost; sailors were losing their lives as land approached before they had estimated – especially at night. When people first pondered the question of longitude, they found that it was closely related to time. Noon in London is midnight half way around the world, half way between these two points to the west of London, say Chicago, it will be 6am. But to the east, in say Irkutsk, Siberia, it will be 6pm. If 24 equidistant lines were drawn from the north to south poles, the time by the sun would vary by exactly one hour from line to line. However, 24 lines were too few for accuracy, so the world was divided into 360 lines of longitude, each being one degree from the next. The imaginary line running from pole to pole, passing through Greenwich, was fixed as nought degrees longitude. The first Astronomer Royal was John Flamstead, who happened to be one of the pioneers in the search for the calculation of longitude.

The imaginary line through Greenwich is still used throughout the world as the point from which all longitude is calculated. In the same way Greenwich Mean Time became the time from which all time in the world was set. An example of how the master of a ship would calculate longitude and time is: the master of a vessel which has steamed due west in the Atlantic, observes the sun when it is due north, which means that at that time it is precisely noon. He has in his possession a very accurate clock, which has been set at Greenwich Mean Time on the day that the ship sailed. He checks the clock and finds that it reads 3 pm, showing that at this spot at sea, there is a difference of three hours between sun time and Greenwich Mean Time. One hour represents 15 degrees, which means that the ship is 45 degrees west of Greenwich, and somewhere to the north east of Newfoundland. A very accurate timepiece can calculate this longitude.

In 1728, John Harrison set off early one morning to travel to London, with a drawing of an instrument which he thought might be useful in calculating longitude. He was certain his idea would work but he required from the government body the finance to produce the instrument. Harrison was still a relatively poor man, but showed terrific strength of character on that morning when he set out. He was driven on by absolute confidence in his idea. It is thought that he walked the full distance to London from Barrow on Humber, carrying his precious life's work with him.

Harrison eventually arrived in London, where he was extremely fortunate to meet up with Edward Halley, the Astronomer Royal. He showed him his drawings. At this time Halley was over 70 years old and on the Board of Longitude. Knowing full well that no advance would be forthcoming from the Board, Halley advised Harrison to go and see George Graham. Graham was reputed to be the finest clockmaker in London and successor to the great Thomas Tampion. He was also a very kind man, a Quaker who believed it was wrong to charge or receive interest on money, keeping all of his cash in a strong box as he did not believe in banks. George Graham liked John Harrison so much that he gave him an interest-free loan of £200 and told him to go back to Barrow and make his clock, and re-approach The Board when it was complete.

Harrison took Graham's advice although his clock was not completed for a further seven years. Visiting the clock at the Maritime Museum, Greenwich, it is not hard to see why it took the time it did, especially since, as well as making the clock, Harrison had to also make a living. The Harrison Marine Chronometer Number One is very large, weighing

70lbs. The movement is very delicate and has an intricate mechanism. It is a clock built to withstand the rolling and pitching of a ship in rough sea, yet still keep the correct time. It was completely made out of metal to the highest standards, each part hand made, and not accepted by Harrison until it actually was perfect, even if its making had to start all over again. It is not hard to see that John Harrison was a genius and his exquisitely accurate workmanship showed in the end product.

The Harrison Marine Chronometer Number One (H1): Harrison's first clock.

In 1735 John Harrison set off again for London with the Harrison Marine Chronometer Number One, the H1, a portable version of his precision wooden clocks. To do this he took a stage coach covering only 20 or 30 miles a day and he had to dismantle his clock completely and reassemble it on arrival in the capital. The journey was a nightmare for him. These were the days of the highwaymen and he had seven years

of hard work packed in a crate. The chances were that he would not have had much sleep at all until his arrival in London but somehow, through sheer determination, all arrived safely.

Edward Halley, still Astronomer Royal, was the first to see the clock working and was very impressed by the quality of workmanship in such an accurate timepiece. The second man to see the clock was George Graham, Harrison's benefactor. Both Halley and Graham gave Harrison certificates of approval and ordered that the clock should be submitted to the Board of Longitude. The other Board members ordered it to be tested at sea. However, the Board took their time in this matter and it took a year before it was put on board a vessel. With the clock on board, *HMS Centurion* sailed for Lisbon in 1736. *HMS Centurion* was a man-of-war and the crew and everyone else connected to the test treated John with great respect.

The H1 made its return voyage on the *HMS Orford,* with the clock keeping time accurately enough for it to correct a misreading of the *Orford's* longitude. A full report was given with Harrison requesting financial assistance from the Board to make a second more accurate time keeper.

George Graham was not very happy at all about the situation, thinking that the prize money should have been paid or, failing that, at least part of it. However the Board were not convinced of the clocks value and only paid out £250. Harrison decided he would accept this even though he was unhappy; he fully intended improving H1 even though it had been as accurate as the Board had required. In 1737 he set out to make H2, for which purpose he moved to London and set about devoting his whole life to the project. It took him three years to complete his work. It was generally thought that he made it in his spare time, as the money given to him by the Board of Longitude was hardly enough to make the clock without having to maintain a living. However, the loan to Graham was still outstanding.

It was 1740 when the second clock was completed. It was smaller than his first and easier to handle. The Board paid him a further £250, then a further £500 for yet another chronometer. Harrison had already started on this even before he received the second amount. It seemed that he felt inside that he could always do better and he *did* do better. Harrison promised the Board that indeed it would be better than the other two. The Longitude Board must have wondered at this statement as it took John Harrison almost 19 years to complete the task. This timepiece was much smaller than the previous two and was extremely accurate, the margin of error being only four seconds a week. This time he was awarded a gold medal for the excellence of his timepiece although he knew in his heart that he could still do better so, he started on a new timepiece.

H2

H3

H4

H5

John Harrison's fourth chronometer was a surprising change from his previous three. This time he commissioned a London watchmaker, John Jeffery's, to make him a watch 13 centimetres in diameter, that looked like a large pocket watch. The experts of the time thought that this timepiece was about as perfect as you could get a watch to be. In his book *The Marine Chronometer*, R. T. Gould said that for beauty, accuracy and also historical interest, 'it must take pride of place as the most famous Chronometer that was ever made, or for that matter ever will be made'.

John Harrison was 66 years of age when he completed the fourth chronometer in 1759. Did he win the prize offered by the Board of Longitude? No! He had been inspired all of his life by this prize, he had bettered his timepiece each time to well within the standards required but they still did not pay him. He had received nothing like the money offered. He had conquered longitude by making a near-perfect timepiece and yet still remained a very disappointed and disillusioned man.

However, John remained extremely confident that H4 would stand up to any test, and asked the Board to give it the most stringent of tests at sea; they agreed and a voyage to the West Indies was arranged. Harrison was by then too old to go to sea on the voyage himself, so his son William went instead. The voyage was arranged for the 18 November 1761. William was on board *HMS Deptford* with his father's precious chronometer. The ship arrived back in England four months later. The timepiece had lived up to expectations, losing only five seconds on arrival in Jamaica 19 January 1762. Over the whole trip, including the return journey, it was accurate to within two minutes, thus qualifying easily for the top prize of £20,000, but the Board of Longitude again refused to pay. The excuses this time were simply amazing. The Board believed it could be a fluke, and that another trial should be carried out, and furthermore, that Harrison should divulge how the timepieces were made. John Harrison refused these demands. Even though he was now old and thoroughly fed up with the Board's behaviour, he petitioned parliament, resulting in a payment from the Board of Longitude for £5,000. Justice, in part, was seen to be done.

John Harrison was now over 70 years old, but his eyes and hands were still perfect. He sent his chronometer to the Greenwich Observatory for testing. He then sent it on a second voyage to the West Indies and Barbados in 1764. Again, William represented his father on the voyage. After seven weeks voyage the results were just as spectacular as on the previous voyage and yet still the Board were not satisfied with the outcome and would still not pay out the full prize money. This time John went directly to the King, George III. On 31 January 1772, via a letter to the King's private astronomer at Richmond, Dr Stephen Demainbray, William expressed his concerns with the Board of Longitude. Harrison's chronometer, H5, was subsequently put on trial by the King himself in 1772, and like the previous timepieces, performed superbly. Finally, John and James were awarded £8,750 by Act of Parliament in June 1773.

John Harrison lived until he was 83 years old, dying at his residence Red Lion Square, London on 24 March 1776, his 83rd birthday; at least his final years were spent in relative comfort.

All John Harrison's remaining clocks can be seen at the National Maritime Museum at Greenwich, London. The Science Museum in South Kensington, London, has many interesting photographs, as well as Harrison's grandfather clock dated 1715; the dial is inscribed 'J. N. Harrison Barrow.' The clock is completely constructed of wood except for the escape wheel. This is Harrison's first clock, and after three hundred years it still works perfectly.

John Harrison died a credit to his profession, with many seamen thankful that he made possible the calculation of longitude with his outstanding engineering techniques and his beautiful clocks.

John Smeaton

1724-1792

John Smeaton was making important discoveries very early on in the Industrial Revolution. He was born in 1724 at Austhorpe Lodge, near Leeds, the son of William Smeaton, a very eminent and prosperous lawyer, who never thought for a moment that his son John would become a great engineer, a builder of lighthouses, bridges, canals, and harbours and eventually a Fellow of the Royal Society.

William Smeaton wished his son to follow in his footsteps and become a lawyer, an occupation that had provided him with a very prosperous life. The difference between John Smeaton and those who followed him like Stephenson, Brunel, Telford, Fairbairn, Rennie and Brindley, was that they had a constant struggle with adversity, having to educate themselves, and scraping by, earning money even to nourish themselves. Brindley, for instance, was more or less illiterate all his life. Whereas Smeaton was different, having education and finance at his disposal, all he had to do was to overcome the pressures put on him by his father to become a lawyer.

Austhorpe was a beautiful house, built by Smeaton's grandfather in the parish of Whitkirk and where John Smeaton was born on 8 June 1724. A brother born in 1727 died at five years and a sister born five years later survived for only one year, making John an only child. There were no other children where John grew up. From a young age he designed and made things. As early as six years old he studied a local windmill then constructed a smaller version of his own, climbing to the top of his father's barn so it got the maximum wind in its sails. Machinery fascinated John.

William Smeaton eventually gave in to his son's obsession, thinking that if the boy was so keen on engineering he should have a workshop and every tool imaginable to further his interest. John used the tools to great effect, making other and better tools for all kinds of uses and complicated functions. He was given tuition in reading and writing and showed an interest in mathematics from an early age. When he was old enough, he attended Leeds Grammar School where it was found he had a natural aptitude for mathematics, in particular geometry. He was also very good at drawing. When he was 16 years old John left school. Knowing fully that his father wished that he followed him in the family legal business he eventually joined the firm, although his love for mechanics and engineering far outweighed his interest in the legal profession.

At this time, one of the main problems with coal mining was that after rain most of the mine would be flooded. Thomas Newcomen invented a primitive steam engine for the purpose of expelling water from the mines and by 1740 more than 150 of these engines were working successfully. Later, larger engines were built on Newcomen's principle. This engine attracted John's interest. He sketched it from every angle, then went home, and produced a working model of the engine. To test the capabilities of the machine he tried it on his father's fish pond. It did so well it killed all of the fish! William Smeaton was not amused, but marvelled at his son's genius in constructing the engine just on sight.

Solely to please his father John continued to attend the office in Leeds, where his tasks were mainly copying legal documents and learning general law. In the evenings he worked until late at night in his workshop. His father began to feel that John would never learn law in Leeds so arranged for him to go to London where he could attend the courts at Westminster Hall – well away from his workshop.

John Smeaton left for London in the autumn of 1742. He loved his father tremendously and no one could say that he didn't give his father's profession a try, working hard in legal circles during the day. But in his own time in the evenings, he attended libraries, reading endlessly on the subjects that interested him – mostly mechanics. Smeaton missed his workshop so much that he wrote a well-presented letter to his father informing him that he wished to give up law and follow a career as a mechanical engineer. William

Smeaton showed that he was a reasonable man and that he also loved his son. He admired the way his son had tried in London and, though disappointed, gave him permission to follow his own interests. He also awarded him a very generous allowance which carried on for the rest of John's life. William Smeaton played a very important part in furthering his son's career. Without his help John Smeaton might never have achieved the marvels he did.

John was overjoyed at his father's support, quickly resigned his lawyer's position and entered the service of an instrument-maker to learn the trade. He also began to attend meetings of the Royal Society and through it met many famous scientists. As early as 26 July 1750, Smeaton read his first paper to the Society, in which he described improvements to the mariner's compass. In 1751, he invented an instrument for measuring the speed of ships at sea. Other papers read to the Royal Society included one on air pumps, another one on pulleys and tackle and yet another on steam engines.

Portrait of John Smeaton 1752.

In 1754, when he was 30, Smeaton was elected a Fellow of the Royal Society, a high distinction for one so young and an indication of the esteem other members held him in. This was also the year that he began learning French, mainly to read books, written in French, on mechanics.

Smeaton also began to take a keen interest in the civil engineering of docks, canals, harbours and drainage and navigation safety. Belgium and Holland were more advanced than England in these fields, so, John travelled cheaply on foot and by canal barge, noting and sketching Dutch dykes and canal systems. He thought the docks and harbours of Amsterdam were amazing. In London, ships had to wait for the tides to go alongside the wharf before setting out to sea. In Amsterdam the tides could be ignored; the docks were kept full by means of locks. The notes and sketches Smeaton made were of immense use, not only to himself but also to the country in general and he used these effectively later in his career.

John always had a great respect for the sea, realising that dock and sea walls had to be constructed with great strength to withstand storms, tides and the enormous power of the sea. This appreciation was to be vital to the success of what is undoubtedly his greatest achievement, the construction of the Eddystone Lighthouse.

If you consider a map of the English Channel and draw a line between The Lizard in Cornwall and Start Point in west Devon, it will pass very near to the infamous reef known as the Eddystone Rock. Most of it lies some 12 to 14 feet below water at low tide and it is covered completely at spring tides. The Eddystone Reef lies across the course of channel shipping, especially those ships heading for Plymouth. It was responsible for the wreck of hundreds of ships with valuable cargoes, not to mention the lives of thousands of seamen. A lighthouse had been built on the rock as early as 1698. Prior to this, ship owners could only place warning lights on the nearest cliffs, scarcely a reliable method. Lighthouse-owners could collect dues from the passing shipping; it was a lucrative business which first attracted the attention of a colourful character called Henry Winstanley, nicknamed 'Whimsical' because of his love of practical jokes. Henry was granted permission to build what was thought to be impossible, a lighthouse on Eddystone itself. However, he defied the sceptics; his lighthouse, completed in 1698 and built of wood and iron and reaching 70 feet high, was regarded as a wonder until it blew down in a great storm on 23 November 1703.

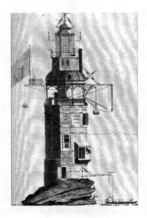

Winstanley's Tower 1698.

The second Eddystone Lighthouse appeared in 1709, designed by John Rudyerd, a Cornishman who owned a silk shop on Ludgate Hill. This lighthouse was made of wood but, unlike Winstanley's, was conical in shape and offered more resistance to the waves. It was built of stout timbers, like ocean-going vessels and withstood storms and buffeting for 46 years, when it suddenly burnt down on 2 December 1755. How the fire started was not clear. A team of keepers worked in shifts to renew the candles used to produce the light. It was thought that the heat from the candles had caused the wooden roof area to become completely dry and combustible. A boat was put to sea to rescue the three keepers. On reaching the shore one of the keepers took to his heels and was never seen again. Another, an old man of 94, insisted that, as he had looked up at the flames in the roof, some molten rock had poured down his throat. Fourteen days later he died, a flat piece of lead weighing seven ounces was found in his stomach.

Rudyerd's Tower 1709.

Mr Robert Weston, who was a major shareholder in the lighthouse, financed the building of a new lighthouse which he wished to be re-built quickly. His first enquiry was made to the President of the Royal Society, the Earl of Macclesfield who strongly recommended John Smeaton for his great knowledge of mechanics and his record of high quality work. The Earl's recommendation was good enough for Weston who sent a message to Smeaton, who was working in Scotland at the time, insisting he build the lighthouse. The message took a month to reach Smeaton. Thinking it was a re-build job he wasn't very keen. However, on finding he was to build a completely new lighthouse, he took up the challenge and hurried back to London.

Smeaton set to work studying the problem of the third lighthouse. He made a lengthy study of the previous lighthouses and considered that the new lighthouses would be built of stone, a thing no one thought possible He studied the London curb-stones, which, because they were interlocked with each other, never moved and decided to dovetail his stone accordingly. The base of the building would be weighed down with heavy rocks. No stone would be able to move on its own; each would be firmly held by every other one. Smeaton experimented with cement until he found one that set quickly and was not affected by salt. He then made a complete drawing of the building even before going to see the Eddystone Reef.

It was March 1756 Smeaton set out for Plymouth from London the journey took him six days. In

Plymouth, he called to see Josiah Jessup, a foreman Shipwright Jessup doubted that it was possible to build the lighthouse of stone but agreed that if it could be done, stone would withstand the greatest of storms. Jessup later gave Smeaton much help with his construction.

Due to strong winds around the channel, it was not until April that John attempted a visit to the Reef. The breakers were battering right over the rock and it was impossible to land due to the ferocity of the sea. Three days later he returned and this time managed to land, staying for two hours. On three other occasions he tried to go back to the reef but found it impossible until the weather changed when, he was finally able to take measurements and make sketches. One evening, he worked by candlelight until 9pm. Eventually he had a working knowledge of every inch of the Reef.

Back in Plymouth at a place called Mill Bay, Smeaton started shaping and storing his stones. He directed the making of a modification to the landing area on the rock, and then set out for London to report to his employer Weston. When he arrived Smeaton constructed an exact model of the proposed lighthouse, making adjustments as he went along. When he showed it to Weston and the Lords of the Admiralty, all were completely satisfied. Smeaton again set off for Plymouth, on the way, ordering the Portland stone that would construct the lighthouse. He engaged workmen, hired transport to and from Eddystone, and finally,

bought all the provisions and tools; Josiah Jessup was appointed his first assistant.

The unique process of making the base with dovetail 1756.

On the 31 August 1756, Smeaton began work. Landing again on the rock, he marked out the centre of the lighthouse. Some days, because of the tide, no work could be done. On other days they managed about six hours, cutting a base into the hard rock where the Portland stone would fit. All had to be done quickly by hand-hammer and chisel, before the start of winter. It was hard work but the dovetails had to be completed exactly. These would be vital to the strength of the base. By November they had completed the first phase and returned to Plymouth. It took them four days and many on the shore thought they were lost, as an almighty gale had blown them as far as the Bay of Biscay. It took tremendous courage and seamanship to get back to Plymouth. The rest of the winter was spent at Mill Bay, dressing the rest of the Portland stones to the exact size. Each one weighed upwards of two ton. Over the winter 450 ton of stone was cut to size and fitted into the next, as they would be on Eddystone. Finally, each stone was numbered, ready for transportation to the rock.

On the 12 June 1757 the first stone was laid on the rock. It weighed 2¼ ton. Next day the first course of four stones were laid, taking into account the slope of the reef. The subsequent courses allowed for this, the second course having 13 stones while the third had 25 and so on. Eventually a perfect, circular course was completed containing 61 stones. Work progressed well because of Smeaton's planning, especially in the stone yard where every stone was first tried in sequence then, within that sequence, transported to the rock, and cemented after fitting within the dovetails. Two holes were bored in each stone and oak tree nails driven to the stone below, nothing being left to chance. After six courses, there was a level platform above the waves.

One day when Smeaton was testing the platform he fell over on to the rocks, painfully dislocating his thumb. He bravely jerked the thumb back into place, there being no medical help, then carried on with the work as if nothing had happened. Nine courses were laid before winter 1757. Before returning to Plymouth a converted boat was left to shine a warning to shipping which more often than not had to seek shelter because of storms. The weather was a good test for the part-finished lighthouse.

It wasn't possible to get to the rock until 12 May 1758. Smeaton and his men found the building had not moved even a fraction of an inch and the cement had set completely. By September, 24 courses were finished, bringing the height to 35 feet. The base being complete they started on the walls of the storeroom and living area which were 26 inches thick. That particular winter was a good one and before retiring they had completed the lower storeroom up to the roof on which they put a temporary cover. The following year, 1759, was very stormy and they did not get to the rock until 5 July. By August, the masonry was finished: there were 46 courses of stones, and the height was 70 feet. The iron work, balcony and lantern came next, ending with the fitting of a gilt ball to crown the whole edifice – which Smeaton fixed himself. He did not leave until everything was complete, including the windows which he fixed himself.

Eddystone Rock lighthouse. On the right: Stump of Smeaton's lighthouse.

On the 16 October 1759, the light shone for the first time and Smeaton breathed a sigh of relief and satisfaction. Inscribed round the upper wall were the following words: 'Except the Lord build the house, they labour in vain that build it'.

Ninety years later, in 1848, the Harbourmaster of Plymouth making an annual inspection of the lighthouse found it had leaned one quarter of an inch towards the northeast. Feeling apprehensive that even a quarter of an inch from the perpendicular was important, he referred to Smeaton's journal of 1759 and found the following entry:

> This day the Eddystone Lighthouse has thank God been completed, it is I believe perfect, except that it inclines a quarter of an inch from the perpendicular to the north east.

Ninety years after Smeaton had completed the lighthouse, it was still standing, as he built it, as a tribute to his skills.

In 1877 it was found that the Reef had been affected by erosion and seawater. Accordingly another tower had to be built 120 feet away which was completed in 1882. Smeaton's tower was taken down stone by stone and re-erected on Plymouth Hoe. The solid stone base still stands on the rock, unaffected by weather and the strong waves of the Channel.

John Smeaton's lighthouse The Hoe, Plymouth.

John Smeaton was awarded the Royal Society's gold medal (the highest award possible) in 1759. He built 40 improved water mills and four windmills in various parts of England, as well as four bridges, three of them in Perth, seven-arch bridges at Coldstream and Banff and one at Hexham in the north of England. The Hexham bridge was reputed to be his only failure, he surveyed and built this in December 1783 and it collapsed. Later in his life he wrote extensively about his work, the main piece being *The Eddystone Lighthouse*. His drawings of the lighthouse are exquisite.

Like most people who put work before health, Smeaton was afflicted with stomach ulcers which may have contributed to his stroke. The stroke was fatal and he died on 28 October 1792, and was buried at the Old Parish Church of Whitkirk. What is certain about John Smeaton is that over the many years that Eddystone Lighthouse stood on the rock, it saved thousands of lives. Now standing on Plymouth Hoe it is a tribute to a great engineer.

Jeremiah Dixon and Charles Mason

1733-1779 & 1730-1787

Jeremiah Dixon was born in the village of Cockfield, near to West Auckland, County Durham, in 1733. His father, George Dixon, was a colliery owner, who, in his own right was a very intelligent and successful man. But it was Jeremiah who was destined to become part of American history as one half of the survey team who laid down the Mason-Dixon line; the dividing line between Maryland and Pennsylvania and the dividing line between North and South in the American Civil War.

Jeremiah was one of two brothers; George was two years older than him and would also make a name for himself but in rather different circles to those of Jeremiah. For a period Jeremiah worked for Chelsea Pottery, painting the finished pieces. Both brothers were self-taught, learning a great deal in the bait cabin at their father's colliery at Cockfield.

Jeremiah was interested from the outset in astronomy, and found great pleasure in using the stars to plot accurate surveys of land and shipping routes. Both brothers attended school at Barnard Castle, the same establishment which Mr John Kipling resided at, as a teacher, a very talented teacher by all accounts. At the school, Jeremiah exceled in astronomy and surveying; while George went on to make his name, not only as a painter of china and engraving, but as a renowned mathematician and mineralogist. George was also heavily involved in the process of dispelling poisonous gasses from mines.

News of Jeremiah's exceptional intelligence quickly came to the notice of William Emerson. Emerson was at the time an acclaimed mathematician and writer. An eccentric who lived at Hurworth near Darlington, Emerson enjoyed drinking in alehouses, especially on market days and was known, at times, to not return home for days. He was also noted for being a peculiar dresser; he would wear a home made shirt back to front, over which he would wear a sleeveless waistcoat fastened at the top, he also wore an old hat which had been in his possession for years. In cold weather he wore shin covers— pieces of sacking tied round his knees. He was also well known for his peculiar sayings. When having a disagreement with anyone he would say without hesitation 'Damn Thee', 'Thou Fule Thou' and the word 'Nincompoops' was in regular use by Emerson! It is reported that one Sunday morning, finding a young boy stealing his apples, he brought an axe and frightened the life out of the boy, keeping him up in the tree for about an hour.

Despite his eccentricities, Emerson produced 13 volumes of

books detailing the various stages of mathematics, such as, 'The Method of Increments', and the 'Doctrine of Fluctuations' and was offered a fellowship by the Royal Society. His reaction was to say 'Damn them and damn their Royal Society too'. Emerson was recognised widely throughout the country, as well as locally, for his genius and the offer of this fellowship was just a small gesture for his contribution to mathematics – of which he eventually went on to accept.

Jeremiah Dixon progressed hugely under the direction of Emerson, not only in mathematics but also in his love of ale! In the Quaker minute book for 28 October 1760, an entry read, 'Jerry Dixon, son of George and Mary Dixon, disowned for drinking to excess'.

During the time he spent with Emerson, Jeremiah met other great men; men like, Thomas Pig, a mathematician from Sunderland, and John Bird engraver and instrument maker, from Bishop Auckland. It was most likely that through men like these, and Emerson himself, Jeremiah was recognised by the Royal Society in his own right, the past presidents of which were people like Christopher Wren, Samuel Pepy's and Isaac Newton.

In 1771, influenced by Emerson and Bird, who were both members at the time, Jeremiah was selected by the Royal Society to go to the island of Sumatra (Indonesia) to plot the transit of the planet Venus. This was the first astronomical expedition of

its kind, backed by the government. This expedition was deemed so important that funds were made readily available from the government treasury, in order to gather the relevant information, in the hope that the findings would measure the precise distance from the earth to the sun. Jeremiah would travel to Sumatra with Charles Mason, assistant observer to the Royal Observatory.

The great Astronomer Royal, Edmund Halley, had previously forecast that the transit of the planet Venus would take place in 1761, so towards the end of 1760 preparations were made for the voyage. The ship commissioned for the task was HMS Sea-Horse. The voyage would be fraught with danger, due to the war between France and England, which had begun in 1756, mainly due to the disputed possession of American Colonies.

Shortly after leaving Plymouth, HMS Sea-Horse was attacked by a French warship, the 34 gun frigate Le-Grande, and badly damaged. Boarded by the captain of the Le-Grande, and quickly recognised as no threat to the French, HMS Sea-Horse was allowed to continue its voyage, with the captain indicating that France was not at war with science. Unfortunately, in the engagement 11 men had been killed and 37 wounded, leaving HMS Sea-Horse so badly crippled it had to return to Plymouth for urgent repairs. This made it impossible to be in Sumatra at the time of the transit. Instead, Jeremiah Dixon and Charles Mason headed for South Africa and the Cape of Good Hope; *HMS Sea-Horse* dropped anchor in Table Bay on the 27 April 1761.

On arrival in South Africa, all of the instruments and equipment were unloaded and the transit was successfully observed on 5 June that same year. During their stay, Dixon and Mason conducted other scientific studies, after which they headed to St. Helena, an island off the south west coast of Africa, where they met with two other astronomers who were also plotting their transit. The astronomers were Robert Waddington and Neville Maskelyne whose observations were unfortunately unsuccessful due to adverse weather conditions.

A portrait of Captain James Cook, RN who visited Jeremiah Dixon at Cockfield.

Mason and Dixon remained in the area of St. Helena collecting data for tidal details and also drawing maps for the Admiralty, after which they set sail for England. On return to the UK in 1762, Mason and Dixon

received £100 each. It is believed that whilst on their expedition, Captain Cook, the great Whitby explorer, had been in their acquaintance although this is still just speculation. However, what is known, is that Cook did study the transit of Venus from Tahiti on 17 June 1769 and that both he and Jeremiah Dixon came from the North of England, and both had similar interests.

After his return to Cockfield in 1763, Jeremiah was requested to go to Kipling Hall, the home of Lord Baltimore whose family had been involved in a long running boundary dispute over possession of land in the developing provinces of America. In 1632 King Charles I had granted to Cecil the then second Lord Baltimore and to his heirs, the province of Maryland. Later, in 1681, a Royal Charter of King Charles II granted the province next to Maryland to William Penn, (Pennsylvania would eventually bear his name). However the Grant of Charter had many indefinite clauses, causing dispute between the two families. This dispute lasted for 100 years; with a long-standing lawsuit in the Chancery Court dragging on way past the demise of the original claimants. Finally on 10 May 1732, an agreement was executed between the heirs of William Penn and the great grandson of Lord Baltimore, and further defined in 1760, to instruct independent surveyors to define a border line between the territories disputed. So it was that Mason and Dixon were appointed to complete this difficult task.

On 15 November 1763, Mason and Dixon arrived in America; it would be some five years before Jeremiah would see Cockfield again. The work for the two men was hard and dangerous; the Native American Indians in the area were known to be hostile. The methods they adopted were partly mathematical and partly astronomical, showing great advances in surveying. In the venture they were assisted by an instrument made by John Bird, Jeremiah's friend from Bishop Auckland, for measuring 'equal altitude'. This instrument helped them to continue a 'right line'. Their work involved forming a straight line, cut accurately through miles of dense forest. The lines laid, measured over 100 miles, although, the path cut through dense forest, actually measured 245 miles.

During their work, Dixon and Mason, along with their party, were subject to Indian attack, the fear of rattlesnakes, especially in the summer months, horse flies, and mosquitoes, along with other bugs, making their task even harder. The actual work was done by chain (a measurement of distance) and checked by statute yard. Stones marked the first 132 miles, each fifth stone having Penn engraved on one side, and the coat of arms of Lord Baltimore on the other side. The line actually cut through measured eight yards wide.

A story recounted from this time, told of how one day, Jeremiah came across a slave-trader fiercely whipping a slave. Jeremiah's upbringing and sense of morality could not condone such treatment and he asked the trader to stop, or he, Jeremiah, would thrash him! The trader retaliated by telling Jeremiah to mind his own business, so, true to his word, Jeremiah went on to thrash the trader, taking away the man's whip in the process. That very whip has been handed down the Dixon family for generations, Jeremiah's sister, Hannah, receiving it first. It is now in the Wilberforce Slavery Museum, Hull.

On 6 June 1768, Dixon and Mason's task came to an end, 245 miles from the Delaware river, taking 1,737 days and costing the houses of Penn and Baltimore £3,500. The Mason-Dixon line was complete; this marked an important event in American History.

Mason-Dixon Line.

Since its completion, some small disputes regarding its accuracy, have occurred, however, later surveys undertaken with modern equipment, have found only a minute miscalculation in the original—John Birds' instrument for measuring 'equal altitude' certainly did its job.

Jeremiah arrived back in Cockfield on 21 January 1769, but on the 8 February 1769 he left again for Norway to observe another transit of Venus for the Royal Society. This was the parting of the ways for Mason and Dixon because Jeremiah would travel with a new companion, Mr William Bayley, and they would successfully observe the transit on the 3 June 1769. This transit would mark Jeremiah's final voyage and he would be destined to spend the rest of his days back in Cockfield, in County Durham. Once there, Jeremiah joined his brother in completing some surveying tasks, and it was said that during this time, he was visited by Captain Cook.

Jeremiah continued to work within his trade, working on the plan of Auckland Castle, for John Egerton, Lord Bishop of Durham; surveying Lanchester Common and working with the entire Mason family to complete a survey for a combined rail and canal coal carrying system.

Jeremiah Dixon died quietly on 22 January 1779 aged 45. He was a bachelor and therefore had no heir to carry on his remarkable work. He was without doubt one of the most ingenious men of his time. It is interesting to note that Captain James Cook died in Hawaii on 14 February 1779, one month after his friend Jeremiah Dixon.

For all the talk of there being no women in Jeremiah's life, in his last will and testament dated 27 December 1779, Jeremiah left premises in Bondgate, Bishop Auckland, to a Margaret Bland, with the profits from the premises going to the maintenance of her two daughters, Mary and Elizabeth until their twenty first birthdays, after which the freehold would be divided equally between them.

Charles Mason returned to America and died there in Philadelphia in 1787.

The Mason-Dixon name became notorious in America and around 1859, a song was compiled, 'Dixieland', by Dan Emmett. During the American Civil War (1861-1865) the Mason-Dixon Line became a dividing line between the North and the South and the song 'Dixie' was well versed by the soldiers marking that line.

Dixieland by Dan D Emmett

I wish I was in the land of cotton,
old times there are not forgotten,
Look away, look away, look away,
Dixie land.
In Dixie land where I was born in,
early on a frosty mornin',
Look away, look away, look away,
Dixie land.

Chorus:
Then I wish I was in Dixie, hooray!
Hooray!
In Dixie land I'll take my stand,
to live and die in Dixie,
Away, away, away down south in
Dixie,
Away, away, away down south in
Dixie.

Old Missus marry Will de Weaber,
Will-yum was a gay deceaber,
Look away, look away, look away,
Dixie land.
But when he put his arm around her,
smiled as fierce as a forty pounder.
Look away, look away, look away,
Dixie land.
(Chorus)

Dars buckwheat cakes an' ingen
batter,
makes you fat or a little fatter,
Look away, look away, look away,
Dixie land.
Den hoe it down and scratch your
grabble
to Dixie's land I'm bound to travel,
Look away, look away, look away
Dixie land.
(Chorus)

William Wilberforce

1759-1833

The Wilberforce family moved to Beverley, in the mid seventeenth-century. William Wilberforce, the great reformers grandfather, was born in 1690. He had a business, which was part of the flourishing Baltic trade and was situated at Kingston upon Hull, a few miles south of Beverley. Hull, the fourth largest port in England was growing rich from the profits of the slave trade, as were. Liverpool and Bristol.

William Wilberforce (grandfather) lived in a magnificent red brick mansion on the High Street overlooking the river Hull, where ships could be seen loading and unloading cargoes of hemp and timber from Riga and St. Petersburg and iron from Sweden. Many Yorkshire products were exported including Sheffield cutlery and even ponies.

In no time at all William was an alderman. He had a vigorous and exciting mind. He owned land in three parishes around Hull. William married Hannah Thornton, whose family were also prosperous Baltic traders.

Robert Wilberforce, William's father, married Elizabeth Bird from London. The Bird family were prominent bankers of the time with premises in London and Hull. William, their third child, and only son of Robert and Elizabeth would ultimately be known throughout the world as the man who freed slaves.

William was born on 24 August 1759, in High Street, Hull. He was blessed with many aunts, uncles and sisters, all financially well off because of the astute business acumen of the family. However, when Robert Wilberforce (William's father) in 1769, died aged 40. William, aged nine, went to live with his aunt and uncle William and Hannah, who had no children and whom he adored, became his guardians.

William's new home was a Wimbledon villa in the lovely Surrey countryside. His second home was a large house at St. James Palace London. William attended boarding school at Putney where he did a little of most subjects, including arithmetic, writing, and reading. He wasn't much impressed with the school and looked forward to his vacations with his aunt and uncle. They took long walks in the Surrey countryside, and during these times they spoilt him. However, his aunt Hannah was afraid that William might be influenced by the Methodist ethos of the school. She was so worried that she took a coach to London removed him from the school and installed him in their grandfather's old school at Pocklington, at the foot of the Wolds, from where on a hill behind the village, York Minster could be clearly seen.

William spent the following five years, from 1771 to 1776 at Pocklington as a boarder. The school, founded in 1514, had links with St. Johns College Cambridge, where William became an undergraduate at the age of 17. At Cambridge, studying came second place to playing cards and other pursuits. William loved entertaining and his unlimited funds allowed him to do this with ease. He enjoyed singing, listening to good conversation, and listening to instrumental music. Later William regretted not being made to buckle down with his studies. It took all of his quick intellect and talent, coupled with his magnificent memory, to get him through his examinations. But while he might have passed with honours, he barely scraped through.

Wilberforce home.

William's uncle died in 1777 leaving the young William very rich indeed. It was inevitable that he would enter politics, and this he did, in the spring of 1780. Wilberforce stood as MP for Hull and the results went extraordinarily in his favour; he polled twice as many votes as the other two candidates put together.

At this time, William became acquainted with some people from the Lake District, one being the uncle of the poet William Wordsworth, another, the brother of Fletcher Christian who led the mutiny against Bligh in the South Seas. William never tired of the Lake District and called it 'England's paradise'. He regularly boated on Lake Windermere, walked the fells, and had a seven year tenancy on a small Manor House called Rayrigg, situated right on the lakeside. The Lakes brought William his greatest friendship, Colonel John Pennington, 30 years his senior and heir to the Muncaster estate in Eskdale.

June 1780 was the time of the anti-Catholic Gordon riots, when mobs burned down a new catholic church at Posterngate, Hull. In the same year there was some movement on anti-slavery when David Hartley put forward a motion in parliament which would lay the foundation for the extirpation of slavery in England. The general feeling in England at the time was that slavery was an unpleasant but necessary trade. Hartley was an eccentric who wore peculiar clothes, did not powder his hair, and secured his glasses by a band on the top of his head. In appearance, he was in direct contrast to William, who also had weak eyes but, dressed strictly to the fashion of the day using an eyeglass hung by a ribbon. Hartley's speeches were said to be long and dreary but he never missed a point. Hartley was the inspiration for Wilberforce's lifetime campaign against slavery; he contacted a friend, who at the time was in the West Indies, asking him to send him details of this formidable trade.

On 31 October, 1780, William took his seat in St. Stephen's Chapel, on the opposition back benches, behind the speaker's chair. Pitt, who was to become a close friend of Wilberforce's, had entered the House in January. Pitt's maiden speech was acclaimed by the whole House. Wilberforce's first recorded speech was made on 17 May 1781, during the committee stage of a Bill for preventing smuggling. He had presented a petition from Hull and spoke against spirits being confiscated from a ship carrying more than the permitted amount.

William Pitt the younger; great friend of Wilberforce and then Prime Minister.

During the recess in 1784, peace had been negotiated with France. Britain had been having sea victories and it looked as though France was surrendering. Wilberforce was invited by Pitt to second the address to the Crown to ratify the treaty.

During this period, King George III, offered the premiership to Pitt, who at 23 was already Chancellor of the Exchequer, but he declined. Pitt resigned his post, allowing the Fox/North coalition of Lord North and Charles James Fox to succeed, and for a time Pitt was free of responsibility. Wilberforce could not match Pitt's lucidity and debating skill, but he ranged his eloquence at Pitt's side. When the India Bill was thrown out by the House of Lords on the direct intervention of the King, Pitt was sent for. The next day, 18 December, the King dismissed the coalition and Pitt became Prime Minister in a hostile Commons at the age of 24.

William Wilberforce was then living in Scarborough, but moved to Nottingham in 1786 and stayed with his cousin Samuel Smith. Here Wilberforce decided to educate himself further and read history, economics, literature, and philosophy. The bible became his favourite book and he learned passages by heart. He had a charming inability to live up to rigid standards and his failings kept him human. It was at this time that William became familiar with an essay entitled, *Essay on the Treatment and Conversion of African Slaves in the British Colonies* by the Reverend James Ramsey, a well known campaigner and anti-slavery writer. His essay tackled the treatment of slaves in the British Colonies and proposed steps of total emancipation, declaring that free labour would yield more profit for plantation owners. Wilberforce was fully committed to an assault on the slave trade, believing that nothing but the complete abolition of this horrifying commerce would do. Thirty years later he explained how he had felt in a letter to Joseph

Gurney, the leading Quaker campaigner for the abolition of slavery. The immediate aim, he told Gurney, was to stop the supply of the slaves; this would force the planters to improve the treatment of their current slaves. Wilberforce hoped abolition might come swiftly and by international agreement. He asked William Eden, whom Pitt had sent to Paris, to negotiate an advantageous commercial treaty with France, to sound out the French on the subject of slaves. Wilberforce told Eden that the annual export from the west coast of Africa, by all nations, exceeded 100,000, only small numbers of whom were criminals or prisoners of war. Wilberforce further informed him that the reception of the slaves in the West Indies was no less than barbaric.

Wilberforce continued gathering evidence. He did, however, realise just what he was up against. Slaving had been a way of life for many powerful traders, who would stop at nothing to carry on with this uncouth business. It had been their source of wealth for centuries. The date for Wilberforce's motion was early February 1788. Unfortunately, on, 19 February William was overcome by sheer exhaustion, fever and loss of appetite; and confined himself to bed. Pitt urged William to get a little country air at Clapham, where he had a room. He returned the following day a little better and his doctor told him to take the waters at Bath. However, before setting out he had a complete relapse. Lord Muncaster and Matthew Montague took on the job of nursemaids. Doctor Richard Warren who treated

the Prince of Wales and later would make more money than any other physician in the country, was also called to aid him. Warren said of Wilberforce, 'That little fellow with his calico gut, cannot possibly survive 12 months'. However, William finally got over the crisis by taking the eighteenth-century cure-all, opium. Bob Smith (Lord Carrington) commented later that his health was restored by that what should have destroyed him. Pitt postponed the debate on the Bill until Wilberforce had gathered further strength.

William Wilberforce.

In 1789, the Bill was eventually debated and William gave a three-and-a-half-hour speech. The speech was free from rhetoric or bitterness. He was easy on the slave owners saying they did not mean to be cruel; he dealt with the arguments of opposition efficiently. He then proposed his 12 resolutions. Pitt said later that this was an error of judgment, having brought the house to a pitch. Lord Penrhyn accused Wilberforce of misrepresentation and Alderman Nathaniel Newnham (a former Lord Mayor of London who had extensive sugar refineries) forecast the ruin of the city if the Bill was passed.

Most of the House was still uneasy, obviously swayed by Wilberforce's facts, put forward so shrewdly, and yet worried in case it would cause economic disaster. The House formed a committee and heard more evidence over nine days that summer, and then adjourned until the next session. On 23 June 1789, the commencement of the new session, William's opponents tried everything they could to stop him— even requesting the House not to allow him to move the Bill, because of the time taken up by cross-questioning witnesses. Wilberforce ingeniously outflanked his opponents by having these witnesses cross-questioned by a select committee upstairs, exposing anomalies and fraud. Eventually, the transcripts numbered 10,000 folio pages (all apparently burned in the fire of 1834). The next year, 1790, Pitt decided to go to the country a year before he needed to and declared an election. William Wilberforce would soon find out if his causes outside Yorkshire had cost him his seat. In the recess, Wilberforce carried out his constituency duties as a good MP.

The General Election was held in June 1790. Wilberforce was returned without the expense of a poll. At about this time he also had a bad carriage accident at Bridlington, which seems to have affected his nerves later in life. He hoped to be able to resume the select committee at once. As it was, the select committee delayed its hearing until February 1791. There was also news of an abortive slave rebellion in the West Indies, where 'Massa King Wilberforce', said they should work only a three-day week for full pay. Wilberforce, again very much up against it was encouraged by the words of John Wesley:

> God has raised you up for this very thing, you will be worn out by the opposition of men and Devils …But if God be for you, who can be against you?

John Wesley.

William greatly admired the Wesleys and had met both John and Charles. When Charles Wesley's widow and unmarried daughter were in reduced circumstances, he and two friends provided an annuity for Mrs Wesley, which shamed the Methodist movement into raising another.

At last the day of the debate came; on Wednesday 18 April 1791 the Abolition of Slavery Bill had its second reading. On Thursday 19 April, Sir William Young said that abolition would lead to the loss of the colonies. He agreed that it must come, but feared that other nations would seize England's share. Matthew Montague uttered a burst of rhetoric in Wilberforce's favour asking 'Is that any reason why we all should be guilty of murder?' Late in the debate Pitt spoke emphasising the injustice, with Charles James Fox making a brilliant speech saying that if the house voted no, it would give parliamentary sanction to 'rapine, robbery and murder'.

The debate continued; on the morning of 20 April, Wilberforce made a brief and short reply to the debate. The House was divided. Only approximately 50% of the members were present to vote; Sir William Dolben, who, as Chairman could not vote, sadly recorded on his manuscript the figures: 'Nos 163, Ayes 88; majority against abolition 75'. In the following year, 1792, an amendment to the Bill by Henry Dundas was passed. Slavery was to be abolished, but only gradually, over a period of seven years.

In 1793 England went to war with France. Wilberforce was not a pacifist; he once refused to join a pacifist movement, saying that the scriptures allowed defensive wars. Wilberforce hated the war for many reasons but mainly because it would slow down his Slavery Bill. During the 1790s, Wilberforce re-introduced his original Bill every year.

Mr and Mrs Wilberforce 1797.

On 15 April 1797, Wilberforce met and fell in love with Barbara Spooner, the lively but serious-minded daughter of Isaac Spooner, an iron-master and banker of Elmdon Hall, Birmingham. Despite troubles in the navy (this was the period of mutinies at the Nore and at Spithead over the appalling conditions for the sailors) Wilberforce could not get the pretty, good-humoured Barbara out of his mind. It affected his eating and sleeping, so much so that he threw caution to the wind and wrote to Barbara and her family requesting her hand in marriage. The marriage of William and Barbara took place on Tuesday morning 30 May 1797. It was a quiet wedding at the parish church of Walcott, Bath, the bridegroom being 38 years old and the bride 20 years old.

Wilberforce bought Broomfield, a house with a long avenue of young trees, situated a mile and a half from Battersea Footbridge. Barbara had difficulties with the birth of their first child, William, who was born 21 July 1798. Wilberforce was a doting father who approved his wife's determination to breast-feed her babies which at the time was particularly unfashionable amongst the upper-classes. Two years later Barbara became ill with typhoid fever while carrying their next child, but survived the ordeal, as did the baby, a daughter whom they named Elizabeth. Barbara bore three more children over the next seven years but it was said that she never really recovered from the effects of the typhoid.

Meanwhile, Pitt attempted to end the war with France but was unsuccessful. Wilberforce, from then on, supported the war wholeheartedly. Britain fought for its very existence, as France broke off the second round of secret peace talks in 1797. They also smashed all the continental allies and Britain stood alone against the brilliant military mind of the all-conquering Napoleon Bonaparte. There was the great worry of an invasion by the French—there had already been incursions into Ireland and an attempt to land in Wales.

These were the years of great generals and admirals, in particular the Duke of Wellington and Lord Nelson. Nelson's sea victories at St. Vincent and the Nile had effectively damaged the French fleet. 1804-1805 was also the time that Captain Bligh returned to the South Seas after the mutiny on the *Bounty*. Wilberforce, who was an ardent evangelical, helped Admiral Middleton secure passages for two missionaries to Tahiti, but they withdrew before the ship sailed. The Missionary Society attempted to get Wilberforce to be president of their organisation but he declined. It was a known fact that Wilberforce, up to

the time of his marriage, gave half of his income to worthy charities and good causes.

Wilberforce thought that the autumn of 1805 would see the climax of the sea war and he was proved right. In the early hours of a November morning in 1805 word was received that Britain had gained a complete victory at Trafalgar, but Lord Nelson was dead. Britain was now in complete control of the seas. The successful naval campaign would have a profound effect on the slave trade and abolition. In January 1806, Pitt died, believed to be mostly of a broken heart from the loss of Lord Nelson. With the death of Pitt, Wilberforce lost a dear and great friend who had stood by him in his fight for abolition. Wilberforce attempted to pay off Pitt's debts by private subscription in order to avoid the controversy of public subscription. Pitt's funeral service was held at Westminster Abbey. John Charles Villiers, the Earl of Clarendon, carried the crest of Pitt with Wilberforce in support.

Wilberforce thought long and hard after the death of Pitt, mainly about the final stages of the Abolition Bill. He was reassured when Lord Grenville was elected Prime Minister and Charles James Fox became Foreign Secretary. The Bill was passed from the Commons to the Lords, Fox and Grenville backing it all the way. Then Fox became seriously ill with dropsy. Wilberforce looked back on the years he had attended parliament with Fox, his arguments for and against issues and how he had stood staunchly behind the Abolition Bill.

He worried that if Fox died the Bill might not be completed even in 1807.

Wilberforce decided to leave his troubles behind him and in the autumn of 1804, set off to Lyme Regis, where Barbara loved swimming in the sea and where he could be with his children. He had much correspondence to answer and was also working on a book about abolition Grenville and Fox now decided to have a General Election, the date was set for October 1807. There was a danger that Wilberforce might lose his seat, as Walter Fawkes of Farnley would stand in opposition against him. He was worried about the final stages of the Bill.

Wilberforce hurried to Yorkshire giving speeches as he went. He need not have worried; the local people carried him shoulder-high to the meeting rooms and it was obvious that they admired him as much as always, and even more so on becoming aware that his campaign for the freedom of the slaves was reaching its conclusion. At Sheffield and Leeds the crowds were also very enthusiastic. Wilberforce was elected easily, but Fawkes was preferred to Lascelles.

After the election Wilberforce returned his focus to his book, which had taken no less than six years to complete. The new Prime Minister, Grenville, had said in the Commons that Wilberforce's Bill must be backed in total but not a penny of Treasury money must be used. Subscriptions came from everywhere; the Methodists and Church of England, Evangelicals, several peers and

magnates, all were in support, saying that Wilberforce was a true independent. There was no shortage of funds to get rid of this ghastly trade. In September 1807, Charles James Fox died just prior to the election after serving over 40 years in Parliament. His successor did well in the election to follow.

In February 1808, Lord Grenville moved the second reading of the Bill with a glorious speech and the House sat all night. The Duke of Clarence defended the trade as did Lord Eldon. Admiral, the Earl of St. Vincent, said that Grenville must have been charmed into backing the Bill by a witch doctor and that he was not aware of the damage he was doing. The peers divided themselves at 5am. The vote was 100 to 36, a majority of 64 in favour of the Bill. Next evening the committee stage was passed swiftly. The Bishops of Durham and London shook Wilberforce's hand warmly, as did the majority of other peers. Most speeches supported the Bill wholeheartedly. As one member sat down, six or even eight were on their feet. The House rose, turning towards Wilberforce, cheering; Wilberforce sat with a bowed head, tears streaming down his face. Then he replied briefly to the debate.

Young Earl Percy, the heir to the Duke of Northumberland, proposed that slavery should be immediately abolished; the House sensed a red herring and called loudly 'Question'. Percy sat down and the House divided: Ayes 283, Nos 16, The majority in favour of the abolition of slavery was an amazing 267. 'What's next?' Wilberforce laughingly asked Thornton 'The Lottery?'

The Abolition Bill came up for its third reading on 16 March 1808 and passed unopposed. On the morning of 23 March, Wilberforce was informed that a clerical error had been found in one of the amendments to be laid before the Lords that afternoon. The Lords had to correct it before it could be debated in the Commons. The procedure was agreed in the Lords, despite protests from Westmorland, and the following day the amendment was agreed. Grenville had already received the Royal assent for the Bill as well as two minor ones. They were actually the last acts of his administration. On Wednesday 25 March 1808, the Bill for the Abolition of Slavery had become law. The problem now would be to enforce it.

Lord Robert Stewart Castlereagh, colonial secretary, at last produced a treaty with Spain in September 1817, immediately abolishing the slave trade north of a line, and within three years to the south of that line. The Spanish treaty allowed British cruisers to search suspected vessels for slaves and if there were slaves on board, the ship could be seized. 10,000 slaves were freed, most being rescued from holds of ships. Most were now experiencing the civil rights of a British Colony. *HMS Derwent* brought 167 slaves into Sierra Leone from a seized cargo ship, conforming to the Abolition Act and providing the prize money, which the navy traditionally received from every capture, be it a 100-gun man-of-war or a slave ship.

In 1818, Wilberforce turned his attention to his family and decided to take them on a long promised holiday to the Lake District. Wilberforce had the poet Robert Southey looking for houses in Keswick, but he changed his mind and sought out Dorothy and William Wordsworth instead, who found two small houses at Rydal near Ambleside. The full party to the Lake District numbered 19 plus the horses and including servants. Wilberforce was still travelling with his two youngest children. As his carriage arrived there was an emotional meeting; Dorothy had not seen William for 25 years and his body had aged somewhat, but he was still stronger than he looked. He was able to walk up Skiddaw, getting wet in the process. The older boys walked a great deal in the fells.

His sons, Robert and Samuel returned to school after their holiday, and William junior returned to Trinity College, Cambridge for his second year. Unfortunately, he was not studying seriously and had, unknown to his father, purchased a second horse at a high price, when his father was trying to cut expenses. He allowed other undergraduates to take advantage of his weaknesses. He was also telling lies and had been drunk at home when Blundell, Wilberforce's great friend lay dead in the next room. Eventually, William was suspended from Trinity much to his father's disappointment. His horse was confiscated and his father prevented him from returning home; an action which almost broke his father's heart. However young William took it well and his love grew for his father. He did not return to Trinity but read at the Bar in the care of John Owen, the secretary of the Bible Society. The following year, on the 13 August 1822, William married Owens' daughter, Mary.

During the years 1823-24, Wilberforce suffered from colds and flu in the chest and his old bowel problem returned. However, three schemes still drew his attention: the creation of a National Gallery; the establishment of the Trustee Savings Bank, and an act against cruelty to animals. He remarked, after hearing the Abolition Bill had passed its final stage on 26 July 1833, that he had lived to witness the day that England had given twenty-million-pounds-sterling for the abolition of slavery. On the following Saturday he suddenly grew tired. On Sunday he fainted and deteriorated rapidly and at 3am Monday 29 July 1833, William passed quietly away.

On Saturday 3 August, thousands of Londoners wore mourning. Wilberforce's coffin entered Westminster Abbey. Two royal dukes, the Lord Chancellor, the Speaker and four Peers supported the pall. Members of both houses walked in the procession. Apart from the choir it was a very plain funeral but exceptionally well attended.

according to his great friend, Reverend James Raine, who was with him at the time.

Bishop Middleham Church.

Robert Surtees

1779-1834

Robert Surtees's most notable achievement was to furnish historians with his outstanding *The History and Antiquities of the County Palatine of Durham*. Robert was born, in the parish of St. Mary le Bow, in the South Bailey of Durham on 1 April 1779; two children had already died in infancy during the 18 years of his parents' marriage. His baptism was registered in St. Mary's the following day and also recorded in the family church at Bishop Middleham. Robert spent his childhood at his parent's hereditary seat at Mainsforth Hall, in the county of Durham. His early memories, which he delighted in talking about, were of happy days spent fishing in Cornforth Beck.

In May 1786, at the age of seven Robert was sent to school at Houghton-le-Spring not far from home. At the time the Reverend William Fleming of Queen's College, Oxford, was a teacher there. Later Robert would acknowledge him as deserving 'a grateful tribute of respect' and on coming upon a monument to his old master in Hexham, he was very moved, speaking of him affectionately,

Robert's first two years at school were spent almost solely studying Latin. He did not start arithmetic until 1788, when he also began Greek. He had an extraordinary memory which stood him in good stead, especially with Latin verse. He also studied general antiquities and the topographical history of his county, even then carefully preserving any documents that came his way. From an early age Surtees also had a great love of old coins particularly Roman ones and travelled to Sunderland and Durham in search of them. When Robert was only eleven years old he was already preparing data for a history of Durham; checking on the ownership of properties, family histories and ancient verse. During his school years, his closet friends were Ralph and William Robinson of Herrington. Robert spent much of his holidays with the Robinson family and would eventually marry their sister, Annie.

Robert left Houghton School in 1793 and was placed under the care of Doctor Bristow of Neasden, near London, who prepared young men for University. It was here that he met Reginald Heber, the Bishop of Calcutta, Sir Wastell Brisco of Crofton Hall, Cumberland and the sons of the Earl of Manvers.

On 20 October 1796, after his time with Doctor Bristow, Robert entered Christchurch College, Oxford as a commoner. A fellow undergraduate was William Ward Jackson of Normanby, Yorkshire. Surtees' tutor was the Reverend M. Marsh, Canon of Salisbury.

During his time at Oxford Surtees was very studious; he read the classics avidly. Besides the college lectures on mathematics, logic and rhetoric, he also attended those of the University in anatomy and natural philosophy. Although his course of study was accomplished with some absences due to his parents' illness, as well as his own, he still exerted himself in the composition of what were called 'Lent Verses'. This was an annual exercise at Christchurch on subjects chosen by the writer. Each Latin verse had to be between 12 and 20 lines long. Six verses were usually expected from the entrants and were subjected to the scrutiny of a censor as to their suitability for a public reading. Surtees produced six verses of which four received the distinction of being publicly read – a great achievement.

Unfortunately, in the spring of 1796 Surtees was called from Oxford as his mother had an alarming illness. She sadly died in her sixty-first year, on 10 March 1797 and was buried close by her home, at Bishop Middleham church.

Surtees and his friend Reginald Heber took degrees in Bachelor of Arts in 1800 and Master of Arts in 1803 and both became members of the Middle Temple. Surtees enjoyed the advantages of good meals with a bottle of 'good old Domus Wine' that this provided. But his time at Middle Temple was sadly curtailed by his father's death on 14 July 1803. His father was buried at Bishop Middleham beside his mother.

Mainsforth Hall, seat of the Surtees family.

Aged 24, Surtees became established at the family home, Mainsforth Hall, where he embarked properly on his life's work. The manner in which Robert Surtees wrote his *History of Durham* was amazing. He never sat down to write but wandered about his garden deep in thought, then returned to his library and hastily wrote down his findings. His mind filled rapidly and his pen could not record his thoughts quickly enough, so his writing was legible to him alone. When he sent a copy to the press, he generally pinned together and numbered the paragraphs but the compositor still had problems deciphering his writing and Surtees was often amused by his efforts. However, with his photographic memory, correction was not difficult.

In 1802 correspondence started between Robert Surtees and the celebrated Walter Scott, Surtees instigating contact because he thought the information in his possession would be useful to the new edition of Scott's *The Minstrelsy of the Scottish Border*.

Through the exchange of letters, Surtees sent Scott information including border ballads, border history and traditions. One particular letter he sent in 1806 starts by quoting a border ballad referring to the feud between the Ridleys and Featherstones, as recited by an old woman from Alston Moor. Surtees accompanied it with explanations and historical notes. Scott was so delighted with the contribution to his collection and satisfied as to its authenticity that he included it in the twelfth note to the first canto of *Marmion* (1808) as furnished by his 'friend and correspondent, Robert Surtees Esq. of Mainsforth'.

Yet, it was all a figment of Surtees's imagination, originating in a desire to find out how far he could identify himself with the stirring times, scenes and poetical compositions, which his fancy delighted to dwell on, and which ultimately, fooled the great Walter Scott. The ballad of *The Death of Featherstone Haugh* still retains its place in *Marmion*, including expressions of obligation to Mr Surtees and commendation of its authenticity.

Surtees and Scott corresponded frequently. In one letter dated 8 December 1806 Surtees discussed the loyalty and spirit of the border clans. Scott's reply, 17 December 1806, describes his own family involvement in border feuds:

You flatter me very much by pointing out to my attention the feuds of 1715-1745; the truth is that the subject has often and deeply interested me from my earliest youth. My great grandfather was out, as the phase goes, in Dundee's wars and in 1715 had nearly the honour to be hanged for his pains, had it not been for the interest of Duchess Ann of Buccleuch and Monmouth, to whom I have attempted, [post lorigo interivallo] to pay a debt of gratitude. But besides this my father, although a borderer, transacted business for many Highland Lairds, and particularly for one old man, called Stuart of Invernahyle, who had been out in both 1715-1748 and who's tales were the absolute delight of my childhood. I became a valiant Jackobite at that age, and I have never quite got rid of the impression, which the 'gallantry' of Prince Charles made of my imagination, and I will preserve these stories.

Surtees was now extremely busy with his *History*. Alone in the mornings, he spent time in the woods or riding through the green lanes or at his favourite Lough bank, beautifully covered with every shade of columbine from seed scattered by him when he was a boy. He had pleasure raising flowers on a garden wall and passers-by would often see the squire mounted on a short ladder weeding the rough grass from wild pinks and stonecrop.

Literary friends made excursions to Surtees at Mainsforth with information for his research. His company was very interesting. As well as being an antiquarian, he was also a great admirer of nature. His thoughts were often on the 'Rising of the North' (1635). He frequently said that many Durham families had suffered severely because of the rebellion, especially at the cruel hands of George Bowes, the Knight Marshal. According to Surtees, Bowes was equal in cruelty to any Duke of Alva that ever existed. Surtees was interested in the part played by the Bowes family in English and Scottish history and sought information from Lord Strathmore of Streatlam Castle.

In 1803 Surtees made a tour to Scotland with his Oxford friend, Sir Wastell Brisco of Crofton Hall, Cumberland. The route taken by them was recorded by Surtees as follows:

> Auckland, Wolsingham, Hexham; Rothbury, Alnwick; Chillingham; Wark; Kelso; Dryburgh; Melrose; Dalkieth; Edinburgh; Perth, Dundee; Glamis, Dunkeld, Blair Athol, Loch Lomond; Glasgow and Lanark, returning through Cumberland and Westmorland, Greta Bridge, and Richmond.

Examples of the kind of observations recorded by Surtees on this trip include the following:

Chillingham Castle: The castle unspoilt by the hand of modern elegance, the residence of the martial family of Grey, guardians of the borders.

Rothbury: Resorted to during the summer and autumn months by invalids for the goat's milk and pure air.

Thumb: A remarkable Waterfall and a walk by the Coquet mollifies the heart of many a Barbara Allen. (This was a very old love song *For the Love of Barbara Allen.* The author of which apparently had to impress his love.)

In a letter dated 4 March 1809, from Edinburgh, Walter Scott wrote to Robert Surtees arranging to call on him:

> I am going to London and if perfectly convenient for you and Mrs Surtees, I am desirous to pass a day at Mainsforth upon our road. I say our, because I believe Mrs Scott will be my fellow traveller.

Robert Surtees replied on 15 March:

Mainsforth

Dear Sir,

We shall be happy to see Mrs Scott and yourself, here for as long as you can spare us. If you come by the High North Road, you need not push on to Rushyford for us, but may reach us in one 9 mile stage from Durham. I believe most of the drivers know the road; you keep the turnpike to Ferryhill and then, are only 2 miles from Mainsforth. If you will inquire at Sam Beardsley's Coach and Horses at Ferryhill on the bank by the roadside, he will take care that there shall be a key lodged for your use of a private road, which is both shorter and better than the public one. If the driver does not know it, anyone will direct you; or if I know your time I would send a person to wait for you.

In the summer of 1819 Surtees and Mr Raine had to make a visit to Scotland, visiting Abbotsford going by way of Coldingham. In Edinburgh Surtees was especially interested in Grey Friars church yard and the chilly tombs of the martyred covenanters. He visited the church yard often, exploring their history. Surtees met the celebrated Scottish poet James Hogg for the first time when he and Raine stayed at the Walkers Hotel in Princes Street; here Hogg visited them regularly. Surtees and Hogg walked hand in hand, as was the custom at the time, deep in conversation about Scottish history and legend. Surtees contacted his friend Walter (Sir Walter Scott) requesting a flying visit to his house at Abbotsford. Scott replied that he would be glad to see him, adding that he had recently been ill, but saying he was better now and was 'using Calomel for prevention sake'.

On meeting, Surtees and Scott were like two brothers and immersed immediately in deep conversation about Border history and Border ballads. On the road to Edinburgh, Surtees had noted a newly published book '*Wolf's Crag*'. Up to that point authorship was secret but Surtees was aware that Scott was the author. The two conducted deep conversations on Douglas and Percy, and the chivalry of old. The flashes of genius from the two men were amazing. Scott listened to Surtees with profound attention and according to Raine, Surtees was at his very best.

Sir Walter Scott.

In 1816 the first volume of *The History and Antiquities of the County Palatine of Durham* appeared. The second and third being published in 1823 and 1829. On publication and at his own expense, Surtees distributed 13 of the large paper copies and seven of the smaller as presents—all of which were greatly appreciated. A copy of the first volume was sent to John Goodchild of Bishop Wearmouth, who had been a senior partner in a bank that had failed. He replied to Surtees as follows:

My Dear Sir,

I hardly know how to express my feelings on seeing the very handsome present made me of your *History of Durham*. Since my misfortunes, I had given up every idea of being in possession of so valuable a work; think then what my feelings must have been on finding it presented to me by you. I shall ever hold it in high estimation; not only as to its real value, but as a proof of your feelings towards me. I was in high hopes I might have seen you at Durham this last week, and could I have spared time, I would of walked to Mainsforth, and paid my compliments, I beg my best wishes and respects to Mrs Surtees; and wishing you every happiness.

I am dear sir, your much obliged and very faithful servant.

John Goodchild

The fourth volume, although well advanced, was not completed at the time of Surtees's death. There was a mass of materials but not in order and it was hoped that it would not remain unfinished. Parts of the Darlington area had remained unexplored by Surtees, although much documentation and oral information had been collected. Happily, the Reverend James Raine, who for years had been a friend and valued contributor to *The History* (in fact responsible for the whole design) was able to complete the fourth volume in 1840 albeit in an imperfect state. Raine laboured without remuneration and suffered great financial loss to complete the work.

As he got older, Surtees did not stray too far away without his beloved wife Annie. On one occasion, leaving Mrs Surtees at home, he returned quickly recording, 'I got home without rain, and my spirits recovered wonderfully as soon as I saw Lough-Bank wood; I found all well and invited myself to dine on a roast chicken; a red herring; and a moderate glass of old Madeira. It is nice to see green fields again; Red Beech and Brown Oaks'. When on an excursion to York where he had fatigued himself on documentary researches he writes to Mrs Surtees, 'I will promise you not to tire myself again, and to rest like a decent Christian on Sunday. I rest in hope to see you soon, which I most earnestly long and desire. I am at times very home-sick'.

Surtees was kindness itself to animals. He never sold his old horses, taking off their shoes and letting them loose in a good pasture and allowing them to die in peace. One summer evening while out walking at Mainsforth, he saw an old pony in great distress. He had the animal taken to a stable, but it got steadily worse and its body began to swell. The Reverend Raine observed, 'If that was my pony I would do it an act of kindness and shoot it'. 'Would you?' asked Surtees, 'Then it will be done'. The pony was at peace within five minutes but Surtees would not act on his own in cases such as this. He once kept a number of sheep but had to give them up as he got attached to the sheep and hated taking their lives. His love for dogs was extraordinary. At breakfast he was always surrounded by his pointers and greyhounds and dogs came from near and far to be fed. When he lost a dog he felt it tremendously; this is evident in his writings on the death of his dog Carlo:

Beneath no high Historic stone,
Tho nobly born, is Carlo laid,
His couch the grass-green turf alone,
And o'er him waves the walnut shade.

Within this still, sequestered garth,
Henceforth shall be his lowly cell;
No more to see the blazing hearth,
No more to range the woodland dell.

Dear, lost companion! Memory oft
Shall bring old Carlo to my view,
And paint, in colours dim and soft,
The lov'd the lost, the kind, the true!

Green Erin gave him gentle birth;
O'er lilied France in youth he strayed
Four summers suns; in English earth
He sleeps, beneath the walnut shade.

Robert Surtees had never had good health. By 1834 it was failing in earnest. After a visit to his mother-in-law and great friend, Mrs Robinson, at Hendon, Sunderland – having ridden from Durham to Ferryhill on the outside of a coach – he appeared to have contracted a cold. Later in the week he complained of a pain in his side. The family surgeon was sent for and administered medicine and leeches. Unfortunately inflammation of the chest rapidly advanced and Doctor Brown of Sunderland was called but gave no further medication. Surtees visited his library with his wife saying to her, 'Annie, I shall never be here again, these books will be yours'. She replied, 'So they may be Surtees, and I would never like to part with them, but don't you think it would be well to send your manuscripts to some public Library, where they would be of some use?' He agreed with his wife, saying that he would make a selection in a day or two. Shortly after he was laid up in his sick bed – a bright sun shining in reminded him of his favourite time of the year and he said, 'I shall never more see the peach-blossoms, or the flowers of spring. It's hard to die in spring', and recalled his favourite lines of Layden:

But sad is he that dies in spring,
When flowers begin to blow,
and larks to sing,
and makes it doubly hard with life to part.

It had been Surtees' morning custom to watch the blossoms as they came out, and the first was usually laid on the table where he breakfasted with friends. God had placed him in paradise where he had everything to make him happy. As death neared he met it with composure, gratitude, and resignation. His mind had always been happy in never feeling a shadow of doubt about the truth of Revelation and he felt, in the hour of trial, the blessedness of that faith which through life he had possessed; nor had his faith been a mere general acquiescence. He was a faithful attendant at public worship and family prayer. Seldom had a day passed without his little green testament being in use.

At about 2am on the morning of 7 Friday February 1834 he said to Mrs Surtees:

Annie, I am very ill. I should have liked to receive the Sacrament, but I am too ill now to send for anyone, but I give it to myself. Don't make yourself uneasy as to my state. I think as deeply as a man can think. You know I am blessed in the power of memory and use it in repeating things to myself, Poor Bradley; he won't like to dig my grave – he knows where I wish to be buried. I pity your mother most, she is an old woman, and has had many sorrows; and she has loved me as I have loved her. I have left you for your life every sixpence that I possess and I hope the sun will go down brightly shining on your latter days.

On 15 February, four days after his death, Robert Surtees was carried to that grave which 'poor Bradley' had dug deep in the rock that forms the brow of the hill on the south side of Bishop Middleham church yard. He was buried close to his brother-in-law, Marshal Robinson, and Marianne Page, the niece of his wife, who had died at school in Durham. Surtees had held both in great regard and when alive, could often be seen placing flowers on their graves.

In the chancel of Bishop Middleham church a monument was erected, in Roche Abbey stone, the design of which was presented to Mrs Surtees by a Mr Edward Blore, friend and architect. On the marble tablet is the following inscription which in the wordy style of the time sums up the man and his work:

Robert Surtees
Of Mainsforth Esq., M.A. & F.S.A.
The only son of Robert and
Dorothy Surtees,
And the author of the History and
Antiquities of The County Palatine
of Durham,
Was born on the first day of April
1779, and
Died on the eleventh day of
February 1834.
He married Anne, third daughter of
Ralph Robinson, of Herrington
Esq., and by her
This monument is erected to his
memory.
His talents, acquirements, and
character
Are developed in his book; and in
the memoir
Of his life prefixed to it by a
friendly but
Impartial hand. His Christian
Faith,
Principles, and hopes are best
described in
His own memorable Words:

I am very sensible to the hardness
of my heart

And of my totally corrupt nature.
My only hope is in the merits of
Christ, but I
Cannot hope for His grace unless I
strive to
Obtain it. What is our business? To
make our
Election sure – to take heed to our
salvation.
Libra nos, Domine Jesu! Audi nos.

A few fields to the south of Cornforth stands a ruined dovecote, haunted by a brood of wood pigeons. Here a poor girl put herself down for love, because of her traitor lover, and her spirit still hovers round the cote, in the form of a milk white dove. The deceiver drowned himself some years later in the Float beck, and is buried where the four roads meet with a stob driven through his body, thus calling the area Stob Cross.

Stob Cross
by Robert Surtees

*Then might the pitying bard the tale
repeat,
Of hapless village love in ages past;
How the pale maid, the victim of
deceit,
Sunk like the primrose in the
Northern blast.*

*See where the ringdoves haunt yon
ruin'd tower,
Where ivy twines amidst the ashen
spray;
There still she hovers round the lonely
bower,
Where anguish closed her melancholy
day.
A dove she seems distinguished from
the rest,
Three crimson blood-drops stain her
snowy breast.*

George Stephenson
1781-1848

Affectionately known in the Newcastle area as 'Geordie Stevy', George Stephenson was born in Wylam, a very small village on Tyneside in the year 1781. From about seven years of age, his time was spent in the pit working as a trapper boy. For only tuppence a day (trapper boys would sit behind a trap door for about twelve hours, opening and closing it for as long as the men worked at getting coal to the surface). As a trapper boy, he simply couldn't leave the door when coal was being transported; not only would he be in trouble with the boss but he would also get a clip across his ear from the putters!

A portrait of George Stephenson.

Working from such an early age meant that most of Stephenson's youth was spent in total darkness either underground, or on his late return home, where he only spent a short time. However, at the tender age of eight, Geordie got a job on the surface, picking stone out of the coal, this job was known as a 'wailer'. For this task he was rewarded with five shillings a week. He quickly established himself as a steady lad and when a vacancy came up at Callerton Pit in 1801, he was given the job of a gin driver, which was a machine for hauling coal tubs from coal faces to the shafts and from there to the surface. Stephenson was found to be very reliable and conscientious. When a pumping engine was erected at the same pit in 1801, he was given the job as foreman, earning 10 shilling a week. From there he progressed to Killingworth in 1804 as engine-man.

When he was about 20 years of age George Stephenson, a hard working but uneducated young man, proposed to a young lady called Miss Elizabeth Hindmarsh, a local farmer's daughter. Unfortunately she believed herself to be above Geordie's class and he eventually married her servant, Frances Henderson in 1802 on 28 November at Newburn Church. Frances turned out to be a perfect wife, but unfortunately did not live long enough to see their son, Robert Stephenson grow up to be a fine young man.

George Stephenson did happen to meet Miss Hindmarsh again and on this occasion she accepted his proposal of marriage.

In 1804, at Wallbottle pit, a banks-man was needed to stop the drawing engine at the moment the coal was drawn over the top of the shaft; Stephenson got the job at 12 shillings a week. In the same year, he was employed in a similar job at Willington Colliery, working on the Ballast Crane.

George Stephenson did not learn to read until he was 23 years of age, education was rare for miners at the time, and later in his life he always encouraged young men to attend night classes. Whilst working as a banks-man at Killingworth Colliery, he studied whenever he could.

Killingworth Cottage 1804.

Whilst at Killingworth, George Stephenson proved to be a genius with machinery and engines not only on paper but also in practice. He worked all the nightshifts at the colliery, knowing full well that this would give him the time he desired for further education and study. He did his sums on a slate hung at the top of the shaft and he got these corrected by a teacher during the day, who then left him more to complete; he gave the teacher four pence a week for doing this. Stephenson cleaned clocks and watches for a small charge,

as well as making shoes. It was said that he was also a first class tailor; he could turn his hand to anything. Today there is still a sundial, he made, hanging above the door at the house where he lived in Killingworth. He took much pride in this until the day he died. It is believed that, as he and an understudy, in 1836, were about to survey the Newcastle to Berwick railway, they took a detour through Killingworth just to get a look at the sundial, little was Stephenson to know that he would die shortly after that day.

There was something beautiful about Stephenson's character and that was his wish to give his son a sound education. He devoted every penny he could spare to achieve this. At Bruce's school, Newcastle, young Bobby received a good elementary education, after which, his father sent him to Edinburgh University. It is gratifying to know that the successes of Bobby would repay his fathers own self-denial. In fact, unlike his mother George Stephenson would witness the greatness of his son.

George Stephenson's rise to fame was not a smooth path. He was at Killingworth Colliery around 1800, when England was engaged in war and taxes were very high. There was general discontent among the working classes with the coal industry and the coal mining population suffering financially. This was the period of the 'dear years' when even a loaf of bread was found impossible to purchase. Geordie and a fellow worker considered going to America to make a living as farm engineers. What a difference to the mining and railway industry's in England this would have made, had they done so. The Great Western Railway (GWR) might never have materialised, and his son may have finished up as a gold digger! However, Geordie stayed in Tyneside and roughed it through, as did a lot more like him at the time. Indeed, a chance incident while walking to work one morning would influence Stephenson's future engineering skills and his life.

On his way to work at Killingworth High Pit in 1810, Geordie passed a newly sunk pit shaft, from which men were drawing water with pumps but they were very slow. Geordie paused and looked at the weary men and eyed the water pumps and told the men that he could do the work in half the time. He was laughed at but they gave him the opportunity to prove himself and he did, he cleared the water in the shaft in no time at all. This incident made him known not only in Killingworth, but throughout the county and he was called upon to service and mend all of the ailing pumps. As the mines started to work better under his care, in 1812, he was appointed as Engineer at Killingworth, and ultimately became a prosperous man.

In the same year, Stephenson busied himself with installing steam engines underground and fixing those above ground. He laid tramways, mended horse gins, together with boilers, for steam engines. One thing for certain, he could now give up his watch cleaning and shoe making. His son grew into a strapping thriving young man, and everything went well

for him. Killingworth became the centre of his activities, and anyone having a problem with machinery came to Geordie; his influence grew and grew around the North of England.

Richard Trevithick.

Steam became a great industrial power in the country and it did the work that just a short time previously was impossible, not only in mines, but also in locomotives, ships and mills. In 1804, Trevithick's engines were working on the Merthyr-Tydfil railway in South Wales. Stephenson, whilst at Wylam Colliery, in 1812, became familiar with this particular engine and set about inventing a more improved version with money supplied by Thomas Liddle, the then Lord Ravensworth and also the owner of Killingworth Colliery. Stephenson improved the engine by adding a further cylinder, Trevithick's engine having only one. Stephenson's version proved far superior and with help from his backers, was patented. By 1814, he had made many improvements and completed his first locomotive, the *Blucher*. George Stephenson was appointed chief engineer for the Stockton and Darlington Railway and in 1821, was given the job by Edward Pease, of constructing the railways in the North of England.

Plaque, first passenger train.

Stephenson can also lay claim to being the inventor of the safety lamp ironically named Davy's Safety Lamp. It was said that Stephenson had been experimenting with this lamp while at Killingworth, even before Sir Humphrey Davy's discovery was made public in 1816. It was also said that he had made tests on a lamp a long time before Davy and that Stephenson was actually the inventor. In fact in January 1818 he was presented with a silver tankard from the public, together with £1,000, for inventing the Safety Lamp. This presentation was indicated as testimony that he actually was the inventor of the lamp – at least in the eyes of the locals.

Still, the eyes of the world were on the development of the railways and in particular the Liverpool and Manchester Railway. Experienced surveyors of the day knew that whoever undertook the contract would have untold and far reaching problems particularly with the rough terrain at Chat Moss and other areas on the route. The emphasis on the Liverpool and Manchester Railway

was more on passenger transport although haulage would become increasingly important. The development of this railway project would set the pattern for rail transport for the next 100 years.

Liverpool and Manchester Railway.

There was tremendous growth at Liverpool and Manchester over this period: in 1790 Liverpool had a population of 55,000 while Manchester over the same period had 57,000. By 1821 Liverpool had a population of 119,000 while over the same period Manchester had 133,000. Transportation has to be given due consideration.

James Brindley constructed a canal with funding from the Duke of Bridgewater, who made a fortune trading via Liverpool and Manchester; Bridgewater was making an annual profit of £100,000 the canal having cost Brindley £250,000 to build. The idea of a horse drawn railway was considered—William Jessop completed a survey in 1797 but did not get backers.

William James early railway promoter 1823.

Liverpool and Manchester Railway, Chat Moss. (Engraving by I. Shaw)

In the summer of 1821 William James, a leading advocate on railways and critic of canal and river monopolies noticed George Stephenson's work with locomotives and described George Stephenson as the greatest practical genius of the age. In 1822 James was given the job of surveying the Liverpool and Manchester Railway with promoters agreeing to pay him £300 and a further £10 for each mile developed. The Liverpool Railway formed a committee consisting mainly of Cotton manufacturers outraged by the exorbitant rates for haulage, which the Bridgewater Trustees were charging. The committee wrote to James putting pressure on him to finish the survey. Unfortunately, James had a few financial problems of his own to contend with: his brother in law had brought a suit in the Chancery court against him and this went through in 1923. This was the first of many actions that was brought against him, finally leading to bankruptcy. William James went to prison for seven month's during which time he retained his precious survey in the hope that the Liverpool and Manchester Railway would re-employ him.

However, the committee fed up with the delays caused by James's personal problems, sent two representatives north to Killingworth to see George Stephenson and his locomotives. A short time after this visit Edward Pease received a very anxious letter from Mr Sanders regarding Mr Stephenson:

Dear Sir

Tho' am aware you are not in town, I take the liberty of addressing this to you to state that the Liverpool Manchester Rail Road Company have appointed Mr George Stephenson as their Engineer and if he be on your line we request you will send a special Messenger to inform him that a letter has been sent to him at Newcastle advising the same. The Deputation had previously engaged him and that engagement has been confirmed by the subscribers at large.

The expense of the special messenger we shall gladly defray. I beg the messenger be sent immediately to prevent him contracting any other engagement.

I shall feel obliged by any person in your absence acting on this.

I am, dear sir, very truly yours
J. Sanders

To Edward Pease, Esq.
Or to the Clerk of the Railroad office in his absence.

Mr Sanders was desperate to contact George in case he signed up for another appointment, prior to receiving the letter. Later William James would claim that George Stephenson had negotiated with the Railway Company behind his back to acquire the job but the letter proves that to be nonsense. A further letter from Mr Sanders was sent to William James regarding the appointment of George Stephenson.

May 25th 1824

Dear Sir,

I think it right to inform you that the Committee have engaged Your friend Mr G. Stephenson. We expect him here in a few days.

The subscription list for £30,000 is filled, and the Manchester gentlemen have conceded us the entire management. I very much regret that by delay and promise you have forfeited the confidence of the subscribers. I cannot help it. I fear now that you will only have the fame of being connected with the commencement of this undertaking. If you will send me down your plans and estimates I will do everything for you that I can, and I believe I possess as much influence as any person. I am quite certain that the appointment of Stephenson will, under all circumstances, be agreeable to you. I believe you have recommended him yourself. If you consent to put your plans under my control and management your name shall be prominent in the proceedings and this, in such a mighty affair, will be of importance to you. You may rely upon my zeal for you in every point connected with your reputation.

James ignored the advice given by Sanders and hung on to his survey and other evidence for dear life. I personally think that if he had trusted Sanders and put his future firmly under his management everything would have turned out well. Instead, Paul Padley who had been acting in the capacity of second in command to James on the project, was asked to compelte a second survey. When Padley arrived, George Stephenson was already there and busy compiling the survey. James was bitter about the way things had turned out. It was a very shrewd move on behalf of George Stephenson but not underhanded and would seem the only viable outcome in order to progress the survey.

Labourers working on the Liverpool and Manchester Railway 1826.

George Stephenson concluded his survey without any further delay. He was living rough in lodging houses and farm houses, some days going without food and water. Most mornings he awoke at 3.30 am to begin his work. Opposition to his survey came from many sources but mainly from the powerful landowners in the district. Some even using guns to try and frighten Stephenson away. Two of these people were Lord Derby and, Bradshaw, the canal proprietor. They tried everything possible to stop or delay the survey but Stephenson and the promoters stood their ground. In a last effort the canal company reduced their haulage rates by 25% and the Mersey Navigation Company did the same.

May 1824 saw Stephenson's official appointment of engineer/surveyor to the Liverpool Manchester Railway Company and the formal registration of the company, with Henry Booth as its treasurer. At this time all was going well for George Stephenson and this is highlighted in a letter sent by him to Michael Longridge:

Michael Longridge Esq.
Chester, November 16th 1824

Dear Sir,

There are nothing but Railways and rumours of Railways in this Country. I am desired to examine Lord Crew's Coalworks in the neighbourhood of Newcastle under Lyme and give a report thereon. As I can make it convenient to do so. Several other Coal-owners in the neighbourhood desire me to give similar reports. How I shall get all ends to meet I do not know. I think your words will come true. I shall have to work until I am an old man. I have a bag full of news to tell you on the defects of your rails. You have got your friends in the north as well as myself. The Indirect secrets are getting out. It astonishes the deep schemes that men contrive for the over throw of their neighbour: and how often does it fall upon their heads? I assure you I have been twisted backwards and forwards as I think a few poor fellows ever were. Not withstanding all those difficulties my spirits are still up, and I think I have got four times as much as I had when I Inhabited the north. I am sometimes obliged to use my tongue like a scolding wife.

My kind respects to Mrs Longridge and your family: also too Mr and Mrs Berkinshaw: not forgetting my friend Mr Gooch. It is now eleven o'clock and a great deal of work yet to do. I cannot get to bed at your time.

I am Dear Sir,
Yours very sincerely
George Stephenson

Stephenson completed his survey of the Liverpoool and Manchester Railway by 1824 and in 1825 produced an estimate of £400,000 to cover all costs of construction and rolling stock. This was £100,000 more than estimated by James, nevertheless a Parliamentary Bill was applied for, followed by an advertising campaign, resulting in the company getting their quota of investors as required by Parliament.

The opponents of the Bill had hired a total of eight counsel to present their case; the cross examination of George Stephenson was the most important. On Monday 25 April, the Barrister questioning Stephenson found a weakness in his evidence namely the speed of the locomotives. At times George was lost for words and his evidence was discredited as more and more anomalies were discovered (and the Bill was subsequently withdrawn). A further humiliation was to come when the Liverpool and Manchester Company decided to dismiss him as surveyor/engineer. They decided to get someone with more experience to make another survey. George, at this time, thought of his son Robert and longed for his expertise.

The Liverpool and Manchester Company engaged the Rennie brothers George and John; they were two of the best engineers of the time

and the sons of John Rennie, the famous engineer who built the old Waterloo Bridge and the Southwark Bridges in London. They further employed another respected engineer Charles Vignoles and a new survey was started. The Rennies estimate was for £500,000 which was £100,000 more than Stephenson's. This survey was passed by Parliament when Vignoles gave brilliant evidence in favour. The Bill was carried by 40 votes on the 5 May 1826.

The Rennies asked for all kinds of concessions for pushing the project forward: they expected junior engineers to do the job and intended to make six visits a year to monitor progress, they asked for £600 a year and would accept no less an engineer than Thomas Telford himself as a junior and on no account would allow George Stephenson any involvement with the project. The rail company refused their demands outright and began looking elsewhere.

The Stockton and Darlington Railway was now progressing well without problems and this was a feather in his cap for George Stephenson. The Liverpool and Manchester Railway Committee had no other alternative but to approach Stephenson again. The approach was made very differently and on their terms. Stephenson was offered £800 a year and was requested to be there for eight months of the year, during which he could not take on any other work. Vignoles was given the job as his assistant, a role that neither men acknowledged openly; each feeling more important than the other. They argued constantly and Stephenson blamed Vignoles for every mistake and error they encountered. Finally Stephenson managed to get Vignoles removed from the job. Charles Vignoles later became President of Civil Engineers.

At this time, George called in all of his old colleagues and assistants from the North east, John Dixon, Joseph Locke and all of the navvies used on the Stockton and Darlington Railway Project. He personally designed all of the bridges and installed machinery as well as his own locomotives. There were a total of 63 bridges on 30 miles of double track line: the most difficult was the 'Sankey Viaduct' with nine arches and the largest tunnel was the Edgehill tunnel at the Liverpool end. To construct the Edgehill tunnel they had to cut deep into sandstone for over two miles, excavating half a million ton of rock, resulting in the tunnel measuring 2,240 yards in length. The biggest obstacle they encountered was Chat Moss. In Parliament, counsel remarked that only a fool or mad man would even attempt lying rail there.

John Dixon arrived from Darlington in July 1826 and on the first day he fell into Chat Moss up to his waist and had to be hauled out. Chat Moss was a complete bog; the more ballast Stephenson put in the more it disappeared. This was a complete civil engineers nightmare. Stephenson tried everything in the 12 square miles of that terrible swamp. George worked round the clock rising at 5 am, riding his horse Bobby, to check on Tunnels and bridges or to just have another go at Chat Moss.

Gradually Chat Moss was conquered, no one believing it was possible; with the causeway eventually to firm up due to the tons of hardcore and other material put in over a period of months. Eventually, the area was strong enough to lay rails.

The Liverpool and Manchester Railway committee had their first board meeting on the 14 June at Manchester and were able to travel there by train. George Stephenson drove the 'Arrow Locomotive', which had newly arrived from Robert Stephenson of Fourth Street, Newcastle upon Tyne. The train took the company directors over the route, travelling 30 miles in 1½ hours and crossing Chat Moss at 27 mph. The Liverpool and Manchester Railway officially opened September 1830. George Stephenson progressed from one successful railway contract to another and the experience gained at Liverpool/Manchester was the most important of all.

Robert Stephenson Jnr. would make far better locomotives than his father, but it was good to see that his were actually improvements on the original engine that his father made. At one time, the whole of Newcastle was proud of the fact that all locomotives made were improvements on George Stephenson's original engine.

In 1838, through his prosperity, George Stephenson, bought an estate at Tapton in Derbyshire and became involved with the Midland collieries. He mixed with all classes of society and he saw his son become an extremely successful man before he died in August 1848 at the age of 67. Previously in a speech he made, 'Geordie Stevy' remarked that he had

...dined with Royalty, and I have also dined with miners, and I also was a boy trapper, I hope that my exertions have beneficial results and that my labour was not in vain. I have been able to use perseverance in my life to get me through.

As I have previously mentioned, sometime before he died, he travelled back to Killingworth again, to gaze at his sundial, which still remained on the door where he had left it years before. His mind must have strayed back to the time he worked as a trapper boy, and then to his inventions, his gifts to society. What an example he must be to young mechanics apprentices and entrepreneurs, especially being a self-taught man. From a trapper boy to the best engineer and inventor this country has ever known.

The Trapper's Petition

Father must I go down with you
Into the dark and dismal hole
And leave the sky as blue above
Buried amidst the blackest coal.

Father I want to go to play,
I've had no play since Monday last,
Oh! Let me have one hour today
And then Ill work and do a vast!

Oh let me play a pretty game
With Tom & Bill upon the heap,
And I shall do my work the same
For then I shall not fall asleep.

Just let me get those pretty flowers,
Down in the field beside the stream;
Then I shall while away the hours
As though I lay in pleasant dreams.

Why must I sit behind the door
So many hours away from you
And hear the putters shout and roar
And nought but shut and open door.

'Tis very dark, and that small low
You gave me, soon will burn away;
And I'm afraid and tremble now,
To think of biding there all day.

They never let me come and sail
My little ship upon the pool,
Or read that pretty little tale
My mother gave me from the school.

But I must go down beneath,
Don't let the putters beat me sore;
I tremble so, it stops my breath
To hear them coming to the door.

Just come and see me now and then,
And bring me little bits of bait
Then I shall tremble at the men
And will all day in darkness wait.

Well father! If I must go down
Just hold me tight upon your Knee;
But get me work in yon big Town,
And let me life and daylight see.

Timothy Hackworth

1786-1850

Like his friend, George Stephenson, Timothy Hackworth was born in Wylam. His father, Jack Hackworth, was foreman at Wylam Colliery. His experience of mining practices was well known as were his skills as a boiler builder although he spent most of his spare-time studying mechanical principle.

From a very early age, Timothy showed an interest in the tools of his father's trade, with his father encouraging Timothy's early interest in all things mechanical. At the age of 14, Timothy was apprenticed as a blacksmith at Wylam colliery. It was during his apprenticeship in 1802, that Timothy's father died and, being the eldest son, most of the burden of caring for his family came to rest on his shoulders. However, Timothy showed strength and hope for the future. He took his responsibilities seriously, supporting his widowed mother and the rest of his family.

On the completion of his apprenticeship in 1807, the colliery manager, Christopher Blackett, was so impressed with his progress that he appointed Timothy foreman blacksmith, the same position held by his late father. Under the direction of Mr Hedley, the colliery viewer, Timothy's interest in locomotives grew, along with his love of Wylam and the surrounding area. In 1818, Timothy moved to Walbottle Colliery, near to Wylam, to undertake a similar posting.

In 1824 George Stephenson was engaged in surveying the route of the Liverpool to Manchester Railway, he had a problem with management at his Forth Street factory; knowing Hackworth's background as an engineer, he asked him to take charge of the factory in his absence. Hackworth readily accepted, with the consent of the manager of Walbottle Colliery. He was also given the opportunity of a partnership with the Robert Stephenson Company, but declined. During his time at Forth Street, Timothy was also offered positions abroad in Venezuela, Trinidad, and New Granada, but rejected them all. One reason for the rejection was his desire to stay in England. The other possible reasons were his religious beliefs and his desire, as a lay preacher, to preach the gospel regularly.

On leaving the Forth Street works later in 1824, Timothy became engaged in building engine boilers for the Tyne Iron Company. He longed to go into business for himself and eventually his chance came. He rented premises solely for this purpose, but just prior to starting on his own George Stephenson asked him if he would accept a post as resident engineer of the Stockton and Darlington Railway Company.

Timothy accepted and started the post in June 1825, three months prior to the opening of the line.

Timothy quickly gained the confidence and respect of his employers. The first public railway had already been laid, but there were numerous important details to perfect for the future running of the project. Timothy revelled in the opportunity to show his skills as an engineer; his main aim being to re-design and modernise the locomotive in time for the coming Rainhill Trials, to be held 1-6 October 1829. Prior to the trials the locomotive had a slight advantage over horsepower for heavy haulage and Timothy was determined to exploit this advantage, whilst at the same time hoping to instil confidence in the early railway system.

As haulage increased with production, Timothy found that to deal with the extra work, a new locomotive would have to be designed and put to work. Permission by his employers at the time, Stockton and Darlington Railway Company, was given for him to work on this project and in 1828, by utilising the discarded boiler of an old engine, the *Royal George* was created. The accuracy and expertise of his design was amazing, and it was far superior to other locomotives of that time. In tests it was found that a 50% saving was made by using the power of the locomotive instead of ordinary horsepower. In the *Royal George* the two upright cylinders worked on separate shafts, placed on opposite sides of the boiler. Hackworth re-introduced this 'two cylinder' design, originally devised by Trevithick, and

discarded as inefficient the design adopted by George Stephenson of the single fire tube. He also made it possible to eject the waste steam through the contracted orifice of the waste pipe in the chimney, the force of the blast was greatly increased therefore the combustion in the furnace was greatly accelerated. Hackworth's improved engine gave speed and power unknown to earlier engines.

Royal George 1828.

As Hackworth was working on his locomotive a deputation was sent north by the Liverpool and Manchester Railway to investigate the efficiency of locomotives and whether or not fixed engines and horsepower were not the better and more efficient option. Their investigations resolved in favour of the fixed engine rather than the locomotive. Messrs Rastrick and Walker completed the report; the findings dealt a severe blow to Robert Stephenson and meant the abandonment of locomotion construction at his Forth Street works, causing him great financial loss. Ultimately, Stephenson sought advice from Timothy; Stephenson knew that the choosing of a fixed engine against the locomotion would have serious financial repercussions for the North Eastern Railway

Company. In addition, he asked Timothy what weight it was possible to haul by a 10 horsepower engine at the rate of 10 miles an hours, and whether this would vary in summer and winter. Hackworth's reply to the younger Stephenson showed his full character and also his knowledge:

Dear Sir,

The statement you allude to, that a complete locomotive will take but 10 tons at 10 miles an hour is quite at variance with facts, as an opinion merely, this I would forgive. Four of our wagons laden for depots frequently take from 12 to 13 tons of coal, exclusive of the wagons. Our engine's never take less than 16 laden wagon's in winter and in the summer from 20 to 24 and 32 laden, they can maintain a speed of five mph except in cases of stoppages by means of horse wagons at the passing places, engines thus loaded have frequently travelled at nine mph sometimes more. It is unsafe to aim at a speed on a single line railway the danger is at passing places. I am verily convinced that a swift engine upon a well conditioned railway will combine profit and simplicity and will afford such facility as has not hitherto been known. I am well satisfied that an engine of the weight you mention will convey on a level, in winter 30 tons of goods at 10 mph exclusive of carriages and 40 tons in summer exclusive of carriages... As to my general opinion as to the locomotive system I think it is comparatively in a state of infancy. Swift engines on a double way, I am convinced may be used to the utmost advantage. Improvements upon anything yet produced, of greater importance in all respects are clearly practical; and I am sure this will prove itself by actual remuneration to such parties as prudently yet diligently pursue the execution of this kind of power, with their eyes open to those alterations and advantages which actual demonstration of local circumstances point out. Stationary engines are by no means adapted to a public line of railway. I take here no account of a great waste of capital. But you will fail in proving to the satisfaction of any not conversant with these subjects the inexpediency of such a system, — I hear the Liverpool Company have concluded to use fixed engines. Some will look on this with surprise; but as you can well afford it, it is all for the good of science and of the trade to try both plans. Do not discompose yourself, my dear sir, if you express your manly, firm decided opinion, you have done your part as their adviser; and if it happens to be read in the newspaper, whereas ropes have strangled the Liverpool and Manchester Railway, we shall, not accuse you of guilt in being accessory either before or after the fact.

Source:'Timothy Hackworth and the Locomotive;' Robert Young, London 1923.

In 1849 Hackworth built the famous *Sans Pareil* the engine that, whilst competing against Stephenson's *Rocket* at the Rainhill Trials, developed boiler problems, causing it to break down. However, the disadvantages under which Hackworth worked are also very well known; the *Sans Pareil* breakdown was entirely due to the bad workmanship of Robert Stephenson and Company who cast and bored the cylinders – the very firm that was competing with him. In many respects Timothy Hackworth's engine was far better than the *Rocket*. George Stephenson himself said that Hackworth's idea for the boiler on the *Sans Pareil* was ingenious. Indeed, at the trials, it proved to be faster than the other locomotives until the boiler broke down.

The Sans Pareil built by Timothy Hackworth, Darlington. Weight 4 tons 15 cwt 18 lb; green, yellow and black, white chimney.

The original *Sans Pareil* could be seen working on the Bolton and Leigh Railway, several years later – not much the worse for wear. The

boiler never required any essential repairs, unlike most of its rivals, which ended up on the scrap heap. The *Sans Pareil* now occupies a position in the South Kensington Museum, London, in the company of *Puffing Billy* and the *Rocket*; all interesting relics of a humble colliery village – Wylam.

Rocket built by Robert Stephenson, Newcastle-on-Tyne. Weight 4 tons 3 cwt; yellow and black, white chimney.

After the trials at Rainhill, most leading engineers started building locomotives; some of which were exported to France and America. In America, William Howard designed a locomotive in 1828 for the Baltimore and Ohio Railroad Company. The locomotive Howard designed was never constructed, but he was credited with the patent. A locomotive that *was* built was *Tom Thumb*, tried in 1829 and in action on the Baltimore and Ohio Railroad by 1830. Designed by Peter Cooper of New York and weighing about a ton, with a single vertical cylinder of 3¼ inches diameter and a stroke of 14 inches, this engine instigated the start of heavy investment in steam locomotives by the Americans. Robert Stephenson and Company built a locomotive called *America* for the Delaware and Hudson Canal Company, which arrived in America about this time. It had outside sloping cylinders attached high on the boiler, one either side of the trailing end, with four coupled wheels.

On his return from the Rainhill Trials, Hackworth was disappointed but not disgruntled. The *Sans Pareil* had displayed well and it had helped Timothy's reputation enormously. Back at his own works at Shildon he came across an engine designed by Robert Stephenson, *Rocket No. 7*. The engine had six coupled wheels, with the cylinders fixed diagonally on either side of the boiler, between the middle and trailing wheels, the same style introduced by Stephenson when he returned from America, in 1827. Over the next two years Hackworth, using this locomotive as his starting block, embarked on building a more streamlined and faster engine, combining steadiness with reliability. Timothy named the engine *Globe*. It had a copper cylinder steam dome to secure 'dry' steam, four coupled wheels five feet in diameter, laminated steel springs to all wheels, inside cylinders with crank axle, and valve motion reversible by a single lever. The cylinders were nine inches in diameter with a stroke of 16 inches, placed horizontally under the trailing end of the engine. The boiler was revolutionary, the power from which was greatly superior to any other engine of the day.

Top: A locomotive built for the Leeds and Thirsk Railway in 1848, which became the original British standard goods engine.

Bottom: A late example of a Victorian 4-4-0 express locomotive dating from 1891 the last of which went out of service in 1930.

The building of the *Globe* was a huge project and in 1830 Timothy moved to Stephenson's Forth Street factory to complete the task. The following extracts were taken from Timothy's diary. They show that he visited a number of towns on his way to the Forth Street works:

He left home on the morning of 1 March 1830, arriving in Newcastle on the 3 March, and in the company of Harris Dickinson, (Robert Stephenson's manager), took a gig to Bedlington, where he ordered boiler plates for the 'Globe' after which he spent the 4th 5th and 6th at the Forth Street Works, explaining the new design, especially the first crank axled inside double, horizontal cylinder, ever designed.

Timothy Hackworth's business card, with a picture of the Globe.

During the construction, there was some opposition to the crank system, by one of the Forth Street engineers saying that it would slow the engine down. Timothy quickly dismissed the comment, saying that all he required from the Forth Street works was good material and good workmanship and that any failure in the design was his responsibility; he also made it absolutely clear he required early delivery. Then on 6 March 1830 he left Newcastle bound for Shildon, thinking the matter resolved. However, that was not the end of the crank system issue. There was no further discussion from the Forth Street works on the crank design, but there seemed a delay in the *Globe's* completion. In October 1830 a crank axled engine with horizontal cylinders, was supplied to the Liverpool and Manchester Railway Company, while the *Globe* was not delivered until two months later.

The delivery journal of Robert Stephenson and Company showed that their engine the *Planet* had been charged to the Liverpool and Manchester Railway Company on 3 September 1830. The Railroad minute book reported the arrival on 4 October 1830, the Liverpool and Manchester locomotive, being ready for trial on 25 October 1830. No mention had been made of why there had been delays with the *Globe* and why the *Planet* had been produced prior to the *Globe* at the Forth Street works.

The Planet, built by Robert Stephenson and Company in 1830.

Along with Edward Pease and his sons, and Colonel Henry Stobart (proprietor of Etherly Colliery), Timothy Hackworth was directly in charge of the engine drivers from Shildon to Stockton, for the Stockton and Darlington Railways. Engine drivers were extremely important in the early days of steam power and their lives were rough and dangerous. They worked long hours and were exposed to all weathers. The drivers were paid on tonnage rate, that is, the amount of goods (coal or other) hauled. Out of this money, they had to pay their assistants, the oil and greasers, firemen and even the coal for fuelling the boiler, as well as the oil and grease needed to run the engine.

Each engine was unique, having their own good and bad points, and sometimes they needed a little coaxing up inclines with a crowbar.

Each driver soon got to know his own machine. One driver, William Chicken, had the reputation of being the only man who could reverse *Globe* in the dark. Having no braking system, the engines had to be knocked out of gear, and the assistants had to break the wagons on banks. Another driver, George Sunter, used to run a train of wagons from Shildon to Middlesbrough, and would take on water at Yarm and Darlington without stopping. To do this he uncoupled his engine from the wagons about a mile from arriving at the two depots, and ran the engine on to take in the water, then restarted his engine and re-coupled without stopping the wagons. Sunter also used to let his fireman go home from the engine on reaching Darlington, on Saturday evenings. He drove and fired it for the remaining 9 miles to Shildon himself. This was not easy as the driver's levers were at one end and the furnace at the other end of the engine.

There was no doubt that driving early locomotives was hazardous. One of the most locally respected drivers was William Gowland, driver of the *Royal George*, and very trusted by Timothy Hackworth. In a statement of monthly wages, for April 1828, for work completed in March 1828, out of five named drivers Gowland had £37 8s 11d, more than double the amount of any of the other drivers. He drove *Sans Pareil* at the Rainhill Trials and afterwards worked on the Bolton and Leigh Railway, he finally made his home in Bolton.

William Gowland 1829.

Timothy Hackworth continued to make quality locomotives, each one more improved than its predecessor. The days of the steam locomotive were certainly here to stay, and it was hard to understand how the coal industry had survived without them. Four locomotives were built in 1838 for The South Hetton Coal Company, the *Buddle* the *Kellor*, the *Wellington* and the *Prince Albert*, all of which were used to transport coal via the incline to Seaham Harbour. They were powerful little engines and could be improvised to act as snowploughs. The Clarence Railway, Hartlepool, was also at its height in 1840 and Hackworth built many locomotives for them; two of which were the *Coxhoe* and the *Evenwood*, they were compact, powerful locomotives with six wheeled coupled engines, wheels measuring four feet in diameter, the cylinder diameter 14 inches and the stroke 22 inches.

The first railway passenger coach built in 1825.

From 1830 onwards, Timothy Hackworth also manufactured and produced stationary engines. These were used for both pumping and winding purposes. One example of a Hackworth engine was at West Auckland Colliery; during the 25 years of the colliery manager's service, the engine worked from 6 am to 4 pm daily without a break, making 1,500 winds a day and lifting 75 score (1 score = 8 tons) which equalled 600 tons from the shaft 324 feet deep. It was noted by the manager and owner of the colliery that the workmanship of the engine was superb, and saved the colliery thousands of pounds.

Other collieries that used Hackworth engines were; Woodhouse Close Colliery, and South Durham Colliery. In 1836 an engine was built for South Church Brewery, along with a pumping engine, for Deanery Colliery, which cost £1086 18s 10d; a 20hp pumping engine for Henry Stobart & Company, costing £346 14s 6d, as well as a second engine for Borough Bridge. A further, large incline engine was supplied for the Durham and Sunderland Railroad—the line, started in 1834, was 16 miles long, and it was decided that this line should be operated by a stationary engine, making it the longest stationary line in England. The engine was 83hp and worked at Eppleton Plane. Including the drums it cost £2,352 19s 10d and was completed at the end of 1836. Although the line was quite satisfactory, overall, it showed the inefficiency of this particular type of haulage. The line was taken over by the York and Newcastle Railway Company in 1836.

In 1836 Hackworth built a locomotive for the Russian Government, it was the first engine ever to run in Moscow and it was dispatched in the autumn of that year. It was a double trunk engine built with a firebox and a smoke box and contained 135 horizontal tubes 1½ inches in diameter. The cylinders were 17 inches in diameter, with a stroke of nine inches, all mounted on six wheels with single drivers, five feet in diameter. The leading and trailing wheels were three feet six inches in diameter. The ledger showed the total cost of the engine being £1884 2s 9d. This included £140 for the wheels, and £330 9s 0d for the tender that was fitted with brakes and a capacious tank.

The duty of taking the locomotive to Russia fell with Timothy's son, John. He was Hackworth's eldest son, 17 years old, and very mature for his age. John was almost as tall as his father and a bright, keen engineer. John had a small staff including the foreman of the Shildon Works, George Thompson. George managed an excellent repair, when the cylinder cracked after only a few days; going from St. Petersburg to Moscow (600 miles) to make a pattern for the cylinder, and having it cast then bored out and returning to St. Petersburg and fitting it to the engine. The locomotive was then taken from St. Petersburg to Tsarskoye-Selo, where the summer Imperial Palace was. The locomotive was started from there, in the presence of the Tsar, in November 1836.

John, who was introduced to Tsar Nicholas, recounted how he talked about a visit to England in 1816 when he observed one of Blenkinsop's locomotives on the colliery lines from Middlesbrough to Leeds. (This was before he was on the throne.) The Russia expedition was a complete success and Hackworth built a further locomotive in the year 1837.

After Timothy was installed as chief engineer of the Stockton and Darlington Railway Company in 1825, a bond grew between him and the Pease family, headed by the father, Edward Pease. A very respectful admiration was jointly held between them and they very much trusted each other. Joseph Pease and his younger brother Henry were held very high in Timothy's estimation, but it was Joseph, to whom he was most drawn. It was Joseph who suggested calling his home and works 'Soho'. Timothy also had a great respect for the father, Edward, but it was Joseph that he completed day-to-day business with.

Joseph Pease was one of those rare people who remained unspoiled by his prosperity. When in Parliament he addressed members as 'members' not 'honourable members', and the speaker as 'Sir', in line with Quaker principles of the day. Prior to 1835

he was the largest and most influential coal mine owner in South West Durham. He also owned coke ovens and had vast interests in Cleveland Ironstone Royalties. On 11 June 1848 Pease wrote to Hackworth asking him to investigate safety lamps, and any improvements that could be made to combat colliery gasses, namely fire damp and choke damp.

George Stephenson was also a very good friend of Hackworth's; he had very influential financial backers himself in the Tyneside area, and recommended Timothy to many of these people. It was also credit to Stephenson that Hackworth got the job as Chief Engineer with the Stockton and Darlington Railway Company.

Although Hackworth invented, produced and supplied numerous locomotives, engines, and other machines, he was never a rich man. Due to his Quaker beliefs, neither was he an ambitious man and the profits from his work were always fair and just. Being responsible for a very large work-force, it was widely known that if a local family was under distress, for unpaid debt, possibly brought on through sickness, he would attend the sale for the furniture, buy it then give it back to the family for nothing.

At the age of 27, Timothy married Jane Golightly at Ovingham Parish Church. They started a family while still based in Wylam; eventually having six daughters and three sons, one boy died in infancy, a great sadness for Timothy. Soho Cottage, their residence, was high in the family's affection and all of them, when married, came home regularly.

Mrs Jane Hackworth.

Timothy Hackworth was well read, and a member of the Advancement of Science, which was formed in 1831. Mrs Hackworth was a tall handsome woman, and in her younger days had been a competent horsewoman. Like her husband she was a devout Methodist. This belief caused an estrangement between herself and her parents. However, by the time she married Hackworth, the rift was healed and she became a great comfort to them in their old age.

When the Wesleyan chapel at New Shildon was built, Jane went of her own accord and laid the foundation stone, then gave an address expressing her thanks to God that he had supplied a chapel for them to worship. Later she rode, at her own expense, to get a minister worthy enough to open the church, and when there was a dispute over the lease of the church, she pleaded, like 'Queen Esther' for God and the people. She loved all who loved God in sincerity, and she helped willingly anyone who needed help, but was a strict disciplinarian of her family. Mrs Hackworth died in 1852; she survived her husband by two years.

Soho Cottage where Hackworth carried out his brilliant early work on locomotives.

Many influential people, especially leading members of the Methodist Church, and their travelling preachers, visited the Hackworth's. Timothy would not at any price work on Sundays, even if there was important work to be carried out. Neither would he work at weekends, keeping that time for attending church and being with his family. His youngest daughter was sent to a Roman Catholic school at Villevorde, near Brussels, to complete her education. Morning and evening prayers were always said by the family. Timothy was an expert dancer, while not doing this in public because of his spiritual beliefs, he regularly taught his children the dances in Soho Cottage, dances like, *The Minuet*, and the *Quadrilles*. He also enjoyed music and had a Baby Grande piano at home and one of his daughters played the harp. When Timothy and his wife died and the house was finally cleared, some of the many books in the house were the *Family Bible; Book of Martyr's*, Bunyans *Pilgrims Progress,* an *Encyclopedia Britannica* and also a great many of Wesley's sermons. Lighter reading was Walter Scott's works, and a translation of the *Odyssey*. All of his daughters had different types of booklets of the day in which their friends would sketch and write. In his youngest daughter's book appeared the following, written by Timothy: 'Blessed are they that do his commandments, that they may have the right to the tree of life', signed Timothy Hackworth 20 July 1848.

Timothy was devoted to John Wesley and he always placed cleanliness next to go Godliness. If it can be called a weakness, he loved fine glassware and china and always had spotless table linen and silver plate. Hackworth enjoyed singing North Country ballads, his favourite being *The Keel Row*. After being placed in sole charge of the Stockton and Darlington Railway Company in 1834, it is significant that Hackworth managed to get the most out of the system. Weight for weight Hackworth's locomotives surpassed any engine on the line. Timothy Hackworth died in his sixty-fourth year, a distinguished mechanical genius.

If Timothy Hackworth were to be reborn in Shildon he would not recognise his hometown. It now has a population of 12,000, and a new Town Square, home to a six foot bronze statue of Hackworth, not very far from his last resting place in St

John's Church Yard. There is also The Timothy Hackworth Museum, opened by the Queen Mother in 1975. Public Houses in Shildon and the surrounding area reflect his life and works: *The Timothy Hackworth*, *Royal George*, *Iron Horse*, *Locomotion No.1* (Heighington Lane Newton Aycliffe Trading Estate), and *Dandy Cart*, Newton Aycliffe.

In September 2004 the National Railway Museum opened in Shildon, and exceeded its annual visitor target of 60,000 within two months. The Museum is the Regions first National Museum and is well on the way to restoring the pride of the area as the 'Birth of the Passenger Railways'.

Since opening, the museum has received the Dibner Award for Outstanding Museum Work by the Society of Technology (Shot). The award was presented to the museum at Shot's annual meeting and official presentation ceremony, in Minneapolis, US, where Dr Graeme Gooday, chairman of the Shot Dibner committee praised the museum for its achievements. He said: 'This is an innovative new museum. It is an exciting exhibit that deserves to be treated as an example of how technological history can be explained by intergrating themes of communal, national and international significance'. The museum, which celebrates nearly two centuries of international rail history in Shildon, including the achievements of rail pioneer Timothy Hackworth, has enjoyed huge success since it opened in September 2004.

The Keel Row

As I cam Thro' Sandgate, Thro'
Sandgate, Thro' Sandgate,
As I cam Thro' Sandgate, I heard a
lassie sing,
Weel may the Keel Row, The Keel
Row, The Keel Row,
Weel may the Keel Row, That my lad
is in.

He wears a blue bonnet, A blue
bonnet, A blue bonnet,
He wears a blue bonnet, and a
dimple in his chin;

And weel may the Keel Row, The Keel
Row, The Keel Row,
And Weel may the Keel Row, that my
lad is in.

'Hail, Tyneside Lads! In Collier Fleets,
The first in might and motion;
In sunshine days or stormy neets,
The Lords upon the Ocean.

Come Englands Foes-a countless crew,
Ye'll give them all a scummin,
And Myek them a'the day to rue,
They Glibb's their jaws at Lunnin'.

Richard Grainger

1797-1861

The Regeneration of Newcastle began after the defeat of Charles Edward Stewart at Culloden in 1746. The English large Military army had major problems moving cannons and stores northwards through Newcastle on route to Scotland. Local developers and business people assessed the possibilities of completely re-designing and re-modernising their town.

They began by dismantling the city walls along the quay in 1763, allowing better access and also an entrance to the upper parts of Newcastle. From 1795-98 the Pandon Close and Sandgates were demolished. In 1811 the Postern and West Gates also quickly disappeared. The town wall from Newgate to Pilgrim Street was removed—this area played an important roll in Grainger's plans for the city.

There was another factor challenging this development and that was Newcastle's coal. The shipment of coal from Newcastle expanded from 15,000 tons of coal in the sixteenth-century to 600,000 tons in 1730. As seams were lowered in the eighteenth-century production increased dramatically and anyone with any vision at all could see gigantic handling problems for Newcastle. Soon, the rivers Tyne and Wear were swamped with tons of extra coal far more than any Keel could handle, and the Northumberland and Tyne Docks were found inadequate.

Large landowners moved away from the city some relocating as far a field as London where they had purchased large houses out of the vast profits that they were now making from the production of coal. As they moved out, professional men took their places: lawyers, surveyors, architects, mining engineers, bankers and industrialists began opening premises.

As this change was taking place, it became apparent that Newcastle's infrastructure was in a terrible condition: 11 out of 12 houses having no water supply and no street lighting in the city at all. In Castle Garth Stairs 200 or even more tenants had to use one public 'netty'. The Corporation and governing body gave themselves wide powers to improve the town including improvements to the dock areas, all public paths and roads and the complete re-generation of the inner city itself. In the years that followed the transformation of Newcastle city was breathtaking, with Richard Grainger playing a huge part in this transformation.

Richard Grainger came from humble beginnings. He was born 9 October 1797 in High Friar Lane, Newcastle, the street between Nuns Field and the Town Wall, leading to High Friar Chare (this area is presently located in the region of Blackett Street). Where, the Grainger family occupied two rooms of an upstairs tenement building. Richard's parents, Thomas and Amelia, had three other children at the time of his birth: George was the eldest, William, unfortunately died at Thirsk in 1823, John was born 17 July 1791 and Amelia, the only girl, born in 1794.

Thomas Grainger was a native of Cumberland, possibly deceased from the Grainger's of Brough. He worked as a humble porter on the Newcastle quay. Amelia, an expert at stocking-grafting and glove making, contributed to the family income during hard times. In 1809 Thomas Grainger died, leaving Amelia to take over the reigns and steer her family on to better things.

Richard Grainger's only education was gained at a parish charity school. At this school he was well remembered for his ruddy smiling face, quiet manner and the green badge coat he always wore. He had an interest in architecture from an early age and became apprenticed to Master Carpenter, John Brown from whom he learnt all aspects of the building trade.

It was not until 1819, when he won the Higham Place contract that Richard Grainger began to see the possibilities of modernising the town of Newcastle. Although the population was only approximately 43000, the town was immensely crowded, especially in the lower areas. These 'lower areas' around Pandon, Close and Sandgates were demolished

in 1811, along with the Postern and Western Gates. The town wall was also removed, from Newgate Street to Pilgrim Street, for redevelopment.

Richard's wife, Rachel, the eldest daughter of Joseph Arundale, a wealthy business man, mainly in leather and tanning, had brought to their marriage a £5,000 dowry. It was with this money that Richard was able to fund his first great enterprise, the erection of Eldon Square.

Newcastle upon Tyne 1870.

After his success with Blackett Street in 1824, in which he constructed houses designed by Thomas Oliver, Grainger undertook the Eldon Square project with a growing confidence. Using John Dobson's designs, work began on the project in 1825 with the removal of some old baron fruit trees and the entire clearing of the area. Grainger built all but three houses in the three sided square. In 1827, the historian, McKenzie, remarked that the completion of the new square was a proud moment to the whole area.

Grainger's next undertaking was the construction of Leazes Terrace and Crescent. In 1829, with Thomas Oliver as architect, 70 first class houses were built in a square, having small gardens to the front and a paved terrace walk. A further 60 houses were constructed, although not as grand as the first. This project took him five years to complete.

In 1834, the Royal Arcade was erected at the eastern end of Mosley Street. This became the town's first indoor retail commercial centre. The area is now occupied by a huge roundabout and new development of luxury apartments, '55 Degrees North'.

Grainger Street, Newcastle 1914.

By 1841 Richard Grainger had enriched Newcastle with property to the value of £200,000 and all of this before embarking on his 'New Town'.

Grainger purchased 12 acres of land in the Middle (Middle Street, at the end of Mosley Street) of Newcastle to the value of £50,000 and for some time he kept his intentions a secret. In 1833, he bought more land to the value of £45,000 and only then unfolded his plans for the huge undertaking of Grainger Street and Market. The Market area was to include the Big Market and the Groat Market.

First, Newcastle would have to give up its old market, for Market Street 'old market' would provide access to the new markets; this cost Grainger £15,000. In exchange for

the loss of their old market and a very modest fee of £36,000, the Council would get a very modern market.

Portrait of Richard Grainger.

The project took five years to complete, with Grainger employing 2,000 people. By 1835, the Grainger Market and Butcher Market were complete and given a grand opening. The opening was celebrated by a public dinner at the market, with approximately 2,000 local people attending. This was the finest market in England, even larger than the Liverpool and Hungerford markets. The Grainger Market had 14 entrances, contained 243 shops all of which could be individually locked, and two water fountains containing 3,000 gallons of water.

Grainger did not stop with the Market. However, in order to undertake his next project a theatre stood in the way. He promised the proprietors of the said theatre a beautiful new building plus £500 cash. Other properties would have to be destroyed too and some tenants were against this and applied for a legal injunction. However, even before the application got to London the contract was signed, and the old theatre chimneys were demolished within the hour. One tenant was holding out in the area, but they were finally persuaded, and escorted to a brand spanking new house lavishly prepared for them. Before morning came, their old house had disappeared.

The task confronted by Grainger was immense but the ground was soon prepared for development. Soil was carted away to the tune of 250,000 loads, each load containing 18 cubic feet, which cost £21,500, paid to only one contractor. People marvelled at Grainger's' genius, especially considering he was a self-taught man; he had amazing powers of enterprise and taste.

Grey Street, Newcastle 1860.

On its completion in 1840, everyone marvelled at the sight of Grainger Street and Grey Street. The ground floor fronts of the buildings were glass; these were for shops and inns. Within three years eight other streets started to spring up, similar to Grey Street. All had uniform colours, and it was said that these houses had an advantage over Regent Street, London, not only in architecture but also in the class of materials used. Grey Street remains

today and is 400 yards long, 80 feet wide; the houses being four stories high and all with basement cellars. The architecture is Corinthian in character, not unlike the Pantheon in Athens; the Ionic columns, 22 feet high. Grainger had created beautiful new buildings, to replace the old and dilapidated.

Central Exchange Building, Newcastle 1940.

During / this period of construction, Grainger built a magnificent new Corn Exchange (1837), at the head of Grainger Street and Grey Street. He offered it to Newcastle Council free of charge just as long as it was used as a corn exchange. Unfortunately, another building, for similar use, was already under contract and so they had to turn the offer down. Grainger's building was instead made into a public meeting place, which included a reading room, a coffee room and conference room. The interior measured 150 foot by 95 foot in a semi-circle with a 75 foot radius; the roof was supported by 14 columns. There were five entrances, with the floor decorated with white tiles. All together the whole building was exceedingly striking.

Altogether, Grey Street, Blackett Street, Grainger Street, with the column to Earl Grey stands as a remarkable monument to the current-day city of Newcastle, where visitors still marvel at the architecture of the buildings. The same can be said of Market Street and Clayton Street, where all of the fronts of the houses are made of polished stone in various designs. In total, nine new streets were added to Newcastle in the space of five years, over 2,000 workmen were employed, and Newcastle showed a growth in its yearly population of some 1,500 a year during this period. Grainger had, without doubt, amazing vision.

Clayton Street, Newcastle 1914.

In just 20 years Richard Grainger had progressed from being a humble joiners apprentice to become a leading and influential builder and property developer. Late in his life on being asked to what extent he was involved in the individual housing development within Newcastle. Grainger simply replied 'a great many'. He did though go on to list some of these improvements; 'Part of New Bridge Street; Carliol Street, Croft Street, Portland Street,

Northumberland Street; 31 houses in Blackett Street, 22 in Eldon Square, 3 in Newgate Street, 9 in Percy Street, 68 in Leazes Terrace, 80 in Leazes Crescent along with other adjoining streets; 14 in St. James St., and Terrace, the whole of the Royal Arcade (used as a Post office shops and excise office), and the Bankruptcy Court. Two banks at Grey Street and the full actual street; 81 houses in Market Street, all of the 38 houses in Grainger Street, 68 houses in Nuns Street, 26 houses in Nelson Street, 26 houses in Clayton Street, 107 in total with adjoining streets, 27 houses in Clayton Street West, 16 in Hood Street, 16 in Shakespeare Street, 14 in Pilgrim Street, 6 in part Nuns Gate, 23 in Rye hill, 19 in Elswick and 20 in Railway Street'.

Grainger gave Newcastle a new heart, his changes revolutionised Newcastle in such a way that manufacturing and other large employers were attracted to the city. The High Level Bridge was constructed in 1850 along with the opening of the Central Station. There was also a high-level road link with Newgate Street and Percy Street, this was an alternative road to the north of the Country and Scotland.

Prior to Grainger's modernisation programme typhus, cholera and other epidemic diseases were common in the area. However, after his improvements they gradually disappeared because of the improvement in the drainage system. A Chief Constables report for 1836 identified 71 brothels, and 46 houses of ill repute in the town. Although they may have moved elsewhere, they appeared to have disappeared at the same time as the improvements to the inner city of Newcastle.

Richard Grainger's home, Elswick Estate.

Later in his life Grainger was harassed by financial difficulties and eventually had to sell parts of his Elswick estate to meet these debts.

He was not impressed by power but as a youth it was his dream to improve his hometown, Newcastle. Richard strived always to make a good impression and always made sure that he could be trusted. People that were familiar with him told how he had never lost his temper and in fact strived to help people where he could. Although being a member of the Chamber of Trade and Commerce he never became an official. He looked very favourable on Charity Trusts especially later in his life when he had more free time. He allowed the development of Botanical and Zoological Gardens on his Elswick estate.

Sir Joseph Whitworth

1803-1887

Joseph Whitworth's early life may have given him the inspiration he needed to build the great engineering business that he did. His brilliant discoveries revolutionised engineering; he was undoubtedly one of the greatest engineers that ever lived.

However, Joseph was barely 12 years old when his father Charles deserted him and the rest of the family to become a clergyman in the Congregational Church. Joseph later condemned his father's decision to foster him and his brother as 'utter selfishness'. Even worse, Charles Whitworth sent his daughter Sarah, to a Bristol orphanage, an extraordinary act for the man of religion he claimed to be.

Charles Whitworth and Sarah Hulse had married when Charles was 21 years old and Sarah 23 years old, at Stockport parish church in Cheshire, on 14 March 1803. The first child, Joseph, was born on 20 December 1803 and their second child, John, was born in 1805. Their home was a two bedroom dwelling house at the top of stone steps leading from a place called Fletcher's Yard in Stockport. Later this house was renamed 13 John Street.

Joseph was scarcely 15 months old when Orchard Street Congregational Church accepted his father as a Sunday School class leader. Even at this relatively early stage of his life it may have entered Charles Whitworth's mind that a full-time position could be an escape from his fatherly responsibilities. The man most to blame, it could be argued, for Charles Whitworth's journey into faith, was the Reverend William Evans, a charismatic preacher who had set out to find young men to spread the faith. Whitworth was waiting to be found and was attracted to Bill Evans like metal to a magnet.

These were dangerous times in Stockport and Manchester. There were regular mill fires and machines were vandalised. In 1812, eight 'machine vandals' were taken to Newcastle and executed. Irish immigrants were taking weaving jobs for low pay. Charles Whitworth was a reed-maker. If the mob had smashed local looms, people like Whitworth were watched in case they repaired them. The Whitworth family was in constant danger of having their windows smashed or of even being assaulted.

In March 1813, Sarah Whitworth gave birth to a daughter whom Charles, baptised Sarah. The baby, though sickly, survived, but her mother died early in 1814 aged 34. The two boys grieved the loss of their mother tremendously, to the point of utter despair. Their father was at a loss as to what to do. His best friend, the Reverend Bill Evans had died three years previously. Charles Whitworth took the extraordinary decision to point the family in four different directions, after deciding to take on a post as a full-time clergyman. Sarah went to an orphanage at Bristol where she stayed for 10 years. The task of finding foster homes for the boys was hard. John went to live in Queensland, Australia, where, in 1830, he married. Joseph was fostered by a middle class family in Stockport He was so desperate to make something of his life that in July 1820, he ran away.

When he approached W. J. Crighton & Company in Manchester for a job, Joseph added a year to his age. He was given a job and stayed there 14 months. From Crighton's Joseph moved a short distance to Marsdon & Walker at Water Street, a firm well known for textile machinery. He stayed there for the same length of time. He was already doing the work of a skilled tradesman and he would not be 21 for another two years. He made a further move, this time as a skilled millwright to Houldsworth & Company, an internationally renowned cotton mill in Lever Street. Later he said that the happiest days of his life were when he was a journeyman at Houldsworth & Company.

Whitworth left Manchester for London on his twenty-first birthday in December 1824. Heading for London via canal, sleeping wherever he could. On his journey, he met a young lady; she was 24 years of age, a bargeman's daughter from Tarvin, Cheshire. Her name was Frances Ankers. It was love at first sight, and soon they eloped, making their way towards Nottingham, having first

called at Ilkeston to get a priest to marry them; on 25 February 1825, Fanny Ankers married Joseph Whitworth. Not being able to read or write Frances, marked the register with a cross. The couple endured some very bumpy years together but Frances ended her days reasonably well-off, living near her sister's home in Cheshire. At the time of this strange marriage, neither Fanny's father nor her sisters imagined it would survive 30, mostly happy, years—but it did.

Joseph Whitworth.

Joseph Whitworth commenced work in London, May 1825, at Henry Maudsley's Machine-Tool Engineering Works, as an ordinary bench fitter. He was one of a 120 employees. He remained there for three and a half years, where he impressed all with his engineering skills. The company was in the forefront of engineering. Maudsley himself had experienced the cut-throat competition in machine-tool engineering when he had worked for Joseph Bramah. Maudsley's was the company where illustrious engineers such as Isambard Kingdom Brunel, James Nasmyth, William Muir and Bryan Donkin later worked.

Whitworth remained in London for eight years. After Maudsley's he went to Holtzapffel, then to Wright's & Sons then Joseph Clements; at each company learning new skills with machinery. However, he longed to go into business himself and could see the potential of mass production, especially in the north of England. The time he spent in London had been invaluable. He had made the best possible use of London libraries and learned societies and he was now prepared to put his knowledge to the test. He and Fanny packed their bags and booked two outsider seats on the Manchester-bound Lancashire Express Mail Coach. Fanny and Joseph had one thing in common: they lived for the future and hoped for better times, which they both knew would definitely come.

Joseph was now 29 and back in Manchester after some eight years—with a wife. It was the start of the cotton boom and Manchester was fast becoming the engineering capital of the world. Before Christmas 1830, Whitworth began searching for suitable premises for a small workshop. He had little money and wanted a place with one or two simple machines. He found what he was looking for in Port Street. He took

over the premises and proudly screwed his name above the door: Joseph Whitworth, Toolmaker from London.

For some reason Whitworth could not get the business off the ground even though he worked from dawn to dusk so he moved on—after only six months. He found new premises in May 1833, at 44 Chorlton Street. Again he screwed his name above the door. Here he sensed he was going to have success. He hated credit either for his own use, or when selling machinery and this slowed down his early progress—he would not allow machinery to leave the premises unless it was paid for in full.

Whitworth's early home, 62 Upper Brook Street, Manchester, 1839.

Whitworth talked openly of the need to standardise precise measurement. People said that it would require new machinery, improved skills, higher wages and it was generally thought that many small engineering shops would go bankrupt. It was at Maudsleys that Joseph had first seen a bench micrometer, (an instrument to measure length, inside and outside diameters) in use. Maudsley claimed that his micrometer gave him absolute truth and humorously called it his 'Lord Chancellor'. Whitworth's early measuring techniques progressed during 1834-36 and it was then he built his first comparator, an instrument used for measuring tight tolerances, mainly in bores. Knowing fully he would also need accurate length gauges, he set about designing these. His measuring system was fully in use at his own premises before the Board of Trade became interested. The simplicity of his system was easy to see, but manufacturing the apparatus took three hard long years.

Towards the end of 1842 Whitworth was producing 50 tons of machinery a week. The number of his employees increased from 277 in 1848 to 636 by 1851. Output increased to over 200 tons a week. It was during the early 1860s that Joseph first had some contact with William Armstrong. For some time now Whitworth had wanted to abolish the use of cast iron for making gun barrels. He helped to introduce his own breech-loading guns made from solid fluid-compressed mild steel. After 1875 the Bessemer and Siemans-Martin methods of steel making (Bessemer steel was a quality and much improved mild steel and could be used for many purposes. It could also be tempered and hardened) would have Whitworth re-think his old engineering techniques.

On 11 June 1855, a Select Committee recommended that Whitworth's standard yard measurement (the same length as that of the Royal Commission) be legalised as the secondary standard for comparisons with local standards of measure throughout the country, and that his standard 'Whitworth' foot and inch should have the same sanction attached to them.

Whitworth became a member of the Small Arms Commission. He insisted on including in the Commission's report a proviso that all government contract work be checked against templates and gauges and that each gauge should be numbered on each drawing. By 1856 his workforce went a little further when they worked to three-dimensional drawings. (First angle is viewed flat as you would a map. A three dimensional drawing is viewed three ways, flat, from the sides and from the bottom. This gave engineers a better idea of the finished product.) They further checked each machined piece against Whitworth's 'Go, and No-go' gauges which consisted of two gauges; if the first gauge is a little tight the machine or lathe operator would slightly touch the control wheel which is turning the product until it fits into the second 'Go Gauge'.

Following the British success with the 1851 Great Exhibition, the Americans decided to go ahead with an industrial exhibition in New York, which opened on 10 July 1853. This effectively set British industrial techniques against those of the United States of America. Two years previously Britain had appeared to be ahead of America especially in armaments. A trio of people attended the American exhibition and reported back to England. They were, George Wallis, Principal of the Birmingham School of Art (which included the only school of rifle design in Britain), Professor John Wilson, a representative of British Industry and Engineering) and Joseph Whitworth.

The three commissioners left the Thames on 10 May 1853, on the steam sloop The *Basilisk*. The frigate *Leander* accompanied them across the Atlantic. They landed at New York two days late after a bad crossing. Charles Dickens described just such a crossing to Boston he and his wife had made earlier: 'The noise, the smell, the closeness, was intolerable, the sea was stupendous, wet, and the decks were rolling'.

The *Basilisk* docked at New York on 26 May. Whitworth and the others quickly went ashore and boarded a train to Washington D.C. On the way Wallis and Whitworth visited some factories at Philadelphia and Baltimore. Whitworth observed that technology and noted that the Americans ideas in repetitive production were far in advance of those in England, although England's tool-making was by far in advance of that of the United States. The proportion of hand-slide lathes was found to be greater in America than England and most had powered cross-slides that were suspiciously like Whitworth's designs. The machine shops were tooled very much as Whitworth's was in England.

As early as 1835 Whitworth had been exporting lathes and other machines to Francis Lowell, the largest textile manufacturer in the United States. Whitworth had also sold machines to companies in Massachusetts and Connecticut. The machines which Whitworth saw were the offspring of his own quick-return lathes and here all the machines were in common use in the factories he visited. Whitworth was very confident of his own engineering skills yet he wondered just how long it would take America to overhaul the lead he himself had given England. Whitworth applauded American management for running the industry as it should be run.

The Crimean War (1854-1856) created a demand for military and naval engineering. Whitworth came up with a hexagonal-bored weapon. The more Whitworth perfected his arms, the more competitions he won – and the more he was castigated. By 1857, after two years experimenting, Whitworth was producing guns to superior quality and yet the British Army were still using the French designed Enfield-Minnie rifle.

In 1861 a Select Committee was set up to examine why the British army had not been supplied with a more efficient weapon than the Enfield. Mr Hussey Vivian, Member of Parliament for Glamorgan asked why Whitworth's rifle had been rejected and declared 'Mr Whitworth's rifle beat the best rifles in the French army by two and three to one.' Mr James A. Turner MP said on 25 June 1861, that Joseph Whitworth 'ended by producing the very best weapons ever invented'. On 23 April 1867, *The Times* reported that the 'Enfield rifle had been completely beaten by the Whitworth, in accuracy of fire, penetration and range. Using only half a charge (35 grams of powder) its lead alloy bullet penetrated through 7 inches of elm at a reduced distance of 20 yards. A steel bullet went through a wrought-iron plate 0.6 inches thick. The War Department representatives were amazed; it was the first time that a rifle bullet had gone through an iron plate'.

Whitworth 12 pounder: Joseph Whitworth third from right.

During the 1860s, Whitworth constructed many field guns with steel barrels designed to act as both muzzle-loading and breech-loading. All were high quality weapons suitable for the defence department including the navy. Although negotiable, the prices were higher than Armstrong's. A 4.5 bore 32-pound gun cost £400, a 5.5, 70-pound gun was £700, his new seven inch 120 pound gun with a hexagonal barrel, cost £1,350. General George Hay wrote in the May 1860 edition of the *Mechanics Magazine*, that there was no other gun in England that functioned as well as the Whitworth rifle.

In 1856, Whitworth was becoming a little fretful. He became quarrelsome and said he was not well. Doctors advised him to rest more but he took no notice. Fanny seemed to get the brunt of all of his troubles. They had now been married 31 years but for the last 10, Joseph had spent most of his time at work or travelling. They were now lonely people, looking for companionship which apparently they could not find in each other. They lived at The Firs, on the outskirts of Manchester, with its long drive and its 52 acre estate and farm. Fanny never enjoyed living in the house at all; in fact she never felt right there. Joseph and Fanny grew more and more estranged. Regular invitations to civil functions arrived addressed to 'Mr & Mrs Whitworth' but more and more Joseph went on his own. Prince Albert himself sent an invitation for Joseph and Fanny to join him and the Queen at Osborne House on the Isle of Wight, in December 1856. Albert wished to try Whitworth's rifle; Whitworth attended on his own.

Fanny and Joseph separated in 1856, but there was no divorce. Fanny never experienced any financial problems at all and settled into a new home, Forest Hall, Delamere in Cheshire supported by an adequate income from Whitworth, she died on 28 October 1870. In April 1871, Mary Louisa Hurst, Whitworth's second wife, became mistress of Stancliffe Hall. Stancliffe Hall was set in a beautiful estate in the Derbyshire countryside, costing £33,850. At first, Stancliffe stood on a bare hillside without any attractions other than magnificent scenery but with the advantage of a bracing atmosphere. Whitworth transformed this bleak setting into one of the most beautiful landscaped garden estates in England. Shrubs were ingeniously planted for effect. *The Chronicle* newspaper described the result of his work: 'The main roads are bordered with wide shrubbery borders filled with a profusion of choice rhododendrons, azaleas and other flowering trees and shrubs, intermixed with spiny conifers, bronze retinas pores and elegant birches. The rocks themselves are light fawn verging into rich chestnut brown and are captured with pernettyas and vacciniums. Of the larger plants occupying pockets on the rocks are glorious masses of white and yellow blooms, gorgeous bushes of gorse, thickets of rhododendrons, daphnes and hollies, conifers are everywhere, mostly flame like or pyramidal in outline'.

Whitworth and his new wife, Mary, shared a common interest in educational issues. Mary was the daughter of Daniel Broad Hurst, onetime Manchester City treasurer. In later years the couple spent their days seeing to the affairs of both their estates, The Firs, and Stancliffe, as well as travelling a great deal abroad.

When Whitworth reached 73 years of age he appeared to relax more and enjoy Stancliffe. The celebrated gardener Edward Mimer and the architect T. Roger Smith rebuilt the house between 1871 and 1872. Whitworth was particularly interested in his stud farm and trotting ponies. He also collected paintings, mainly watercolours. His favourite water-colourist was William Etty but he also liked Thomas Creswick and landscapes of the Lake District and Derbyshire.

In 1873 Whitworth's health was deteriorating and realising that his latest heart palpitations were a warning, he started to attend the Saxon church of St. Helen, in Darley Dale but rather unfortunately he had a disagreement with the vicar about village education.

Whitworth devoted only a small part of the last twenty years of his life to engineering. He set out his Articles of Association in 1874. These were amazing in their philanthropy and include the following provisions:

The establishing, managing and assisting of schools, libraries, banks, dispensaries, infirmaries, provident societies and clubs for the benefit of persons employed by the company.

By these Articles he wished to supply education for his employees and apprentices. He also wanted to supply the services of a works doctor and medical room. The Articles were passed in the spring of 1874 when Whitworth employed 780 people. His company was also one of the first to issue shares to employees; the £25 shares could be paid for from wages. If, because of sickness, workers were forced to sell the shares, or if they were leaving, then the shares could be re-sold to the company plus interest, at the price they originally paid.

Whitworth Hotel with the Institute on the right, at Darley Dale, after opening in 1890. The object being to give his workers the chance of further education.

Sir Joseph Whitworth died on Saturday evening of 22 January 1887, at the English Hotel in Monte Carlo. Whitworth was a great benefactor; in his will drawn up in December 1884, it was clearly indicated that he wished the bulk of his estate to provide an educational foundation capable of carrying forward eligible pupils, both male and female, to become superior workmen or teachers. The amount left by Whitworth and his wife was £1.8 million sterling, estimated today at £95 million. Taking into account the undervaluation of the two estates, it exceeds even Lord Nuffield's magnificent legacy.

Lady Whitworth died unexpectedly in 1896 and this allowed a complete takeover of the Whitworth Company by his old rival, William G. Armstrong of Elswick. This new company was called Sir W. G. Armstrong Whitworth and Company Limited.

Joseph Whitworth was buried in the churchyard of Darley Dale, Derbyshire, near a great yew tree which some say is 1,000 years old.

Henry Bolckow and John Vaughan

1806-1878 & 1799-1868

Henry William Ferdinand Bolckow, the Middlesbrough ironmaster, was born to Caroline and Henry Bolckow in Sulten, Prussia, on 6 December 1806. Sulten stands near the river Recknitz, not far from the Prussian border. Most people in the area were employed in agriculture, mainly in the production of wheat, which was transported via Rostock to the rest of Europe. At the time of Henry's birth, Napoleon with his powerful army, was ravishing the country. The Bolckow family were fairly prosperous and members of the Junker class, that is, they were country squires. Henry's father owned a large estate; he had his son educated privately, after which he was placed in a merchant's office in Rostock where it was thought he would have every chance of following a commercial career befitting a member of the Bolckow family.

Henry laboured for six years in this office, learning as much as he could of the corn and agricultural business. He made friends with Christian Allhusen, who had a brother in the corn trade in Newcastle-upon-Tyne, England. Christian, on joining his brother in 1827, invited Henry Bolckow to Newcastle where he began employment as a clerk for C. Allhusen and Company. In a short time Henry gained promotion to junior partner, due to his experience and business acumen. C. Allhusen and Company were merchants based on the quayside in Newcastle, and also owned a granary in Pandon Street. The main object of corn companies at the time was speculation, the companies holding back the corn until the prices expanded. During his time with C. Allhusen and Company, Bolckow made himself a fortune of £50,000 through speculative dealings. At the same time, he met Miriam Hay, a widow who owned a tobacconist shop on the quayside. This was also the beginning of his friendship with John Vaughan; Vaughan was courting Miriam's sister. Both courtships proved successful, with Henry and John becoming brothers-in-law.

Portrait of Henry Bolckow.

John Vaughan, of Welsh descent, was born 21 December 1799, making him seven years older than Henry. Vaughan's father was an ironworker in South Wales. He himself had been a foreman at Dowlais Ironworks in South Wales before moving to Carlisle in 1825. John married at Carlisle in 1840, where his only child, Thomas, was born. In 1832, he moved his family from Carlisle to Walker-on-Tyne, accepting the job of manager with Losh, Wilson & Bell at the Walker ironworks. Fate seemed to bring Bolckow and Vaughan together, forging a formidable partnership that would completely develop Middlesbrough and Cleveland; turning Middlesbrough into the iron capital of Europe if not the world.

Portrait of John Vaughan.

Bolckow being a man of capital hated the annual fluctuations in the corn trade. In 1839, seeking a new commercial venture, Vaughan, with his experience in the iron trade and knowing the potential growth in the railways, encouraged him to invest in iron. Bolckow, particularly after a further meeting including Joseph Pease, was convinced of the commercial value of iron and terminated his partnership with C. Allhusen and Company. Pease advised the partners to purchase cheaply six acres of land close to the river Tees; he also provided them with a letter of introduction to the coal owners of South Durham.

Joseph Pease believed that without the financial interest in iron ore, Middlesbrough would not survive economically. He seemed desperate for the partners to develop the area. But Bolckow and Vaughan, both rational thinkers had already fully considered the area for their headquarters, taking into account the deeper sea and better facilities for exporting heavy goods.

Another influence on their decision making was James Harris, an engineer on the Stockton and Darlington railways, who informed them that Middlesbrough was a better prospect than Hartlepool or Stockton and ideally situated for coal from Durham and limestone from Cleveland. Subsequently, in 1841, their partnership began with the opening of an ironworks at Middlesbrough. It processed pig iron, for rail, bar, and rod, with rails of 73lb per yard being rolled for the Stockton and Darlington railroad.

Bolckow and Vaughan lived next door to each other in Cleveland Street, Middlesbrough, which is today part of Queens Square. The partners formed an ideal business team, Bolckow a man of capital and Vaughan an expert in iron management. By 1846, 20,000 tons of iron was being processed at their Vulcan Street works, importing the pig iron from Scotland. Bolckow had hopes at the time of being totally self-sufficient, owning iron mines, railways, ships, blast furnaces, and coalmines. In 1843, on gaining the contract to build engines for the steamship *English Rose*, they indeed felt that they were taking a step in this direction. It was absolutely essential that adequate supplies of Scottish pig iron were maintained, but during 1845 it fluctuated and rose from £2 to £6 per ton. The partners felt it was important to look for a local supply which they found at Whitby. This located, the partnership decided to erect a number of smelting furnaces at Witton Park, 20 miles to the west of Middlesbrough.

One of the most important days in Cleveland's history was 8 June 1850. This was the day an exciting discovery was made by John Vaughan and a geologist, John Marley from Darlington. They found the existence of a bed of ironstone to the south east of Middlesbrough. A tramway was built down the side of Eston Hills to a local track, resulting in 4,041 tons of ironstone being transported to Witton Park. The following year a branch railway was added to Middlesbrough so that even more iron ore could be taken to Witton. Marley estimated that the partnership needed initially 1,000 tons a week, but before the permanent railway had been completed, this figure was increased

to 1,000 tons a day. The Middlesbrough blast furnaces were eventually opened, with Vaughan introducing the Bell and Hopper system invented by Parry, of Ebbw Vale. This allowed the closure of the top of the furnace. This iron making practice became common throughout the world in the second half of the nineteenth-century.

In 1840 the district of Cleveland had been an agricultural centre of little importance. By 1870 it had grown from obscurity to a position of renown in the world of the iron trade. The discovery of the Eston ironstone acted as a catalyst and also a stimulus for the future economic expansion of the area, as well as the rise in the fortunes of Bolckow and Vaughan, whose expansion after 1850 was incredible. After the exciting discovery of ironstone at Eston, hopes were high that further ore would be found. Two branch railway lines existed into the ironstone area: one opened by Bolckow and Vaughan to get ironstone from Eston mines, the other from Upleatham (owned by the Derwant Iron Company, who were rivals to the Stockton & Darlington Railway Company).

By now Joseph Pease had his very able son, Joseph Whitwell Pease, to assist him in business and in November 1851 they issued a prospectus for a new Railway Company, which would run from Middlesbrough to Guisborough with two branches to the Cleveland Hills. Prior to its new-found wealth with iron ore, the Stockton and Darlington Railway Company had undergone an economic downturn. The present proposal was seen as an attempt by the Pease's to monopolise the freight in the new boom area. Many thought that the line was a bad commercial venture, John Vaughan among them, and the subscription list was filled slowly.

The line was completed in 1854, and the Pease's gamble with the line seemed to be paying off when negotiations were opened with Robert Challenor for permission to survey estates in Guisborough. Permission was granted and iron ore was found in abundance. Later there would be wrangling over mining rights, but in February 1855, an agreement between Bolckow and Challenor was made and signed, granting the iron magnates the ironstone rights in, upon, and under lands north of the Middlesbrough to Guisborough railway. They were also granted the rights to sink pits, set up machinery, construct railways and erect houses, workshops and offices for agents and engineers, as well as 20 cottages for workmen near to the mines. Challenor retained the rights of any other mineral found on the land. The partnership had to undertake not to destroy fish and game, nor to underlet or assign and promise not to spoil the scenic beauty of the estate and that Challenor would be allowed to inspect the workings at any time.

Bolckow and Vaughan agreed to pay surface rent of not less than £2 per acre and a rent of £300 in the first year, rising to £1000 in the third year and every subsequent year. The agreement held until 1877, when about this time, Challenor brought a civil action against Bolckow and the 1855 lease saying they had wrongly deducted property tax. By then general rates for the mines had been assessed and Bolckow had rightly deducted these from the rent. He pointed out that royalties and rent were to be paid free of taxes, rates, or impositions laid on the property by Government. Challenor's objection was defeated locally and on taking it to the House of Lords, was again defeated. However, the action did not embitter relations because the lease lasted until 1921.

Gunnergate Hall, John Vaughan's home.

In the 10 year period between 1851 and 1861 ironstone production increased from 13,000 tons to 609,000 tons with the proportion of finished products just as significant. By 1857 more than seven million tons of iron ore was being mined in Cleveland and by 1861 Bolckow and Vaughan were the largest and wealthiest iron masters. Their degree of self-sufficiency could be seen from the diversity of their holdings, before they were transferred to a limited company. Hematite mines at Eston, Guisborough, Upsal, and Skelton supplied ore. Coalmines at White Lee, Woodifield, Shildon, West Auckland and Byers Green, all which had been sunk by the Coulsons, supplied over a million tons of coal each year. Their own quarry at Bishopley supplied limestone. Their own railway went to the docks, and loaded finished products onto their own ships. Ten thousand people were employed and £1million paid out in wages.

Well before 1864 Bolckow had achieved his dream of self-sufficiency and in 1864 both partners, wished to convert their holdings into a limited liability company, mainly to enjoy some of the fruits of their labour. An act had been passed in Parliament in 1862, which absolved shareholders from being personally responsible for company's debts. Accordingly they converted their company at the end of 1864, and on 1 January 1865 they, commenced trading as a limited company, with 10 directors, among whom were, Henry Bolckow, John Vaughan, Benjamin Whitworth a Manchester MP and Alderman Pochin, the Mayor of Salford; each member having to submit himself for re-election every three years. Henry Bolckow however remained as Chairman until his death in 1878.

The limited companies first Annual General Meeting was held at the Memorial Hall, Albert Square, Manchester in November 1866. With shares totalling 25,000 of £100 each, 8,000 being held by Bolckow and Vaughan. The subscribed capital was £1.5 million and the paid up capital amounted to £1.2 million. In his report to shareholders Bolckow revealed that their interest in the new company was assessed at being £1.5 million, but the new directors refused to accept this valuation, after which an independent valuation was carried out during 1865, when the purchasing price was fixed at £995,000. After forwarding some cash to the ex-partnership, the new company still owed them £280,000. This was to be paid in six half-yearly instalments. Thus the deficit, which would show on the accounts, left the ex-partners in full control of the company. Henry Bolckow commented that the new company had inherited a valuable property at a very modest price, consisting of three large works, five collieries and various ironstone mines. All would have to be sold to the new company for approximately £700,000.

Although 1865 was marked by a series of downturns including 10% bank rate, a strike lasting 18 weeks and war on the continent, Bolckow was still able to report a profit of £134,914, which entitled the shareholders to a 10% dividend. As the years progressed the company kept abreast of technology and continued to expand until the original capital rose to £3.5 million; a shining example of a company surviving all kinds of pressures and still making a profit.

Marton Hall, Bolckow's home.

Bolckow and Vaughan, both represented Middlesbrough in politics; Bolckow was Lord Mayor in 1865, and often entertained dignitaries and public representatives at his residence at Marton Hall. He also represented the town as a Liberal

MP in 1874. His hold over the electorate was overwhelming. He polled 3,719 votes. Kane, the Labour candidate got 1,541 and Hopkins, the Conservative 996.

Bolckow although a Prussian by birth, amassed his vast fortune in England. He wished to be as British as possible. As early as 1841 he made numerous attempts to naturalise himself, buying Marton Hall in Middlesbrough to develop an interest in the area around him. Captain Cook, the famous explorer had been a native of Marton which was part of Bolckow's estate and because he admired Cook and all that he achieved, Bolckow completely restored Cook's home, making it a place of local interest. When anything connected with the great man came up for auction, he was one of the keenest buyers. Over the years he collected important journals and dairies which had been assumed lost.

In 1868, a group of ten manuscripts were auctioned by Messrs Puttick and Simpson of 47 Leicester Square, London. Lot 640 was the most important of the documents, being the Holograph Journal on the charting of New Zealand and Australia between 1769 and 1771. A dealer called Massey sold them to Bolckow, for £14 15s 0d. The journals ended up in the library at Marton Hall, where they were discovered by the trustees of Bolckow's fortune. They came up for auction at Sotheby' in May, 1888, making £71,387, which was for some time a record for sales in one day.

Bolckow and Vaughan had brought prosperity to Middlesbrough and Bolckow wished to give something back to the people of the area. Subsequently, in 1868, he bought 97 acres of land for £19,600, to provide a park for the people. He shunned calling the park after himself naming it Albert Park after the late Prince Consort, who was a Prussian himself; her Majesty was in full agreement with the name. Before the park opened the cost had mushroomed to £30,000, but was paid gladly by Bolckow. At a banquet held at Marton Hall, the Archbishop of York praised Bolckow tremendously and the press also sang his praises calling him a 'philanthropic donor'.

Statue of John Vaughan in Victoria Square, 1906.

Sometime after Vaughan was Mayor of Middlesbrough (1858), his health began to deteriorate and by 1864 he took little interest in the business. His doctors ordered him to go to London and in 1867 he died there on 16 September 1868. In 1879 Joseph Dodds, the MP for Stockton presented to Middlesbrough, on behalf of some subscribers, a portrait of John Vaughan which is in the Council Chamber. A statue of Vaughan was unveiled on 29 September 1884 near the Albert Bridge which was moved to Victoria Square on 23 October 1904. His son, Thomas, served as Mayor of Middlesbrough in 1871 and died in 1900.

Statue of Bolckow in Exchange Square, Middlesbrough 1986.

Bolckow remained healthy until 1877. However, by August that year, suffering severely from a kidney disorder, his health deteriorated and he was confined to his London home, 33 Princes Gate. Bolckow's doctor recommended a change of air and in May he went to Ramsgate where his health improved at first, but later deteriorated again and on Tuesday 18 June 1878, at the Granville Hotel, Ramsgate, Henry Bolckow died. A wish that he be interred at Marton cemetery was carried out and a special train brought the coffin and mourners from London to Middlesbrough, with the cortege proceeding by carriage to Marton Hall on 22 June. A huge cortege left Marton Hall for the parish church where the Reverend J. K. Bailey conducted the service. Bolckow was buried in a grave overlooking the road, between avenues of lime trees. An inscription on the now-neglected tombstone reads: 'Blessed are the peacemakers, for they shall be called the children of God'.

However, all the railways he built where successful and Hudson became known as the 'Railway King'.

George Hudson
1800-1871

On 30 December 1833, a group of tradesmen met in Tomlinson's hotel in York. Amongst them were solicitors, owners of small businesses, and small shopkeepers. The Sheriff of York, a coal merchant named Meek, chaired the meeting. The Liverpool to Manchester Railway had recently been shown to be a complete success and now South Yorkshire coal owners had come together to discuss building a railway line from Leeds to Selby, with the possibility of proceeding as far as Hull. It was hoped that in a short time south Yorkshire coal could be transported cheaply and swiftly to the south of England. This meeting was the beginning of George Hudson's amazing quest to develop the railways in the north of England.

Hudson was a linen draper of College Street, York. His beginnings were rather obscure, but by his own exertions he became a millionaire. He provided the whole of the north of England with railways which were carefully planned, built quickly and at the same time supplied work for thousands of men. Both he and his friends became very rich, though later the methods he used to raise money for the projects would be questioned.

Top, Hudson's old shop in 1821 and below, how it is today.

George Hudson was the son of a prosperous yeoman farmer from the tiny village of Derwant which lies between York and Malton. George was his father's fifth son, born in 1800. His father, who had intended him to be a farmer, died when George was only nine years old.

George left school aged 15, and was bound apprentice in William Bell's linen shop in College Street, York. In 1821 he married a solicitor's daughter, Elizabeth Nicholson, who occasionally worked in the shop where the couple also lived. When William Bell retired, George renamed the business Nicholson and Hudson. Later, Hudson said that his days at the shop were the happiest of his life—running a business with an annual turnover of £3,000, a quarter of which was profit.

In 1827, however, something happened which would change Hudson's life, bringing him extreme wealth but eventually financial ruin. Hudson's rich great-uncle, Matthew Bottrill, died, leaving most of his fortune of £30,000 to his nephew George. Bottrill had made the will on his deathbed where Hudson had been assiduous in attendance on the old man in his final hours. The will was not contested and Hudson became one of the richest men in York, using his legacy to invest in the North Midland Railway.

The linen shop gradually disappeared into the background and Hudson rose in society as a member of the Conservative Party. During the autumn of 1832 he stood as Conservative candidate in the council elections, progressing from organiser to treasurer of the Party. At the same time, He became interested in banking and formed the York Union Banking Company, which began trading in 1833 with a capital of £500,000. Deposits were forthcoming from Sir John Lowther MP for York and other wealthy men and the company began trading with Glyns, a London bank, the chairman of which was also chairman and chief promoter of the London to Birmingham Railway. Hudson's bank would soon play a major role in the financing of railway companies.

At the meeting at Tomlinson's Hotel at the end of 1833, Hudson was appointed treasurer of the York Railway Committee. The committee would undertake the development of a railway to link York with towns in West Riding. Hudson bought up most of the shares offered for the York to Leeds Railway and secured a famous engineer, John Rennie, to survey the line. His report was ready in early 1834; with Rennie actually proposing the use of horses, on the grounds of economy! Hudson visited Whitby later that year where he met George Stephenson. Stephenson and Hudson struck up a formidable friendship which lasted throughout both men's lives.

Around this time, there was a lull in the progress of the railways in the north so Hudson took the opportunity to advance his political career. In 1834 the first reformed parliament was dissolved and there was a general election. With help from financial deposits from Sir John Lowther and the York Union Bank and also from James Richardson, the Conservative agent, Hudson supported Sir John for one of the York seats in the election; £2,000 being spent on the poll and a further £1,000 to reward 'those that voted Tory'. The seat was secured despite objections to the bribery used by the Conservatives in securing it. However, in August 1835 Hudson and over 60 prominent citizens were summoned to London to testify before a Commons Committee on Election Petitions. Hudson, as party treasurer, was cross-examined for two whole days and forced to make a number of damaging admissions: the Conservatives had been guilty of gross bribery, but Hudson, although guilty of impropriety with funds, was welcomed home a hero and a true blue.

During the autumn of 1835 there was a public meeting in Doncaster with a deputation headed by its richest citizen, Edmund Becket Denison, to beg Hudson to build a railway to Doncaster. Hudson decided to be guided by Stephenson, who advised the use of engines rather than the horses Rennie had recommended. Stephenson's plan was to put in two railways right through the Midlands, one from Derby via the hilly country to Leeds, to be called the North Midland Railway, and one from Rugby to Derby called the Midlands County Railway. He had secured the agreement of the Derbyshire and Nottinghamshire coal owners, as well as a group of capitalists from Liverpool, so success was virtually guaranteed. Hudson had already made his own promises to link Leeds to London and begged Stephenson to make the terminus of the North Midland line at York rather than Leeds: 'Mak all t'railways cum t' York', he pleaded. But Stephenson, thinking of fixed gradients on his lines, refused to change his original plans. So, Hudson thought up a clever variation of his original plan: the York line should connect with Stephenson's line at Normanton. This was common sense and it meant that they could also enlist Stephenson as engineer and use his prestige to raise capital.

The plan quickly took shape; Hudson's strategy proved sound. A group of Quakers who had originally been involved in the Stockton and Darlington Railway had proposed a line from Newcastle to York; (the Great North of England Railway) and the two groups agreed to collaborate.

George Hudson at the height of his fame.

Hudson wholeheartedly took the lead and the committee was transformed into the North Midland Railway Company with Hudson as treasurer, James Richardson as solicitor and one of Stephenson's assistants as engineer. A survey of the line was carried out and the Bill drafted for introduction to parliament. Capital of £300,000 was required; there were few investors from York but a group of London capitalists added their weight and by 1836 the £50 shares began to sell. The York MPs, including Lowther, ensured an easy passage for the Bill. By August 1836 the new committee was able to hold its first formal meeting, register the shares and elect a board of directors. Sir John Simpson, the Lord Mayor of London topped the poll. Hudson, beaten by a single vote was second. James

Richardson, Alderman Meek Robert Davies the Town Clerk and Richard Nicholson, Hudson's brother-in-law were all elected. Later Hudson was chosen as chairman and his friend George Baker became secretary.

It was early in September 1836 when Stephenson staked out the first few miles of the new line, saying that it would be completed in 18 months; he was however, proved to be over optimistic. In order to speed the Bill through the House of Lords, Hudson had made an offer of £5,000 to Lord Howden, who owned some of the land en-route. Later Hudson attempted to get out of the deal but after litigation, Howden was paid £5,000 by the committee. Hudson had overreached himself.

In April 1837 Hudson set the contractors to work on the line, which was due to run from York, and across the Leeds-Selby line at South Milford at Altofts. The company's stock rose together with Hudson's prestige in York. Stephenson had promised that the line would be the cheapest yet constructed and actually invested £20,000 of his own money in shares. He encouraged his friends to do the same. The Quakers in York were a little suspicious of Hudson, but still invested their money, mainly because of their confidence in Stephenson. York City Council gave permission for a tunnel under the city with space for a station.

In April 1839 the first engine arrived from Stephenson's factory in Newcastle and was christened *Lowther*. It was decided to have the opening ceremony on 29 May, when all York

celebrated the occasion. A large crowd of distinguished guests consumed early morning breakfast, then, after a short speech by Hudson, 400 passengers packed themselves into 19 carriages serviced by two engines and made the journey to South Milford. Resplendent in his glory was Hudson, with Stephenson at his right side. A long round of speeches and toasts followed with the crowd streaming back to the state-room of the Mansion House, where the mayor led the dancing which lasted until four o'clock in the morning.

The opening of the York Railway was indeed a huge achievement. Hudson's prestige was at an all-time high but in both politics and business he had made many enemies; The Quaker businessmen in particular did not trust him. However, the Great North of England Railway Company did not prosper. The company engineer had not constructed adequate bridges and Robert Stephenson had to come to the rescue. In fact Stephenson became their engineer, but on his own terms, one condition being that the company drop all thought of proceeding further with the northern half of the project between Darlington and Newcastle.

On 26 February 1841 there was a half yearly meeting of the North Midland Railway Company. Hudson was nominated for election to the board of directors but declined the offer. He was too interested in the Great North of England Railway and the Newcastle to Darlington route. People wondered at the time why the North Midland, with Stephenson as engineer fared so badly against

Railways in 1843.

Hudson's line. In hindsight the answer is clear to see—the company had paid far too much for their land whereas Hudson had not.

In September 1843 Hudson succeeded in a triple amalgamation of the Midlands railways. People were now realising how astute a businessman Hudson was. The people of York were fully aware of this and nicknamed him 'Gumsher Hudson', while in London he was called 'The Yorkshire Balloon' 'Jupiter' and even 'The Railway Napoleon'. And a journalist for *The Railway Times* wrote, 'I consider Hudson to be a shrewd and honest man' and compared his power to that of the Prime Minister, William Gladstone.

After the hard-won victories at the Midland meetings in August and September 1843 a lesser man would have taken a holiday but not George Hudson. He and Robert Stephenson bought the Durham Junction Line in late autumn 1843, for less than its original cost of construction. The next project was extending the line to Newcastle and then to Berwick. Finance was forthcoming from the shareholders of the Darlington to Newcastle line. But an obstacle stood in their way—the river Tyne.

Until 1843 the line ran only as far as Gateshead, on the south bank of the Tyne. George Stephenson devised a scheme for a great bridge at a high level across the river from Gateshead to Newcastle. The project was priced at £100,000. The High Level Bridge over the Tyne and the Berwick Railway progressed slowly. Rivalry was developing between the York and

North Midland and the Hull and Selby Railways. North of York there was towns with undeveloped docks; Hudson imagined the cargoes of coal and iron ore entering these docks. He also wished to build a line of watering places between Hull and Hartlepool by connecting up Filey and Bridlington with Scarborough, via a coastal railway line. This brought Hudson into conflict with the Selby and Hull Railway Companies who naturally thought it was their territory. The directors could not sustain a fight with Hudson unaided, and tended to stick close to the Manchester to Leeds Railway Company, who were also hostile to the York and North Midland Company; sooner or later there would be a mighty conflict in eastern England.

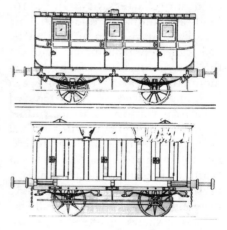

Carriages used for conveying 'Parliamentary' passengers, 1845. The upper carriage had glazed windows (marked A) in the doors; in the lower carriage, the spaces marked A could be closed in bad weather.

Rumours of Hudson buying the Great North of England Railway Company were rife in the autumn of 1844, but it wasn't until May 1845 that Hudson made his move. The company was invited to lease their line to Hudson's group of companies for five years at a guaranteed 10% on all their shares. Thereafter, the Newcastle and Darlington Junction Company would buy the whole line out at the rate of £250 for every £100 share. The Great North of England Railway Company shareholders would be paid off in 4% stock, continuing to receive 10% in perpetuity on their existing capital. They stood to make an enormous profit. Total capital so far extended on the line was £1,300,000 and it would take a further £344,000,000 of new capital to purchase it. The total income of the line to date was only £75,000 a year, yet the guaranteed rent he promised was £109,000 a year until 1847, and even more after that. In 1846, Hudson admitted in evidence before a Parliamentary Committee that he had paid more than market price for the line. He justified this by having more efficient management between York and Berwick; he then reduced prices on the line gaining public goodwill. Hudson added that he had no personal interest in the purchase, not holding a single share in the Great North of England Railway Company at the time of its purchase. He maintained that his interest really lay in raising shares in order to pay for the purchases.

About this time Hudson raised a testimonial subscription for George Stephenson in the form of a plate and the erection of a statue on the projected High Level Bridge over the Tyne. Since Hudson was closely connected with these projects, two testimonials were planned. One story, advocated by Bridges Adams

tells how Hudson drafted the appeal for his own testimonial, drawing up a list of subscribers with large sums next to their names, including contractors and engineers. He then instructed his secretary to send the list to the press in the hope that those people now publicly named, would not refuse to support his testimonial. He then requested all of the donations to be paid directly to his bankers. George Stephenson denounced this procedure, saying that he intended writing a letter of refusal to the press, but other directors convinced him that this might affect the railway shares so he backed down.

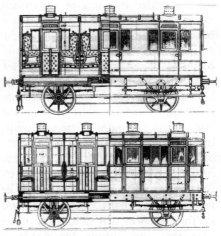

First and second class railway carriages, c. 1860, used on the Great Northern Railway.

Hudson travelled south to Westminster to monitor progress with the Railway Bill. On 11 July Lord Brougham complained that Hudson was working with a 12 counsel power before the committee on the London to York Line with obstructive purposes, and that he had interfered with the committee. The merits of the London-York Bill had now being argued *ad nauseam* and the committee's duties were finishing. Speculation in company shares was rife. On 23 July, with the casting votes of the chairman the Railways Bill was approved. When the Bill had passed the standing-order stage in the House of Lords without challenge, it was found that a lot of the names and addresses of share-holders were fictitious. A petition to enquire into allegations of forgery was mounted, but the bill still passed its third reading.

Later the charge was found to have been well grounded. At the very last stage of the bill, the Lords Committee recommended that it should proceed no further until investigations could be made. The 70-day committee, the counsel, witnesses and promoters in parliament, together with outside speculators, found that the veto had fallen. The Midlands Railway was safe for another year when it could consolidate the east of England with its own railway system.

In 1845 a series of celebrations took place throughout the east of England. On 16 August, a reception at York Station was held. The Lord Mayor, Sheriff, with the Dean of York attending. The Minster bells were rung, cannons fired and deafening cheers and music welcomed the 'Railway King'. After celebrations at Whitby, came Sunderland where there was a conservative banquet on 21 October. For years businessmen had striven to increase the importance of Sunderland as a port, but had not succeeded – now Hudson was doing it in no time at all.

However, the London-York Railway Bill still haunted Hudson. The York and North Midland Railway Company was charged with £30,000 and The Midland Railway Company £50,000 as their share of the costs. The Bill's passage through the Commons was assured if there were no changes. Hudson proposed to create a north-south line of his own. To do this he would have to move south to London. He therefore took on the chairmanship of the Eastern Counties Railway. This railway was 150 miles long, one of the longest in the country and carried more goods than passengers but it was badly managed although it had a London terminus. Three million pounds had been spent on the line with only a return dividend of 1% in July 1845.

Prior to moving to London, Hudson bought the Durham and Sunderland Railway for £270,000, double the market value as well as building a new dock for £200,000 at Jarrow Slake on the Tyne. Hudson also leased to the Newcastle and Darlington Company and the Hartlepool Dock and Railway Company, which linked the town with the main line. *The Times* declared Hudson had secured almost entire command of the northern railways in the county of Durham.

It was said that one of the major blunders of Hudson's career was his chairmanship of the Eastern Counties Railway. Strategically this railway was an unusual partner for the Midland and York and the North Midland Railways and because of the alliance, Hudson's companies were vulnerable.

By the end of 1843, railway mania increased and engineers such as Brunel, Locke, Rennie, and Vignoles were in great demand. George Stephenson was now retired and living at Tapton House but his son, Robert, was connected with 34 separate lines and Hudson often called at Stephenson's offices at 24 Great George Street, Westminster.

The demand for labour of all kinds increased. The price of iron doubled. Solicitors, stockbrokers and estate agents were all in demand; 16,000 people ranging from bankers to clergymen had bought railway shares of £2,000. Even such unlikely figures as Emily and Ann Bronte invested small amounts. Their more famous sister Charlotte failed to persuade them to sell when the market was high and they lost their money in the 1848 slump.

George Stephenson said, from his retirement at Tapton, that Hudson had became too great for him. Stephenson had made Hudson a rich man but he would soon care for nobody unless they could make him money.

The amalgamation of the lines north of York was accomplished in two stages; the first of these was the ratification by parliament in 1846 of the purchase of the Great North of England Railway Company by the Newcastle and Darlington Junction Company, which was renamed the York and Newcastle Railway in September 1846; 159,000 new shares at £25 each were issued, making the new company £6,625,000. Hudson made a pledge to buy out every holder of shares worth £100 in the Great North of England, for £250 before 1851, so confident was he of success.

On 5 July 1847, the young Queen Victoria and Prince Albert her consort travelled on the Eastern Counties Railway to Cambridge where they attended the installation of the Chancellor of the University. Hudson seized the opportunity to put on a flamboyant display. A special train was fitted out for the occasion. The Queen appeared in a transparent cottage bonnet and peach-blossom satin dress. She bade Mr Hudson good-morning whereupon he guided her into a pavilion filled with elegantly dressed women. From there he escorted her to the royal carriage and presented her with a beautifully executed map of the line and illuminated copies of the timetable of the royal train. The carriage was coloured white and gold outside. The linings and furniture were of French grey satin. The roof was fluted with the same material and the carriage hung with the fairest and freshest favours of flora. On arrival at Cambridge, Hudson leapt out and quickly opened the royal carriage door. The Queen took his arm and he escorted her into the pavilion, preceded by the Earl Marshall, the Duke of Norfolk. Later, Prince Albert, conveyed Her Majesty's satisfaction in her comfort and well-being to Hudson.

Hudson's calculations about the success of the enterprise were made on the expectation that the year 1847 would turn out to be the worst year of the trade depression. He thought that after a slump, trade would revive and prosperity would follow. However, revolution and riot were rife throughout Europe and like most of the population, he had not anticipated the political upheavals of 1848. Anxiety affected his health and in April of that year Hudson was confined to bed with a digestive problem, which later affected his heart and caused attacks of angina.

May 1848, Robert Davies retired after completing 20 years as Town Clerk of York. Hudson missed his old friend whom he could trust to guide the machinery of local government. Between August and September of 1848, Hudson had to repay £400,000 that he had borrowed from banks on behalf of his various companies. He managed this, but it left his reserves seriously deflated and future dividends were in jeopardy. Rumours leaked about the massive repayment, causing panic throughout Hudson's shareholders. By 27 October the York and North Midland £50 share had fallen from £62 to £46, the York Newcastle and Berwick £25 share from £30 to £23, the Midland £100 stock from £93 to £73, the Eastern Counties £20 shares to just over £12. Railway stock throughout the country was also affected. Hudson again suffered with digestive problems and his financial statements were delayed until 14 November. For the moment the shares were checked but there was an obvious storm brewing and investors settled down to await the next set of accounts.

The Stockton and Darlington Railway Company had rather declined from its original glory and the directors wished Hudson to place it in his care which he agreed to do in November 1848. A notice appeared in the press that the line was to be leased to the York, Newcastle and Berwick Company at guaranteed a return of 9% on capital. The North British Railway had also changed their minds and approached Hudson, but now conditions were different, and Hudson could not raise the capital necessary. The 'Railway King' had spent enormous amounts on his four northern railway companies. Approximately £30 million went to guaranteed dividends on leases and shareholders. Now no more capital was forthcoming from any source. Each of the four half-yearly meetings in 1849 spelt trouble for Hudson. He had loaned £150,000 of the shareholders money to the Sunderland Dock Company without parliamentary sanction. He also had trouble with the strangulation of Hull shipping with a fishing blockade by the Danish fishing fleet. In January there was a rumour of his impending resignation. Matters went from bad to worse when on 12 August 1848, George Stephenson died aged 68. Stephenson had been associated with Hudson since the railway mania had started in 1835, but he had lived more or less in retirement since 1845. The passing of Stephenson proved an ill omen. Hudson was put further and further under pressure, as one after the other of his financial indiscretions surfaced. His accounts were a shambles, with dates and times of transactions missing; signatories for the North Midland Railway Company, James Richardson and Robert Davies had signed any cheque laid before them.

Eventually the Prance report (two representatives from the Stock Exchange, Haratio Love and Robert

Prance held shares in one of Hudson's companies and subjected the company to scrutiny) was published which blasted any good name that Hudson had left. Many wished the 'Railway King' to be prosecuted for the violation of the Companies Act. The press was very hostile, 'Mr Hudson will not escape us' and 'Mr Hudson has duped thousands' were some of the comments.

In September 1845 Hudson was hauled in front of a tribunal of the Eastern Counties Railway, where Mr William Cash, the chairman questioned him relentlessly, 'Didst thou ever, after the accountant had made up the yearly accounts, alter any of the figures?' asked the Quaker William Cash, to which Hudson replied, very subdued and after hesitation, 'Well, I may have perhaps added a thousand or two to the next accounts'. 'Didst thou alter the accounts to say £10,000 or even £40,000?' the chairman added. Hudson replied nervously, 'Maybe not as much as that'. William Cash ultimately did not press the point, but decreed '...thou should go home and write down these amounts', much to Hudson's relief.

Out of £545,714 distributed in dividends from 4 January 1845, to 4 July 1848, £115,278 was procured by the alteration of traffic accounts and £205,294 by wrongly charging capital accounts, making a total of £320,572, which was not subject to dividends. Out of £545,714 only £225,142 had been earned and therefore subject to dividends. *The Observer* recorded at this time that for four years £13 million had been at the disposal of George Hudson and John Waddington to do with as they chose, making and unmaking dividends, acquiring traffic capital and revenue, pocketing cheques with no authority, re-directing sums to their own accounts and even charging hotel bills to the company.

Hudson's friends at Sunderland rallied loyally behind him, but to no avail. On 4 May 1848 he sent a letter of resignation to his companies. His brother-in-law, Richard Nicholson, was also implicated by the Prance Report and on the night of 8 May he left his house at Clifton and walked along the bank of the Ouse to Marygate and was never seen alive again. His body was recovered from the river the following day.

The news reached Hudson at Newby Park where he was struck with grief. Within days he had to attend the House of Commons where, on 17 May he faced charges of bribery of his fellow company members. At first he was unable to speak. He stood, his large head lightly covered with grey hair, his broad forehead and penetrating eyes looking pathetic, like an overgrown schoolboy. He began hesitatingly to say that he had never signed company cheques, but merely presided over them. He went on to say that he had taken a sanguine view of everything. If it were determined what should go to revenue and what should go to capital, there would be a clearer picture.

The majority heard his speech in stony silence. An investigative committee uncovered a web of deceit. One item alone showed Hudson himself had kept £37,350. Other accounts had been manipulated.

Early in January 1850 Hudson consented to pay in instalments, a sum of over £100,000, in settlement of all claims made against him by the York, Newcastle and Berwick Company. Subscribers were at least getting some of their investment back, but it appeared to be an admission of guilt.

Nevertheless, on 20 June 1850, the Sunderland Dock opened, one of Hudson's greatest achievements. There were 50,000 spectators, cannons were fired and there were scenes of rejoicing. Hudson was in his element making speeches, referring to the High Level Bridge at Newcastle and now this magnificent dock. But the glitter of the occasion was short lived for the 'Railway King', as one after another the Chancery cases came to court. The Solicitor General and the Master of the Rolls decided against him and Newby Park had to be sold. Hudson negotiated a settlement with the directors of the York, Newcastle and Berwick Company in 1854, after which no more claims would be pressed against him.

Unfortunately, no sooner did he get this debt settled than another charge that he had bribed Members of Parliament emerged. On 18 February 1854, a French Count sued him for £4,000 damages in connection with a contract to supply iron. This latest repayment meant that by the autumn of 1854 he had fallen into arrears with his payments to the York, Newcastle and Berwick Company. His parliamentary immunity protected him from his creditors while the Commons was in session, but in recess he had to resort to all kinds of evasive action to stay at liberty. He found it impossible to retrieve any of his fortune or do business with foreign rail companies, and the pressures of merely living were enormous. For a little peace he decided to go abroad and on 12 August 1855 left for Spain. On reaching San Sebastian he became violently ill and was confined to bed for months. Very despondent, Hudson returned to England and Sunderland where he promised to attend better to his constituent's problems as their MP, if re-elected. He was indeed returned and worked hard on their behalf. In recess he went to Paris to avoid his creditors.

Hudson's wife managed to salvage a little money out of their wrecked affairs, living in lodgings in Belgravia. In November 1857, she was robbed of clothes and jewellery to the value of £200 and became traumatised with grief. Her second son, John, enjoying a brilliant military career as an officer in the 6th Carabineers serving in India, had been killed in the Indian Mutiny earlier that year. This was a terrible blow to the family. There was a further setback when their one remaining enterprise, the Sunderland Dock Company, in which Hudson had £60,000 invested, was reported to be doing badly. Lord Londonderry and other coal-owners appeared jealous of the docks and started boycotting the facilities. Seaham Harbour, Jarrow, Middlesbrough and Hartlepool were all touting for trade, so the dividend at Sunderland could not be maintained.

Hudson lost his seat at Sunderland in 1859 and had to go quickly to

Paris where he lived in exile to escape his creditors. In the autumn of that year Robert Stephenson died leaving his seat vacant at Whitby. The Whitby people loved Hudson, but he dare not venture back to England as his creditors would have him, and besides he was penniless. His old enemy H. S. Thompson of Moat Hall carried the seat.

Hudson travelled from one channel port to another living in cheap hotels, eating where and when he could. Creditors still hounded him relentlessly wishing to foreclose on his Whitby Estate. The Sunderland Dock Company was wound up and Hudson's shares were worthless. In 1863 Charles Dickens came across Hudson when he was travelling to France and remarked, 'I feel I should know that man'. Hudson, who was taking leave of a friend, was shabbily dressed and waving his high hat in a desolate and sad manner, Dickens, informed that it was Hudson, was amazed and recalled the incident in his autobiography.

Hudson failed because of his own faults, but we must also remember what he accomplished. In the early nineteenth-century. England required an efficient rail system, quickly, to take advantage of the next 25 years, when most other countries in the world were struggling. Hudson succeeded with the help of Stephenson and other engineers to do just this. Together he and Stephenson produced a very efficient system capable of keeping England ahead of the other countries. Hudson was a rogue in many ways but a scrupulous, unselfish man might never have produced the railway. It perhaps needed a man whose ambition overrode moral considerations.

An interpretation of the 'Railway King's' character was given in a report by Dr Robert Saudek, Europe's leading graphologist who, on sight of a specimen of Hudson's handwriting, and without any knowledge whatsoever of whose it was gave the following analysis, 'Here is a man of tremendous temperament, nervous, irritable, neurotic and impatient – with himself, as well as others – gifted with farsightedness, grasping things at a moment's notice, ever ready for combinations, lacks the ability to make himself easily understood, as his thinking would be faster than he could speak, and his instructions could be misinterpreted'.

On 8 June 1865, Hudson finally returned to England and Whitby to contest the Parliamentary seat there. In an address to a large public meeting, he promised to take West Cliff Estate back out of the hands of the railway company and develop it for the town. Early on Sunday morning 8 July and 48 hours before the poll, the Sheriff's officer entered Hudson's bedroom and arrested him for debt. Hudson was placed in the unsanitary old town prison at York Castle, where he stayed for three months. His creditors, mainly due to campaigning by the Whitby people, eventually released him. However, by now his health had completely deteriorated. Subsequently he and his wife were allowed to live quietly in retirement at 87 Churton Street, London. To his last day Hudson's spirit was fresh and alive and he quite enjoyed talking of his experiences and eventual downfall.

His death came in the winter of 1871. He had come north to York to visit some old friends, staying at the house of J. L. Foster, one of the oldest of them when he became very ill with angina. Returning back to his wife in London, Hudson died on 14 December. His remains were returned to York where they toured the city. Hudson's family and friends were in attendance, including Close, his faithful secretary, Cabrey, the engineer and J. L. Foster the editor of the *Yorkshire Gazette*. The procession toured the valley of Derwent and the Yorkshire Wolds. Hudson's body was interred in the churchyard at Scrayingham.

Today, the tall grass hides the grave and the words carved on the gravestone of the once-mighty 'Railway King' have been obliterated.

There's a bad time going, boys,
A bad time going!
Railway shares have seemed to be
A sink fore! Men's property
In the bad times going.
Lines, which used to quarrel then,
To prove whose purse was stronger,
Shall be controlled by honest men...
Wait a little longer!"

Punch, 1848

Robert Stephenson

1803-1859

Robert Stephenson was born 16 October 1803. A weak and sickly baby, he was christened at the school house at Willington. Unfortunately at only the age of three his mother died of consumption and never witnessed his rise to fame. People predicted Robert would not survive (he had his mother's weak chest all his life). However, the strong Stephenson blood flowed through his veins and he grew into a slim wiry boy – strong and full of energy, mischief and humour.

When Robert was 11 years old in 1814, he attended the 'Bruce Academy', at Newcastle leaving in 1819. Robert and his father George were very close and he made sure that Robert got opportunities, especially in education, that he never had. On returning home from school Robert had a great deal of work to do. His father often questioned him on his school lessons; he also had him read from books loaned from the library on science and inventions. On other days he and his father might repair clocks and watches and both worked on the sundial that would hang on the door of the family cottage.

Robert commenced work at Killingworth Colliery in 1819 where he was indentured as an apprentice engineer to the Manager Nicholas Wood who was himself a brilliant mining engineer. Robert's father, George, had been assigned to survey the Stockton to Darlington Railway and it was not a surprise when Robert joined his father in this project in 1922, after completing three years learning the main aspects of colliery maintenance and engineering with Nicholas Wood at Killingworth.

About 1823 George encouraged Robert to further his education by attending Edinburgh University but by the end of that year, Robert was back with his father at Fourth Street, Newcastle.

Robert Stephenson.

In the early 1820s, the most popular method to 'get rich quick' was to find gold or silver and many companies were formed for this purpose, particularly to look for gold in South America. In these early days of gold and silver exploration though, there was a scarcity of good professional men to manage the projects, and so young mining engineers with limited experience were made very tempting propositions by big companies. One such company was the Columbian Mining Association, who had interests in two mines named Santa-Anne and La-Manta, these mines were situated about 12 miles from Mariquita, a fine old city in South America. At this time it was deserted and run down, but still showing signs of being a noble city. Very near to the mines was the village of Santa-Anne.

In October 1823, George Stephenson was approached by the directors of the Columbian Mining Association to act as their consultant, in Columbia, engaging miners and inspectors, as well as shipping iron. However, it was Robert Stephenson that their confidence really lay in and it was soon made known to George Stephenson that they wished Robert to be Engineer in Chief for the project.

At the same time, the Stephenson's Fourth Street works in Newcastle was quickly expanding along with the growth of the locomotion, Robert Stephenson had shown strength of character and perseverance as manager of the works and it had obviously not gone unnoticed. Indeed, the works seemed as if it would not run without him, even so, romantic travel at the time fascinated Robert and he agreed to take the job.

George Stephenson strongly opposed Robert's venture to Santa-Anne, he even questioned it on medical grounds, because of Robert's constitution, but Robert's physician said he would thrive, especially with the change of climate. George Stephenson reluctantly gave his consent, and after an emotional departure, Robert sailed from Liverpool on 18 June 1824. The voyage lasted 35 days and after a pleasant trip Robert docked at La-Guaira on the north coast of Venezuela. From Venezuela he travelled to Caracas, 15 miles inland and stayed there for two months, which he spent investigating the strata in the area.

As the roads were in a very bad state he was not able to travel immediately. It was not until October that he commenced his journey to Bogotá. The route was through very rough terrain and there was known to be outlaws in the area who preyed on unfortunate travellers. Robert rode on a mule and progress was very slow but he did make sure that he was well armed. He took with him an interpreter, and a servant. Robert checked on strata and ground conditions whenever he could while travelling, and the guide pointed out old mining shafts that had at one time yielded deposits of gold.

Robert appeared to have enjoyed the mule journey very much, in fact, everything about the journey fascinated him – the local dress, the beauty and panoramic scenery; he found it all breathtaking. Nights were spent in the open air with his mosquito net hung from the branches of a tree. Robert always wore an under garment of white cotton with a cloak of blue woollen material, which doubled as a blanket at night. On his head he wore a high hat of plaited grass which was circled with a wide brim. He certainly did not look anything like an engineer's son from the north of England.

Robert Stephenson carefully logged the route taken on his journey, paying particular attention to the best possible route for the machinery, which he knew, would have to follow. He carried out his observations very carefully. In 1825, his party finally reached their destination. Before them were two long abandoned mines, La-Manta and Santa-Anne, they had become lost in vegetation. They were previously Spanish owned and worked. Robert soon got to work on opening the mines and his unstoppable energy meant the mines would be ready for the Cornish miners already on their way from England.

Roads had to be cut to the mines and overgrowth removed, good workers were hard to come by in the area. Many obstacles were put in his way, especially from rival companies. Robert longed for the arrival of the Cornish miners, whom he knew he would get a fair day's work from. Unfortunately, when they did arrive, the Cornish miners were nowhere near as good as those he was used to from the north of England. They were always under the influence of alcohol and would not respond to any kind of discipline. To add to the disappointment, the machinery he had ordered from England was far too heavy and awkward to get to the mines at Santa-Anne. Robert had to make do with lighter machinery, and then send for machinery in England which he knew could be transported and still carry out the work required.

By October 1825 there were enough men in Santa-Anne to do the work required. However, it was thought that the wages for the contract were far too high and some miners even returned home because they had made enough money. It was also thought amongst the miners that the youthful Robert Stephenson would not be capable of carrying out this difficult project and his connections with the northern coal fields caused Robert to be treated with contempt by the Cornish men.

One night early in December 1825, Robert retired to his house totally exhausted. As he drifted into a deep sleep, he suddenly heard loud yelling; the Cornish miners had entered the front room of his house, and were shouting abuse. Robert lay for a while working out what his approach to the miners should be. He wanted to avoid an all out stoppage. The miners insulted Robert in their drunken stupor to such an extent that he knew he would have to confront them or they would think he was afraid. Robert was taunted further by the men, 'let's put this clerk in his place', he heard just as he decided to finally confront them. He strode directly into the room and keeping as calm as possible approached the ring leaders of the mob saying that it was unfair, on his part, to fight at this time as they were drunk and he was sober. He challenged them to come back the following day. They could not believe their eyes, here was a young clerk confronting hard Cornish miners in a calm and collected manner.

The following day Robert had further trouble with the miners. He contacted London and the Columbian Mining Association, checking on his authority in disputes. An urgent message was returned confirming that he was in overall control of the miners' interests, and informing him to demand prompt obedience. Robert let this be known to the miners, but tried a new approach with them. He had always been good at games such as throwing the hammer, quoits and lifting weights, he suggested to the men that they would have a better social life doing these things and he challenged them to contests. This led to friendly rivalry among the men, as well as having the desired effect of keeping them temporarily away from alcohol. Robert had now spent a full year on the project in Santa-Anne, Mariquita, striving to make it a success for the Columbian Association. Unfortunately, some of the directors of the Association were putting extreme pressure on him to get better results. Robert, aged only twenty-two, took these experiences in his stride, knowing he would have similar situations on his return to England.

Letters from his father and other directors informed him that the Columbian Association had lost a great deal of money on this venture. As soon as Robert reached the end of his contract period, July 1827, he suggested the Association appoint another engineer in his place. Robert felt that he should return to Newcastle so that he could face any criticism that may be circulating at that time. The company, in retaliation, requested Robert to stay on the project. Ultimately, he rejected the offer and made ready to return home.

Robert Stephenson left Santa-Anne and made his way to Carthagena where he thought he would find a ship heading for England. Unfortunately, he was disappointed; instead he found a ship making ready to sail for America, docking at New York. He booked a passage on this hoping to get a connection from there to England and home. On arrival at Carthagena, Robert met up with Trevithick the Welshman and inventor of the first passenger locomotive; he joined Robert's party travelling to America. On the voyage the ship was hit by a hurricane before arriving at New York. From New York the party travelled to Montreal, Canada. Finally, he returned to New York where he boarded a ship for Liverpool. On returning home in 1828, he found his father doing very well and laying his second public railway.

Robert's spell in South America did him the world of good, as his physician said it would, making him self reliant, and broadening his mind. On his return, he was bronzed and looked extremely well for his trip and, if anything, the experience had refreshed and strengthened his resolve ready for the work that lay before him.

By 1828 Robert now fit and full of enthusiasm from his adventures in South America began work on the famous *Rocket* locomotive, which would win outright at the Rainhill locomotive Trials. However, before the trials, he proposed to Fanny Sanderson, the daughter of Mr John Sanderson of Broad Street, London. They married 17 June 1829 at Parish Church, Bishopgate.

In 1830 at the start of the Trials there was three different locomotives that were able to compete to the standard laid down by the rules of the Competition. They were from London, Shildon and Newcastle. The rules stipulated that locomotives should be mounted on springs weighing no more than six tons including water. They must consume their own smoke. A six ton locomotive must show that they are capable day by day of drawing a gross load of 20 tons at 10 mph. Steam pressures were not to exceed 50 lb. The Company reserved the right to test the boiler up to 150 psi. Nicholas Wood and John Kennedy were judges for the event.

During the summer of 1829, Robert worked hours on his locomotive *Rocket*. Mechanically he copied his previous locomotive *Lancashire Witch*. This machine had proven satisfactory; the locomotive did not have coupled wheels but it had single driving wheels, 4.8 inches diameter and the rear wheels were 2 feet 6 inches. The engine was a three-way invention, incorporating the skills of Henry Booth, (treasurer of the Liverpool & Manchester railway) George Stephenson, and Robert Stephenson; the roller had two straight flue tubes with a furnace in each—there was also a number of small ones, drawing hot gasses from a separate firebox, thus increasing the heating surface. The emphasis was on sustained power output over long distances. This design is generally credited to Henry Booth.

At this time one of the main problems of the steam engine was how to secure the tubes to the tube plates to make them steam proof. Robert tried many systems, one being, threading them in with a fastening nut to tighten them down. However, this was eventually dispensed of and he finally riveted the pipes in place. The only trouble was when the pressure rose above 70 lb—the pipes bulged out. Eventually he put in a series of long stay rods, between the two tube plates and on 5 September 1830 he was able to report to his father and Booth that the locomotive was now able to sustain the requirements of the test when the pressure was raised to 150 psi.

After making some adjustments to the locomotive it was all taken apart and lifted on to wagons on Saturday 12 September 1830 and sent on its way via Carlisle. Later it was loaded onto a barge on the Carlisle canal and conveyed to Bowness where it was transferred to the *Cumberland*, steamship and transported to Liverpool. On arrival it was carefully unloaded and taken to the Railway workshops at Crown Street, ready for assembly. In letters to Booth, Robert had mentioned that Hackworth was a serious exhibitor, with his engine *Sans Pareil*.

On Tuesday 6 October, crowds began to gather at Rainhill. They were from areas around Liverpool, St. Helens, Warlington, and Manchester.

There were officially five entries, the *Novelty*, from London, the *Sans Pareil*, from Darlington, the *Rocket*, from Newcastle upon Tyne, the *Cycloped*, from Liverpool, the *Perseverance*, from Edinburgh. There were 10,000 spectators each waiting in anticipation for a competition of which they were unsure of what to expect.

The course for the competitors was one eighth of a mile to terminal points. There were also Blacksmith's shops and other repair facilities available on the premises. As well as a point where water and fuel could be drawn—a weighbridge was also evident to make sure everything was perfectly legal. The trial commenced by each machine attempting to haul a train three times its own weight for a total of 20 runs, to and fro over the one and a half mile course.

Tests were carried out on how long it took the locomotives to build up steam. Along with checks made on just how much fuel and water was used, even how much evaporation was evident.

However, two of the machines were not eligible; the *Cycloped* (which depended on a horse) and *Perseverance* (met with a mishap before the event). The owner, withdrew on watching the other locomotives perform, Mr Burstall accepting that his machine was not up to standard. The Competition started with Braithwaite & Eriksson's *Novelty* (the favourite). Mr Vignoles, the engineer, had come especially to see this locomotive perform. The *Novelty* started well and clocked 28 mph, covering a mile in one minute 35 seconds. However, suddenly there was an explosion with sparks and flames coming from the engine. This put the locomotive out of the competition. *Sans Pareil* with Timothy Hackworth was struggling with a leaking boiler; like *Novelty* Hackworth asked for extra time to get the engine prepared. The *Rocket* exhibited but the crowd were not very keen on it. The weather changed very quickly to rain which brought the day to an end. The judges asked the Stephenson's and the *Rocket* to return the following day to exhibit further.

On the morning of 8 October the *Rocket* was weighed in the presence of judges. The machine weighed 4 tons 2 cwt more than originally declared but well within the permitted maximum for a four-wheeled engine. Steam was raised to 50 lb from cold in 57 minutes using 142 lb of coke. The two wagons of stone were coupled to make a weight of 12 ton 15 cwt. The two timekeepers with watches at the ready then took their stations. Rastrick at post no. 1, Wood at the other. Robert McCree of Killingworth was the *Rockets* regular driver but evidence shows that George Stephenson himself drove the locomotive on this occasion.

The *Rocket*, performed brilliantly, the east bound run was covered in 6 minutes, 15 seconds. As the test progressed George Stephenson increased the engine speed and on the tenth run he completed the measured distance in 4 minutes 12 seconds. To achieve this gallons of water was used and George completely oiled the machine including greasing the pistons.

Before the second half of the contest was progressed all locomotives were filled again with coke and water; during the break period, steam blew off from safety valves. When the Killingworth locomotive trials were held years previous the Stephenson's allowed the coke to get down thus losing steam; this took too much building up again. Thus, the second half of the trial went even better than the first; Stephenson kept one eye on the pressure gauge and found it averaging 50 psi. Nicholas Wood one of the judges checked the time of the machine which was 3 minutes 44 seconds, for the 60 miles the *Rocket* had travelled, it averaged 14 mph, 4 mph more than the speed required for the test with evaporation at 114 gallon per hour and 217 lb of coke had been burnt. The performance of the *Rocket* surpassed any other machine in the competition.

The following day it was the turn of Timothy Hackworth and *Sans Pareil*. Hackworth's time taken for raising steam could not be checked because Timothy had been working all night and the boiler was still hot. The engine was weighed and found to be 4 ton 15 cwt and above the weight he had declared—actually 5 cwt over the maximum for 4 wheel engines. This was a terrible blow for Hackworth who had worked all through the night and now faced exclusion from the contest. One other point overlooked was that the machine was un-sprung. Hackworth

as usual had mounted his cylinder vertical and this gave a direct drive by short connecting rods. This system stopped the use of springs on the drive axle. However, the judges were determined to let him compete.

Sans Pareil had its load attached and began its trial—red-hot coke came from its chimney; the machine took 5 minutes 9 seconds for the beginning run and Timothy never improved on this. Driven by Tommy Grey, the locomotive worked well and reached its eighth eastbound journey with Timothy working hard to keep the boiler fired and the feed pipe working. Unfortunately on one of its return journeys just in front of the stands there was a large cloud of steam—the lead fusible plug above the fire had melted due to lack of water. The *Sans Pareil* had to be manually pushed by the crowd to the Blacksmith's shop. This was the end of the *Sans Pareil's* challenge on the *Rocket*. However, it had averaged 14 mph and for the 22.5 miles it travelled with a load of 19 tons, it had consumed 692 lb of coke; the *Rocket* only consumed 217 lb. The judges had no other alternative but to judge that Stephenson's *Rocket* had displayed every laid down requirement of the Trial and that it was the best locomotive to exhibit at Rainhill.

Today, both *Sans Pareil* and the *Rocket* are displayed at the Science Museum. The *Sans Pareil* was strong but the *Rocket* was made with vast improvements in mind especially in power and speed and this was necessary for the advancement of the railways. The *Novelty* as George

Stephenson had said, 'lacked guts' and disappeared from the railway scene.

Top, Sans Pareil: Bottom, Rocket.

John Dixon when writing to his brother at Darlington summed up the Rainhill Trials:

Dear James,

We have finished the grand experiment on the engines and G.S. or R.S. has come off triumphant and of course will take hold of the £500 so liberally offered by the Company: none of the others being able to come near to them. The *Rocket* is by far the best engine I have ever seen for blood and bone united....

Timothy has been very sadly out of temper ever since he came for for he has been grobbing on day and night and nothing our men did for him was right, we could not please him with the tender or anything; he openly accused all G.S.'s people of conspiring to hinder him of which I do believe them innocent, however he got many trials but never got half of his 70 miles done without stopping. He burns nearly double the quantity of coke that the *Rocket* does and mumbles and roars and rolls about like an empty beer butt on a rough pavement and moreover weighs above 4.5 tons consequently should have six wheels and as for being on springs I must confess I cannot find them out.... She is very ugly and the boiler runs out very much, he had to feed her with more meal and malt Sprouts than would fatten a pig....

Robert's abilities began to be well known after the trials; and it was not a surprise that he was appointed Chief Engineer for one of the most important sections of the Railways. This was the Birmingham to London line, the first railway into London, which he completed in 1838.

On 28 May 1833 the London and Birmingham Railway officially came into being: with rich subscribers of the company offering landowners £750,000 on land valued only at £250,000 and Stephenson gained this valuable contract even though some of the best engineers had shown interest. At the time, Robert was just 30 years of age and responsible for laying the railway through rough terrain for 112 miles—to date, the most responsible position he had undertaken. Robert set about the appointment with confidence and accepted full responsibility for the massive masonry work, bridge and tunnel work and also the viaducts and embankments at Tring and Blisworth. Robert and his young wife reluctantly moved south to London where they rented a furnished cottage at St. John's Wood. They rented this until they could move into their house at Haverstock Hill.

Robert split the Rail Company into four divisions and appointed sub-assistants to be responsible for each part. They were divided as follows: Camden Town-Aldberry (John Birkenshaw); Tring-Castlethorpe (John Crossley); Brisworth-Kilsby tunnel (Frank Forster); Rugby-Birmingham (Thomas Gooch). For the purpose of the contract each stage was split into six mile sections.

After Robert engaged his staff he began to stake out the line; this work began in November 1833. Even with the terrible weather that particular winter the stake out was completed in February 1834. From his daily observations, drawings were completed by draughtsmen, three copies were completed—one for the District Engineer, one for The Management Committee and one for himself. The Rail Company eventually purchased the Eyre Arms Hotel that was on the route at Swiss Cottage, turning its large dining room into a drawing office.

All of the sections of the railway were let out to different sub-contractors of whom Robert kept tight control. Robert was a perfect delegate, he was always full of charm and very much liked by everybody and rarely lost his temper but when he did he was direct and to the point. Robert had youth on his side but was always respected if not adored by his staff. It was said that the responsibility of being head of the Birmingham Railway shortened his life, he seemed to be at the beck and call of everyone.

The original Act of the London & Birmingham Company stipulated that the terminus of the railway should be in a field on the West side of the High Road, leading from London to Hampstead. The land beyond the road was owned by Lord Southampton one of the leading opponents of the Railway in the House of Lords. Robert had actually heard that he was having a re-think on his opposition to the Railways, mainly because of the success of the Liverpool & Manchester Railway. On the strength of this Robert proposed that the line should be extended to Lancaster Place, Strand. This would have direct access to the London River. Its proposal was initially refused but later the terminus was extended to a vacant piece of land at Euston Square.

The building of the line between Camden Town and Euston Square was an entirely different, if not difficult, operation. The Regents Canal had to be crossed without interrupting traffic, sewers had to be avoided, bridges had to be added to allow for urban development and the roadway had to be wide enough for four lines of railway because it was anticipated that the new Great Western Railway would form a junction and use the same Euston terminus.

At Wolverton in December 1834, Robert ran into problems he did not envisage. To form the long embankment across the Ouse Valley to the north of Wolverton he proposed taking material from the workings at Blue Bridge and Loughton to the south. To do this he had to build a temporary bridge over the Grand Junction Canal. The canal company disputed this, as the job entailed driving large piles into the canal sides. However, Robert taking advantage of the seasonal period, on the night of 23 December he encased a large group of engineers and navvies and began building the bridge by torchlight. The work carried on through Christmas Eve and was completed on Christmas Day. The canal company did not take this lightly and arrived with a larger group of workers and pulled the bridge down. Ultimately, the Railway Company applied successfully for an injunction in the Chancery Court and this allowed the bridge to be rebuilt.

In developing the line, two most awkward earthworks were undertaken when cutting through the oolite and clay between Roade and Blisworth. The contractors had to cut through unstable rock and water springs. Pumping engines were brought in and installed. However, the contractor failed to complete the work that he was commissioned to do and Robert had to take over the contract personally. Robert managed to progress the section until meeting large problems at Kilsby Tunnel. This area is well documented, with Robert fighting through quick sand and other major problems, thus taking four years to complete. Further problems were also evident from land

owners and Northampton residents—all these problems Robert gradually dispensed with.

On completion, the tunnel was approximately 2,400 yards long. Public doubts about ventilation prompted Robert to sink two shaft, both 60 feet in diameter, and more than 100 feet deep. This was extra work that he had not been envisaged and so increased the project cost. The work in this region involved 1250 men and 200 horses.

The total initial estimate for the completion of the railway was £2,400,456. The actual cost was £5,500,000 this was £50,000 a mile as opposed to £21,736 initially estimated. Robert Stephenson was able to complete the London & Birmingham Railway on Sunday 24. June 1838. This completed Robert Stephenson's contract with the Company but they still engaged him as a consultant.

Outside of locomotive and rail construction, Robert Stephenson served many years as MP for Whitby and was returned as their representative on the 30 July 1847. Robert chose not to carry out duties as Member of Parliament and subsequently did not attend the House of Commons. Robert Stephenson had many downturns in his life, but he also had many great and successful periods, especially in bridge building. His crowning achievement was his work as a structural engineer. Some of his greatest being the Tubular Britannia Bridge, across the Menai Straits to Anglesey (1845-1850), the High

Level Bridge, Newcastle (1849) and the Royal Border Bridge Berwick, (1850).

In 1838 George Stephenson had made a survey of the Menai Straits and at this time two alternative railheads were under consideration—Holyhead in Anglesey, and the new Harbour at Porthdynlleyn on the Lleyn Peninsular. Taking everything into account George Stephenson decided at this time on Holyhead, which offered better facilities and a more level line. There was one big problem and that was the 'Menai Straits'. Telfords famous bridge over the Straits was just not meant for modern trains and George Stephenson in his report suggested a one track line with the engine pulled by a horse. Although overall it was a good report everyone knew that in the age of the train this was not feasible. No discredit to Telford his bridge had been the marvel of the period but the years had now advanced.

An act was finally passed for the construction of the Chester and Holyhead Railway, in June 1845 and Robert Stephenson was appointed Chief Engineer. Again, the current suspension bridge proved inadequate for current day rail travel, leaving with no alternative but to construct a new bridge over the Straits, to everyone's satisfaction.

At first Robert thought a cast iron bridge would suffice but then abandoned the idea, finally coming up with an idea that would be his greatest achievement but would also be his greatest professional failure. The Chester end of the railway was completed first—this included a bridge over the River Dee, just outside the city. Robert intended putting in a five-span brick bridge, but reduced it to three-span. The rest of the river was spanned with cast iron girders reaching 98 feet; four to each span, 12 in all. Robert was not pleased having to use the cast iron girders but at this time did not have many options.

Robert Stephenson with the Britannia Bridge in the background.

The Dee Bridge was completed September 1846 and on 20 October it was inspected and passed for Traffic by Major General C.W. Pasley who was the Board of Trade Inspector General. Passenger trains began using the bridge immediately and the bridge continued as normal until the 24 May 1847, which proved a disastrous day for anyone using the bridge. A passenger train bound from Chester to Shrewsbury met with a terrible disaster. It reached the last of the three spans of the bridge when the outer of the three girders directly below broke into three pieces. The locomotive driver sensing trouble accelerated the engine forward, saving his own life, but his fireman was killed outright. The coupling had parted and the rest of the train cascaded into the river, killing a guard, two coachmen and one passenger and injuring 16 others. It was remarkable how the rest were saved.

Engineers throughout the world viewed the accident with curiosity and quiet caution and waited for the results of the inquest; Robert Stephenson was the most eminent civil engineer of the day. The inquest was held at Chester.

One good thing that did come out of the disaster was the reconciliation of Robert and Joseph Locke. Some years previous, Robert's father, George Stephenson had had a dispute with Locke and Robert had taken his father's side. Locke was a brilliant engineer who for the last few years had been working in France. Joseph Locke, Brunel, Charles Vignoles, Tom Gooch, Tom Kennedy all respected engineers had arrived to give evidence on Robert's behalf. After this Locke and Robert were reconciled and again firm friends for the rest of their lives. Others, such as, Robertson the engineer of the Shrewsbury & Chester Railway, actually said that Robert's design was at fault and said that he should be charged with manslaughter. Major General Paisley who had checked the safety of the bridge and issued the certificate could hardly speak for fear of repercussions.

Robert had been persuaded by the solicitor of the Chester and Holyhead Company to defend the action by stating that the girder had fractured after receiving a heavy blow caused by the train becoming de-railed due to the wheel breaking. The argument was strengthened by the success of Robert's similar bridge at Stockton— this functioned very well. The jury returned a verdict of accidental death but they added that they considered the bridge unsafe and recommended a Government enquiry into the safety of similar bridges.

Other bridges using cast iron girders were immediately strengthened. Cast iron girders were superseded by the use of wrought iron, even though this was the first time any accident had been recorded by the use of this type of girder.

The Dee Bridge disaster, cast a shadow in Roberts direction for a short period but Robert had inherited his father's gift of perseverance and was determined to put this right. By constructing the Menai Bridge, he intended to show the world just what he was made of.

Robert selected a point about a mile to the West of Telford's Suspension Bridge. Here the Britannia Rock was a good foundation for a Pier. He intended to erect a bridge of two cast iron arches, each covering a 350 feet span with a roadway height of 105 feet above high tide. The Admiralty rejected this. Immediately Robert introduced a completely new type of suspension bridge. This would not be a platform like other uspension bridges but a deep-trussed girder construction. Trelliswork on the bridge would be vertical and its members would be made out of wrought iron plates. Stephenson explained it would be like a box without a lid on it; this would increase the bridge strength enormously and would be progressed in stages and when finished would look like a great wrought iron tube, being so large that trains could pass straight through it.

Robert contacted his father's old associate Fairbairn and also Professor Eton Hodgekinson, an expert on iron beams. Both gave different reports but both recommended the use of wrought iron for strength. Fairbairn went further saying that if the correct thickness was properly riveted it would withstand any pressure. At the same time a report that the iron ship *Prince of Wales* had slipped its launch chains at Blackwell and its hull had not been warped, damaged or strained in any way even though its overall length was 110 feet greatly encouraged Robert Stephenson. Robert Stephenson admitted to Tom Gooch that for weeks the bridge and its tubes had been constantly on his mind; at times he even dreamed of the bridge.

Robert Stephenson's Conway Bridge.

Stephenson proposed the same type of bridge for over the Conway which would consist of a single 4,000 foot span of two tubes. Having settled on the design the next problem was how to build the bridges. The first idea was to prefabricate the tubes in small sections at the iron works. However, this could not be done due to the amount of handling problems. Instead the tubes were built on staging near to the site and floated into position between the two piers on pontoons. They were lifted by means of a powerful hydraulic press housed on the pier. Brunel had used the same system with success at Chepstow and Saltash. Twenty years previous, Telford had actually floated the chains for his Menai Suspension Bridge. The difference was Telford's chains were 23.5 tons the main tubes for the Britannia Bridge was 1,500 tons and the Conway 1,000 tons. Stephenson appointed Edwin Clark his resident engineer for both bridges; Edwin later wrote a definitive account of the two bridges, which was extremely informative.

By the end of February 1847 the first of the two Conway tubes were ready for floating. The plan was to float them on the spring tide on 20 February. There was a delay and it was put back to the 6 March. The six pontoons were moved into position. In charge of the pontoons was Captain Claxton; Brunel's old friend. Brunel was actually there with his hands in his pockets and cigar hanging from his mouth. On the day the weather was good. The floating went ahead until one of the pontoons slewed slightly and fouled a rock. The tide on the Conway began to ebb before the tube could be freed and floated safely into position. The job had to be completed the following day. There were repeated attempts that week and many near accidents; some pontoons were swept out to sea. Finally on 11 March the tube was put into place. On the 8 April the hydraulic presses began to lift. After the initial lift the work was progressed with speed and the first locomotive passed through the tube with Stephenson on the footplate. On the 1 May 1847 the bridge was open for single traffic. The second tube was floated then lifted into place without a hitch on the 12 August. A terrible accident was narrowly avoided when the tube was within two feet of its height and a crack was noticed on the cross head of one of the lifting presses. The tube was quickly chocked up and the press lifted slowly with caution. Gradually it came into place. Robert and other visiting engineers watched in awe fearing a catastrophe. The atmosphere was full of anxiety and tension; gradually the tube came into place.

Having completed the task at Conway, Evans the engineer responsible for the floating of the tubes; now brought the pontoons and tackle round to the Menai Straits. The only difference this time; there was four tubes to be floated over treacherous waters of the Menai and raised to a height of over a 100 feet above high water. Arrangements were made to float on the Anglesey side of the Britannia Tower on the 19 June 1849. The decks of the remaining three Tubes were full of spectators. There were some delays but at last the crowd were rewarded with the tube gliding smoothly into the tide. The Britannia Bridge being the central Pier was now at the height of 230 feet; the two side piers being slightly lower. The additional height was necessary to house the hydraulic gear for lifting. On the 19 June 1849 it was arranged to float the first tube. Again spectators lined the decks of the other tubes; Brunel again stood side by side with Robert Stephenson.

Locke was also there to offer encouragement; all waited in anticipation. Late afternoon the tide lifted the pontoons and the long awaited signal was made at 6 pm. One of the pontoons gave way and the operation was cancelled until the following day. On the 20 June Stephenson decided to float again— the spectators held their breath. There was a period when it looked as if the engineers were losing control and that the 1,500 tons of iron would be swept away. The success of the operation depended mainly on guiding the Anglesey end of the tube so it would butt against the Anglesey Pier and, once lodged it could be swung into place. At one point supporters helped to steady a pontoon. All kinds of problems and near calamities were somehow just avoided. Finally amid deafening cheers the great tube struck the base of the Anglesey Pier and the battle was over; the Caernarvon Capstans went quickly into action. Within minutes the other end of the tube was drawn in safely under the Britannia Tower. Bands struck up and crowds cheered loudly. Robert Stephenson heaved a sigh of relief and remarked; 'Now I can go to bed'.

Early next morning Sir Francis Head one of the many distinguished visitors strolled at leisure down Lian Fair village and on reaching a good vantage point, he gazed at the new wonder of the age and the work that was completed on the previous day. He sensed someone else was already there gazing at the sight—it was Robert Stephenson. Head remarked, 'This great work has made you ten years older'. Robert had not slept soundly for three long weeks and now the tension was at last receding. The present success meant so much to him after the terrible disaster of the River Dee Bridge.

The success of the Conway and Menai bridges encouraged Robert Stephenson to design other tubular bridges. Two of these were built for the Alexandria & Cairo Railway; one to span the Damietta branch of the Nile at Benha and the other the Karrineen Canal at Birket-El-Saba. One of the largest of Robert Stephenson's bridge projects was the Victoria Tubular Bridge over the river Lawrence at Montreal.

During all of this success, Robert encountered much heartache, particularly in 1842 when his wife Fanny died of cancer on 4 October. In the same year he was also threatened with insolvency. His life continued to have many ups and downs: Whilst acting as a consultant for the Stanhope and Tyne Railroad Company, Robert took payment of 10 shares, not realising the implications. When the company was making losses the creditors would come to him for payment of anything over and above these shares – this very nearly ruined him. Luckily, this was the expansion time for the railways and another company Pontop and South Shields Company, bought all of the shares in the troubled company. A further upheaval came in 1848, with the loss of his father, George Stephenson. Robert and George had been more than father and son, they had also been partners in business and life, and they loved each other a great deal.

Early in 1859, Robert was advised to retire by his medical advisers. Sadly on 12 October 1859, aged 67, Robert Stephenson died. He had been visiting the opening of the Norwegian Railway, and was returning home in his yacht, *Titania*. His health deteriorated on board the yacht, and his friends feared for his life. Robert rallied and managed to get home to Gloucester Square, London, where he eventually died. The cause of death was aggravated jaundice followed by dropsy of the whole system.

So ended the life of one of the greatest engineers of all time, who together with his father left an infrastructure of bridges, engines and a railway system for which England will always be indebted. Unfortunately, Robert always regretted having no children to pass on his worldly possessions. Robert Stephenson's remains were interred in Westminster Abbey.

Robert Smith Surtees

1803-1864

Robert was born in Milkburn, near Hamsterley, in 1803. His father was Anthony Surtees, the original foxhunting squire of the nineteenth-century. Charles James Appleby (1779-1843) the sporting writer who used the pseudonym 'Nimrod', said of Anthony Surtees, 'he was as good a judge of a horse, hound, a bottle of port, or an oak tree, as any man in England'.

Having settled in Hamsterley Hall, Anthony Surtees kept his own hounds and hunted both hare and fox. Robert was raised with the horse and the hounds and when he was old enough he hunted with the South Durham foxhounds, the Master at this time being Mr Ralph Lambton, who was Member of Parliament for Durham and uncle to the first Earl of Durham. Roberts' early life consisted of writing and hunting.

In 1815, when the war with France was at its height, Robert started school, attending a private school at Ovingham run by Reverend James Burkett. All his life Surtees closely observed peoples' characteristics which he would adapt and use in his later novels; the characteristics of Reverend Burkett would become one of his fictional characters.

Burkett was a man of many occupations, as well as being a schoolmaster he farmed, dealt in cattle, and was involved in horse breeding. At the time Robert attended his school, Burkett's particular hobby was carving 'gibby sticks'. Made from ash plants or blackthorn, one end of the stick was carved with the head of a famous person of the day. Later, in Roberts' book *Mr Sponge's Sporting Tour* (1853), it is easy to recognise Reverend Burkett in the characters of Mr Jogglebury Crowdey and Slooman. The schoolmaster of *Hillingdon Hall* (1845) is also a portrait of Reverend Burkett.

Portrait, Robert Smith Surtees.

Ovingham School was not bad, as far as schools went in those days. The washing arrangements were primitive, four roller towels for the use of the whole school, and the soap just refused to lather. There were also no tooth or nail brushes and no facilities for changing the water, so the last one to wash used dirty water. The food however, was amazing, home fed beef from the farm, fresh milk from the dairy, and fruit from the garden. The boys, as well as learning and attending lessons, were also expected to work on the farm or in the garden and earn their keep; all in all, Surtees was well looked after and treated fairly. He never referred to bullying, which was commonplace in those days, and something Dickens frequently mentioned.

Robert Surtees stayed at Ovingham until 1818, when he left to attend Durham Grammar School, staying for only one year. This was more or less the end of Robert's education, he never claimed to have learned anything at all while attending school, but it was apparent that he must have learned at least some Latin or Greek and was well-read in Shakespeare (evident from his books). Ultimately, his family was not much interested in education; their main interests were, rearing horses and hunting. In fact the real scholar of the Surtees family was the other Robert, of Mainsforth, who became the antiquary and historian, of Durham. There is no record to suggest that the two Roberts ever met, but they seemed to have something in common in that at Hamsterley Robert wrote novels while at Mainsforth Robert wrote Border Ballads – which apparently fooled Sir Walter Scott.

Robert of Hamsterley was the second son to Anthony so would not have a positive claim to Hamsterley, but he did succeed some years later

when his older brother died. Prior to this inheritance though, it was necessary for him to make a living. At this time, careers for the sons of gentry were usually confined to the church, law, or the services – unless there was an obvious special talent. Often, gentry would work their own farm, or even a small estate. A lot of upper-class men were articled to solicitors, where they learned the law of trespass and also became acquainted with the general law of the land.

Robert Smith Surtees at Hamsterley Hall.

In 1822, Robert Surtees was articled to Mr Robert Purvis a solicitor in Newcastle, where he remained for three years. He was later articled to Mr William Bell, of Bow Church Yard, London; in the spring of 1825, he left Hamsterley and set out for London. Surtees travelled on the famous *Highflier* coach, as the railway was not available, other than some narrow track lines which were in use at some mines and the occasional passenger train. Surtees was not keen on railways at the time. He remarked in 1825 that the dirty appearance of the system reflected the passengers who travelled on it. However, later he would speak out in favour of the railways.

The *Highflier* worked between Newcastle and The White Horse Inn in Fetter Lane, London; a single fare costing £6. London was entered by the never ending Tottenham, which today is Tottenham Court Road, ending at the White Horse. Robert was forever complaining about coaching inns in some of his books, and it was the White Horse that made him think in this way. He always complained bitterly of dirt and discomfort, but on his first day in London, he arrived at the White Horse in style; the horses wearing the hollyhock flowers, which were always added for decoration in the final leg of the journey. Robert arranged lodgings at Lincoln Inn's Field and two days later reported at Mr Bell's solicitors, Bow Church Yard, London as promised.

As well as Robert there were other articled people learning law, and there seemed to be two categories 'saps' or working pupils, and gentleman pupils – who were learning very little. It is not certain which category Robert fell into but, on reading his later novels, it is apparent that his knowledge of general law was certainly pretty good. One example of this was 'The case of Doleful and Jorrocks', in *Handley Cross* (1843), this was known as one of the most amusing court scenes, anyone had ever read, and certainly the best in literature at the time.

In 1825, Croyden was the southern hunting centre and at this time, Surtees was given the chance to ride with the harriers, stag hounds or fox hounds. As in most hunts the fox was taken to the country in a horse box, and set free, this was a little unfair in that the fox would not know the lay of the land. Hunting at Croyden was nothing like hunting in Hamsterley, but Robert enjoyed it anyway, and it gave him extra insight into characters he would use later. It was on one of these hunts that he found an ideal character for *Mr Jorrocks MFH*, grocer and tea dealer. In a lot of ways it was sad that the original inspiration for Jorrocks was not known, he would certainly recognise himself from the book because Jorrocks was such a strong character. Jorrocks would become increasingly famous and actually survive his creator as one of the immortals of English literature.

John Leech, who did most of the illustrations, for Surtees' books, used as one of his models a coachman who he saw asleep in church one Sunday morning. Indeed, Leech's pictures of Jorrocks would become familiar to most people at the time and were the chief means of ensuring the lasting popularity of such a humorous character.

Surtees never divulged the name of the man whom he saw while hunting with the 'Old Surrey' and who started the trail, which led to *Handley Cross* and *Hillingdon Hall*.

Surtees did not think much of cockney hunts, and he started to go further a field to indulge in his sport. In those early days this wasn't difficult as hunting was just as popular as football is today. Every village seemed to keep its own hounds; there were very few other sports. Manchester and Birmingham had their own pack of hounds—one Epping Forest hunt was said to have attracted hundreds of horsemen, with 4,000 foot followers.

The only means of transport to the 19th century was stage coach. Surtees often used this transport. The travellers endured terrible weather conditions and usually the stage coach carried more than twenty people more outside than in.

After some time Surtees chose Brighton for the centre of his hunting activity. Coaches ran regularly from London, and he hunted with both the Southdown Foxhounds and also Brookside Harriers. Brighton was also the place 'to be' outside London and it was where the Prince Regent regularly attended the hunts. Robert met the Duke of Wellington out with his hounds on one of these occasions. Hamsterley still remained the hunt he enjoyed most but he always spoke highly of Brighton and attended their hunts whenever he could.

Whilst in Brighton, Robert always stayed at the Bedford Hotel and spoke very highly of the care and service he received whilst staying there. He also stayed at the Mutton although alas, this would be the place of his death, shortly after which it closed; the Bedford Hotel survives into the present century. Brighton supplied Surtees with a host of characters, which he later used. The master of the Southdown hunt was one Captain Eld. The self-styled master of ceremonies of Brighton, re-appears in *Handley Cross* as Captain Doleful, with his seedy militia coat and white hack, which 'went up and down like a yard and a 'alf, of pump water'.

In 1829, Surtees visited France he went to Bologna for a holiday and succeeded in getting mixed up with a pack of hounds, and in fact ended up owning them. They had been the property of Mr Sackville Creswell, who had just been arrested for debt. This gentleman gave the hounds to Robert—so at the tender age of 24, he became Master of the Hounds. The French didn't have much idea about fox hunting, and the French farmers were not amused when their lands were invaded, subsequently Surtees received more summonses for trespass, than his hunts killed foxes.

Robert's companion in these experiences in France was Colonel Charitee. One day they came across a French hunt and decided to join forces with them. Obviously, not happy with the encounter, the following day the French turned up with muskets, blunderbusses, and all kinds of strange instruments. Bullets were flying all over the place and Robert felt that he was lucky to get away with his life. Another incident happened when on one of his hunts, the fox ran to ground in the shed of an old soldier of Napoleonic times, who defended his property with a broom.

In 1829, Surtees returned to England never to go abroad again. It seemed an odd coincidence that his return to England coincided with the opening day of the South Down hunt! Unfortunately, this particular year suffered an exceptionally harsh winter, keeping Robert indoors and preventing him from attending any hunts and so he turned to his talent for writing. There was of course the option to return to Law, but he did not feel like doing this. A few months prior he had begun a novel based on his hunting journal. After completing a few pages he showed them to two friends who laughed at the result, not the reaction Robert had hoped for. Later he tried again, this time taking advice from an editor of the *Sporting Magazine*, Mr Shury. The editor liked Roberts work and gave him the opportunity of writing a series of articles on the Hunting Scene. It was quite fortuitous for Robert that he should seek Mr Shury's advice at this particular time because the magazine had only just parted company, with its hunting correspondent, Mr Charles James Appeley, Nimrod. Everyone, at this time, was familiar with the work of Nimrod, even people outside hunting circles, read his column. Nimrod was without equal, as a hunting correspondent, but he was also headstrong, and always in debt. He constantly pressed his employers for increases in his salary and expenses. His salary at the time was £1,500 a year, with the additional cost of five hunters being kept for his sole use.

After the magazine proprietors refused Nimrod any further money, Surtees stepped into his position. This started an all out quarrel with Nimrod, with apparently all of the spite coming from Surtees. When they met, Nimrod treated Robert with respect and courtesy, which was not returned by Surtees and for some reason Surtees hounded Nimrod even when he went abroad. Surtees taunted him through his column and in his novel, *Handley Cross*. Some people feared that this would undoubtedly lead to a libel action or even a duel, his taunting was so vicious, but the untimely death of Nimrod put an end to it. Nimrod was flamboyant, self-opinionated, and a snob, but did not warrant the attack by Surtees. In a book on the life of John Mytton, Surtees wrote the preface in an attempt to correct this wrong but it was far too late for that.

Surtees spent the following year, 1830, working as a sporting correspondent for the *Sporting Magazine*, whilst still managing to follow the hunt in Brighton. Cockney hunts and the hounds of the Bologna hunt were both used to inspire Surtees. In 1838 Mr Jorrocks was born. The *Jorrocks's Jaunts and Jollities* are nothing compared to some of Surtees' later work. However, this was the material that the *Sporting Magazine* was getting and the readers enjoyed. Unfortunately, Surtees didn't much enjoy working for other people and did in fact try to buy into the magazine, thus hoping to have a say in the policy, but he was refused.

Surtees liked doing things his own way and ultimately resigned his position with *Sporting Magazine*. In 1831, after making an arrangement with a printer, Ackerman, he launched the *New Sporting Magazine*. Mr Jorrocks continued to run riot through its pages for the next five years. Surtees acted as his own correspondent, and started to hunt in the Midlands. 'Editing', Robert wrote, 'is very good fun for a time' but after five years with the magazine he tired of it, and in 1836 put the *New Sporting Magazine* up for sale. After it was sold he continued to contribute to the magazine for a number of years, but he grew tired of the endless travelling, and poor inns, about which he never stopped complaining. Indeed, it was at this time that he embarked on a vicious attack of the Lemington Inns. The proprietor of one of the inns brought an action against him, which was heard at court. Surtees lost the case, but the damages were assessed at only one farthing.

In 1831 Robert's brother, Anthony, died at Hamsterley and he became heir to the Estate. Both of his parents were in poor health and he returned to Hamsterley in 1836 just in time to be there when his mother died. His father died the following year and he succeeded to the Hamsterley seat at the age of thirty-two. Robert formerly adopted the roll of 'country gentleman'; he also sat as a magistrate and was for a time an officer in the Yeomanry. In 1856, he became Deputy Lieutenant, for the County of Durham, where he made a reduction in the expenses for the post, which was very welcome. Gradually Surtees contented himself with Hamsterley and he began to keep hounds and hunted the country around his estate. Previously, Mr Ralph Lambton had hunted there, but he had been crippled after a fall and the area had been neglected. However, for no apparent reason, two years after putting together a good set of hounds, Robert gave them up without any explanation. He continued to hunt with the South Durham Hunt, and some time later he was offered Mastership when Lambton could not ride, but he had to decline this because he had his own estate to run.

After being approached by Mr Lambton in 1838, Surtees ran for Parliament; this was more or less an exercise to split the vote of the two Liberal candidates. Mr Lambton was Conservative MP for Durham, and he persuaded Robert to stand in the Gateshead constituency. Robert Surtees did well and attracted good backing, which would have undoubtedly upset the Liberal vote in the area, but Robert thought it was all a farce and withdrew from the contest before the election. However, like most of his life experiences, he captured this event in one of his novels, when Mr Jorrocks in *Hillingdon Hall* stands as a candidate himself. However, unlike Surtees, Jorrocks is elected.

Surtees initially entered politics to help a friend, but ultimately never intended getting himself elected; Hamsterley was more than enough for him. He continued writing sporting columns, one in particular, *Bells Life*, and still attended hunts for this purpose. He did change his opinion on the railways, because trains were able to transport him and his horses to distant meets and he was spared having to use coaching inns. He also, eventually, turned his attention to getting his novels published. In 1838, *Jorrocks's Jaunts and Jollities* was published, followed by *Handley Cross* in 1843 and *Hillingdon Hall* in 1845. The first editions of the novels were illustrated by Hablot K. Browne, under the name of 'Phiz'. Surtees never put his name on any novels; the early novels he signed as 'A Durham Sportsman', and when Jorrocks' trilogy came out he insisted on being anonymous. Surtees was obsessed by not adding his name to anything except legal documents and horse sales.

On 10 May, 1841 Robert Smith Surtees married Elizabeth Fenwick, daughter and co-heir of Field House, Co Durham, and also of Pallion Hall. They had three children, two daughters and one son, Anthony, who succeeded his father in 1864, but died in 1871, passing Hamsterley to the eldest daughter, Eleanor, who married the fifth Viscount Gort. Their other daughter died unmarried at Brighton in 1916. At this point the Surtees line, descendant from Robert, ceased; the present owner of Hamsterley Hall is Viscount Gort, who also married a Surtees but of the Dinsdale line.

Initially the Jorrocks series of books were not all together successful. Yet, when serialised in the *Sporting Magazine*, it was a complete success. In *Handley Cross* Jorrocks is at his best, together with James Pig, the North Country Huntsman, and 'The Boy Benjamin'. Mr Jorrocks was a marvellous character.

Surtees also wrote some hunting articles called *Analysis of the Hunting Field* (1829) and wrote a further novel *Hawbuck Grange* (1847). At this time Phiz was still illustrating for him. However, he met John Leech, following an introduction by Thackeray, whom he knew from his London days. Leech started illustrating Roberts' creations, and carried on doing so until his death. Surtees and Leech became great friends, and very much enjoyed working with each other. Their first book together was *Mr Sponge's Sporting Tour* (1853) and it was an enormous success. The hunting public loved it, and the change of illustrator was just what *Mr Jorrocks* had been waiting for; the early novels were re-marketed with Leech's drawings. Everything in Surtees' life was rosy, but alas could not last.

Unfortunately Robert had a very unpleasant quarrel with Harrison Ainsworth. At the time, Ainsworth was an author in his own right, as well as editor of the *New Sporting Magazine* and accepted *Mr Sponge*, as a two year serial. After this had run its time, Surtees offered him a further novel, *Young Tom Hall,* to take its place. Ainsworth liked the story immensely, and immediately started advertising it, with Surtees as the author. Initially, Ainsworth was given *Mr Sponge* on condition that Surtees' name was *not* divulged as author, which, at the time, Ainsworth accepted.

Surtees had managed to keep his name out of his writing all of his life, so when his name was divulged to the public by Ainsworth, Surtees was understandably deeply upset. He wrote to Ainsworth asking him to withdraw the advertisement, but Ainsworth, known for getting his own way just as much as Surtees was, refused. After all the fuss he later asked Surtees to wind down the *Tom Hall* story; this was a complete and utter shame, as it may have been one of Surtees' better stories in the series. Surtees ceased writing about the character in disgust; he put *Tom Hall* away and he would not be re-introduced until after his death.

The incident with Ainsworth seriously affected his work because his next books were not quite up to the standard people were used to. Some material he intended using for *Tom Hall* was used for other books like *Ask Mamma* (1858) and *Plain or Ringlets* (1860). Surtees spent more and more time managing his estate at Hamsterley, he always found the estate and farming more important than his novels, he wrote a short book on farming during this period, but did not bother to get it published. He was busy at the time with his memoirs, for an autobiography, and his farming book was going to be combined with his autobiography in one book called *Sporting and Social Recollections*, and published under his own name, for once, but he broke off to write *Mr Facey, Romford's Hounds* (1865), which sadly was to be the last book he and Leech would ever write together.

Leech died prior to the publication and 'Phiz' had to finish it. The publishers, Bradbury and Evans, had decided to bring out the first volume in 1864, but it was very sad that Surtees would not live to see it. Surtees and his wife had gone to Brighton after an exceptionally hard and cold winter. They stayed together until May, just before *Mr Facey* was due to be published. Robert went to bed early, not complaining about being ill but, during the night, he complained of a pain around his heart, and then passed gently away. Surtees never claimed to be the greatest of authors, but he was a brilliant novel writer; his characters were so alive and vivid.

The Works of Robert Smith Surtees

Jorrocks's Jaunts and Jollities (1838)

Handley Cross (1843)

Hillingdon Hall (1845)

Hawbuck Grange (1847)

Mr Sponge's Sporting Tour (1853)

Ask Mamma (1858)

Plain or Ringlets (1860)

Mr Facey Romford's Hounds (1865)

it printed, at his own expense, and issued copies to all of his friends. Although this was her first publication, it is believed that Elizabeth was writing perfectly good poetry from the age of eight.

Elizabeth Barrett Browning

1806-1861

Elizabeth Barrett was born at Coxhoe Hall, in the County of Durham, in 1806, the eldest of 12 children. She was baptised at St. Helens church in Kelloe, where the records can still be seen. Her father was Edward Moulton-Barrett who had made his fortune in Jamaica where he owned a sugar plantation. At the time of Elizabeth's birth, Coxhoe Hall belonged to his brother and was a beautiful house with stables and gardens spaciously set out. There were walks through the woods to the back of the Hall and Elizabeth must have walked these regularly with the rest of the family. Within the estate, there was a gamekeeper's cottage, along with a mill for grinding corn. On entering Coxhoe Hall, there was a magnificent marble staircase, leading to the upper floors, of which there were three. Coxhoe Hall was a beautiful Manor House and could be seen for miles around, framed in surrounding trees, it was very picturesque.

Elizabeth started writing poetry from a very early age and it was when she was only 14 years old that she wrote and completed her first important piece, *The Battle of Marathon*, which she dedicated to her father. He was so proud that he had

Coxhoe Hall, Elizabeth Barrett Browning's birthplace.

In 1809 Elizabeth, and her family left Coxhoe Hall and moved to a new house that her father had designed and built, called Hope End, near Malvern, Herefordshire. The house had a Turkish theme where everything seemed odd, all nooks and crannies. It also had very spacious grounds, where Elizabeth and Edward, her brother, rode their ponies. This would be their family home for the next 23 years.

The parish church of St. Helen, Kelloe, Co Durham, in which Elizabeth Barrett Browning was baptised.

At the age of 15, Elizabeth suffered a fall from her pony. Many believe that this was the start of her health problems. However, Elizabeth advocated that it was after suffering a bad chest cold the problems with her health began. Her primary ailment lay with her lungs and chest. During periods of illness, Elizabeth enjoyed reading more than ever. When still a child Elizabeth had studied Greek and Latin, and during her bouts of illness was encouraged by Mr Hugh Boyd, a local classicist, who often visited Hope End, to continue her studies especially Greek as well as her knowledge of the Classics. Therefore it is no coincidence that in 1833, her first published poem was a translation of *Prometheus Bound*, by the Greek dramatist Aeschylus.

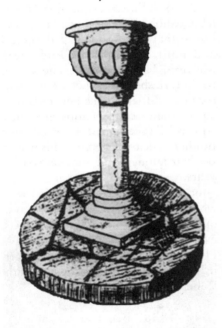

The font in the church of St. Helen, Kelloe.

Elizabeth's father, Edward Moulton-Barrett was born in 1785, the second child and first son of Elizabeth Barrett and Charles Moulton. He had an extremely privileged childhood. In the Caribbean, Edward's early home was a beautiful house and estate on Cinnamon Hill; the house stood halfway up a hillside on a glorious part of the coastal plain, stretching from Montego Bay, to Saltmarsh Bay.

The savageries of slavery were well known at that time in the Caribbean, and Edward would be fully aware of it even at the early age of seven. Slaves, often treated no better than animals, harvested the sugar cane. A standard punishment being, 39 lashes of thick cattle whip, for some inconsequential offence and a spiked collar worn by those slaves who had tried to escape.

Edward was sent to boarding school in England at the age of seven. On his trip to England and school Edward was very sad and sent his mother a tear-stained glove as a souvenir of his trip. In later years, Elizabeth, requested this glove, and was given it by her mother and it is now, in the Berg Collection, in the New York Public Library.

There has always been a question in people's minds regarding why Moulton-Barrett did not want his children to marry. One reason was the desire to keep his children at home, and under his control; he also wished his daughters to be pure and therefore spinsters. Another, raised doubts regarding his children's sexuality. However, the most likely was that he did not want any legal heirs to the Moulton-Barrett dynasty or any 'mixed blood' marriages. This particular fear was rife in the days of the British Empire. Moulton-Barrett was constantly reminded of this by his experience on the bench. He was present at many court hearings when wills were contested – 'mixed blood' was always a possibility when people had sugar plantations in Jamaica. There was later to be some erroneous comments regarding Elizabeth's own racial origins. The Barrett's were half Creole and Elizabeth herself was very dark skinned.

Moulton-Barrett was a concerned father, very upright, of high, but narrow virtues, he always felt he should be obeyed and had a God given right to do as he pleased. Elizabeth always called this cruelty 'unkindness'. Mrs Barrett had no influence over her husband at all and seemed to be constantly having babies. After the birth of her youngest child Octavius in 1828, she died, and sadly this appeared to go unnoticed by her husband. Elizabeth wrote about her mother a month before she got married. She said that 'scarcely was I a woman when I lost my dear mother. A gentle sweet nature of a woman, whom the sweetness had been soured slightly by thunder (thunder being Moulton-Barrett) everyone in the household bowed before it'.

After the death of his wife, Moulton-Barrett found himself in the position of sole parent to 11 surviving children. He came to the conclusion that his financial affairs abroad would not be concluded for some time and so put his largest asset, Hope End, on the market. After finding a suitable family home overlooking the sea at Sidmouth, in the summer of 1832, he moved his family there—everyone

was very happy there. However, in 1835 Moulton-Barrett made the decision to move his family once again and this time to London. He made this decision primarily because of the career paths his sons had chosen to take; George wished to be a solicitor and Moulton-Barrett thought that London would accommodate this choice. So, the family moved to a house in Gloucester Place where they would remain until somewhere permanent could be found. Mr Moulton-Barrett at this time was involved in the City, and living anywhere near to his work was a bonus. There was a family rumour that if everything went well during their father's work in the City, they would be really very rich again.

Due to her continued ill health, Elizabeth spent most of her time confined to bed. Her father loved her dearly and fussed over her, calling a never-ending number of doctors, but with no improvement in Elizabeth's condition. She constantly read books and wrote poetry. She also wrote to other writers and poets and made good friends with Mary Mitford, who was a brilliant writer of plays, opera libretto, and fiction. It was Mary who gave Elizabeth her spaniel, Flush, who would play a huge part in her life and her relationship with Robert Browning.

In 1838, because Elizabeth's health was not improving, her doctors recommended that her family take her abroad to a warmer climate, or by the sea, to live. In that same year the whole family moved to Torquay, with her father commuting to London. Elizabeth was very close to her father and the torture of parting every week was tremendous for both of them. In 1839, Elizabeth wrote to Mary Mitford saying, 'my beloved father has gone away and his spirits are far worse than mine'. Every time that Moulton-Barrett went away he feared that he would not see his beloved daughter alive again. As time passed Elizabeth became weaker and again, writing to Mary, in the year 1840, she said that she had not dressed since the previous October.

At this time her doctors started giving her laudanum, which she continued taking for most of her life. For some reason Elizabeth always paid for her own medicine, she did this out of a small income that her mother had left her. Apparently, in those days opiates could be paid for over the counter. It was not clear if her father was aware of the extent of laudanum that his daughter was taking, but after five years of use, Elizabeth needed 40 drops a day. Under this medication, Elizabeth struggled through the winter. As the weather became warmer she got a little better. In July 1840 she was overcome with grief, learning that her beloved brother Edward had been drowned. The tragedy happened in one of her father's absences from Torquay. Edward's friends had gone out boating, and the boat had failed to return in the evening. Two days later the boat had been found drifting with two dead bodies in it. A fortnight later, Edward's body was washed up on the shore, the shock of this nearly killing Elizabeth. What made it worse was that she blamed herself, for Edward had stayed at Torquay because Elizabeth had begged him

to, when his father had wanted him to return to London.

In November of the same year, Elizabeth's health started to improve. Her father's reaction was, to move the family back to London. They moved to the street that would become part of Elizabeth's fame and where she would find love, 50 Wimpole Street. Elizabeth spent the following five years there as a virtual invalid. For almost nine out of every 12 months, she never left her room but was more or less confined to her bed. Her bedroom window was kept permanently sealed. A fire burned constantly in the stove, even at night, and she always slept in the company of her personal maid, Wilson, as well as one of her sisters and her dog, Flush.

Robert Browning and Elizabeth Barrett.

Elizabeth's father insisted that she eat large meals, saying that toast and obstinacy was the cause of most of her health problems. In the spring time of her confinement, she would sometimes be allowed into an adjoining room, and in full summer she occasionally, painfully, descended the stairs and had a little carriage exercise in the park. But the preparation for this venture did not warrant the small good it did.

When Elizabeth was young, she was always very lively, a 'tom boy' in fact. She loved the outdoors. When she was fourteen, her two other sisters came down with the same illness she appeared to be suffering from. Henrietta and Arabella, recovered from this illness, while Elizabeth never did. Doctor after doctor was summoned to try to treat Elizabeth, but to no avail, and by the time she was 15 she had a pain in the head, then in her right side, near the ribs, then in her back, right shoulder, then finally down her arm. There was an average of three attacks each day, and she was unable to rest on her right side. Her stomach and bowels seemed fine and her doctors were surprised at her love of spicy food. It was thought that because her other sisters were also ill at the same time as Elizabeth, it must have been caused by something they had eaten. Opium, for a time, relieved the illness, but this lost its effect with constant use. The Doctors were sure that Elizabeth had an illness of the worst kind in that it could not be diagnosed, and that she may have a 'de-arranged organ', but they treated her for spinal disease. Her illness continued to be a cause of concern, her lungs were weak, and she haemorrhaged. She had congestion, but it did not point to tuberculosis, which at the time could have been diagnosed. The final conclusion was a possible abscess on the lungs. The symptoms were: racking cough, pain, lack of breath, phlegm, complete loss of appetite, and bronchial problems that could now be treated with antibiotics.

Elizabeth survived with great courage, and perseverance. Miss Mitford called regularly, keeping her spirits up, and Mr Boyd, the blind scholar, read Homer and Aeschylus, with her. She also had letters from other friends. Mr Boyd once sent her a case of Cyprus Wine, which she treasured, and she always imagined Greece as being a beautiful green country. She offered her father a glass of wine, saying it must be good, because it was Greek, her father did not like it and spat it out, saying, 'it may be Greek but it is nasty'. When life became too much to bear Elizabeth took her laudanum.

Her real joy was her poetry, it put gladness back into her heart. She wrote endlessly, and she soon completed a volume of poems and arranged with a publisher called Moxon to publish them. One of the poems from that particular collection was published in Blackwoods Magazine in 1843 and became famous as *The Cry of the Children*. Elizabeth had written this poem, after reading about the plight of young children working in mines and factories as young as six years of age – even her own problems did not let her forget the plight of these children.

Moxon thought there would be repercussions from industry and powerful people, and there *was* a delay in getting the poems published for a full year, but finally they did come out. The dedication was to her father, 'To satisfy my heart while I satisfy my ambition'. The volume was a complete success, in England and more so in America, for the slave abolitionists were very touched by, *The Cry of the Children*, and begged her to write more material for their cause. She sent them another poem called *The Curse of a Nation*, which was printed in the *Liberty Bell*, in 1845.

Elizabeth regularly corresponded with other literary people of the day, and on 17 January 1845, she received a letter with handwriting she did not recognise. On opening it she saw that it was from Robert Browning. Part of the letter puzzled her; it read, 'I love your verses, and I also love you too'. She did reply to his letter, resulting in a total exchange of 572 letters over a period of 20 months. Elizabeth and Robert's was a romance that in 1930 would be immortalised in the play *The Barrett's of Wimpole Street* by Rudolph Besier (1878-1942).

Moulton-Barrett encouraged Elizabeth to have her own visitors, as long as he didn't have to meet them. On 20 May 1845 Robert Browning first met Miss Barrett, and on this day he completely lost his heart to her. He wrote asking if she would marry him, as he loved her dearly. This letter happens to be the only one missing from their correspondence. Elizabeth embarrassed by this open display of emotion, wrote back, saying that she didn't wish to see him ever again.

Robert Browning apologised somewhat humbly, and was allowed to call on her again; first, once a week then twice a week. On one of these visits, Flush bit Robert's leg tearing his trousers. It was also at this time that Flush was stolen by a con-man named Taylor, who offered to return him for a price. Taylor apparently stole respectable peoples' dogs and returned them on payment of a ransom. In some cases he stole the same dog twice from unsuspecting people, increasing the payment each time; these people obviously loved their dogs. He was reputed to earn £2000 a year doing this. When Taylor first called, Moulton-Barrett answered the door and quickly sent him on his way. The second time Moulton-Barrett was away and Elizabeth managed to get Flush back, only to loose him again to Taylor. She mentioned this to Robert and he said that she must not give in to extortion, but Elizabeth thought that it was because of Flush biting his leg that he made this remark and they quarrelled about it.

Elizabeth was determined to get the dog back again from Taylor, who had told her in no uncertain terms that he intended to send Flush back, paws first, and then his head, if she did not collect him at the time stated, and also that she should collect the dog herself. The request was an impossible one, apart from Elizabeth's health, London at that time was very dangerous, full of thieves and criminals. She was determined to get her dog back and asked Wilson her maid to go for him. Even though Wilson came from Sheffield and was somewhat street-wise, she still refused to go, and neither would she allow Elizabeth to go. Elizabeth made it quite clear that she fully intended to get Flush back; she thought so much of the dog and just couldn't bear to be without him. Even though she could hardly walk, Elizabeth struggled out of her sick bed and, accompanied by Wilson, went to get her dog.

In the summer of 1845 Robert begged Elizabeth to go abroad with him to Italy, saying it would greatly improve her health. Robert continued to urge her to go, not really being aware of the physical effort this would entail. Elizabeth finally agreed. Her father, again getting restless, suddenly decided to move once more, saying that the family should decide between, either Tunbridge Wells, Dover, or Reigate. This quickly made up Elizabeth's mind, she knew in her heart that if she didn't marry Robert now it would have to be put off indefinitely. She did not relish the thought of living in Dover or Tunbridge Wells, especially without the company of Robert, so she told him that she would marry him and go to Italy.

Over the following weeks nothing seemed to go right with the travelling arrangements. Wilson helped her pack essential things, which could be carried. Flush and Wilson were also going with them on the journey. On 12 September 1845 they left the house and Robert and Elizabeth were married at St. Pancras Church. After the wedding she stayed for a while with Mr Hugh Boyd, her old friend. She ate some bread and butter, and had a glass of Cyprus wine, which her father had very much disliked. The same day she found out that they could not travel for a further week, and for this period stayed at home, further deceiving Papa. Robert did not call this week at all, saying he dare not ask for Mrs Browning, and did not want to ask for Miss Barrett. However, everything at long last came together. They all met at Victoria Station, where they caught the train to Dover. In a matter of a few hours they watched the coast of Dover disappear in the distance, as they left the Dover coast and headed for the continent. The Browning's

had a rough channel crossing and on arrival in France, Wilson, Robert, and Elizabeth were exhausted. A carriage was hired to take them to Rouen and, writing later, her description of the carriage ride in the moonlight was that of someone in love.

Elizabeth, for a time, was overcome with exhaustion and had to lie down in the coach with her feet raised until she recovered. They stayed for a while at a hotel for a rest and something to eat then continued their journey to Paris. At 10am, Monday 20 September 1846 they booked into the first hotel they came to, making sure that the coffee was good and the bedrooms were clean. In Paris their marriage was consummated. Elizabeth writing later of the occasion, saying, 'All is well ...I thank God... And I am well ... Living as if in a dream, loving, and being loved better every day'. They spent many pleasant hours in Paris, dining with friends, in the evening, as the Parisians do. Robert romantically carried her up stairs to their room, and they watched the stars rise over Paris' tall buildings, whispering sweet nothings to each other.

After their visit to Paris, time lapsed and Ba (Robert always referred to Elizabeth as Ba) became pregnant, in fact she was five months pregnant before she realised. However, in March 1847, at 5pm one Sunday Elizabeth miscarried. She had felt perfectly well until six weeks before the due date, when she had violent night pains. She took a little brandy and Robert rubbed her stomach, after which her pains would subside.

However, the pains continued and the baby was miscarried; Ba was used to pain in her life, but this was *real* pain. At times she and Robert felt they had brought this wrath on themselves, because of deceiving Papa.

On 12 September 1847, the Browning's celebrated their first wedding anniversary. As time passed, Elizabeth suffered two more miscarriages until 9 March 1849 when she gave birth to a gorgeous little boy. He was healthy and fair skinned. Ba informed her sisters after a fortnight. She had also given up the use of morphia during her pregnancy, showing 'the strength of a thousand men' according to Browning. Her labour with the baby lasted 21 hours and the rapture of the first cry was simply unspeakable. Browning told his wife, he could not love a child like he loved her.

The birth of Robert Wideman Browning was witnessed with incredible relief by all, and nurses reported that Robert danced instead of walked. The caps Ba had made for the baby did not fit, as the baby was very large. Ba cut three strands of hair from the hair of the baby to send to relations, one being to Robert's mother but, unfortunately, she did not live to receive it. Ba hoped and prayed that her father, because of his grandson, would relent and want to see him, she again wrote to him at Wimpole Street, but again another letter was added to the pile of unopened ones. The boy, for some unknown reason, was referred to as Penini by his mother and Ba spoiled him, especially since doctors had told her that she could have no further

children. The boy grew up to be a natural painter, something his father always wanted to be.

When Moulton-Barrett heard of the wedding and their subsequent trip to Italy, he was livid; he ordered all of Elizabeth's clothes to be packed and put into a warehouse, sending the bills on to her. He forbade any mention of Elizabeth at home by any one in the family and it appeared that his senses had left him when he said, that he would rather see her dead at his feet, than alive and happy. Moulton-Barrett never saw his daughter again, Elizabeth wrote to him constantly, begging forgiveness and ceaselessly informing him of her love for him. The letters multiplied, unopened for a full five years; culminating with Moulton-Barrett sending them to Robert, enclosing a violent letter of abuse.

Just prior to Moulton-Barrett's death, Robert wrote to him hoping for reconciliation but this was not to be; this was Elizabeth's final hope, and she was overcome with grief and remorse. On 17 April 1857 Moulton-Barrett died, Elizabeth was again overcome with grief and remorse. She had never felt like this since the death of her brother and to the end of her life she protested her love for her father.

Prior to these events, the birth of her son and the death of her father, Elizabeth had enjoyed her time with Robert, basking in the sunshine of Pisa, then later Florence. The sunshine suited both Robert and Ba and her health improved steadily and dispensing with her morphia, her appetite automatically came back. One day for dinner she had a meal of sturgeon, turkey, stewed beef, and mashed potatoes and finished off with cheesecake.

Both Ba and Robert were writing again during this period and they were doing this in relative peace. Ba was working on a collection of sonnets, and Robert felt he had something to offer all of the arts so, in-between modelling in clay and painting, he strummed a piano, which he had hired. It was not long after the birth of their son that Ba presented her husband with her completed volume of sonnets. She had become much bronzed with the sun and Robert called her 'his little Portuguese', hence the name given to the sonnets: *Sonnets from the Portuguese* (1850). Ba was a little diffident regarding the sonnets but Robert was very enthusiastic. They were printed and published as collected verse. Later, critics would consider the sonnets to be her best work.

Although very much in love, Elizabeth and Robert did have many differences of opinion; one area in particular was spiritualism. Ba attended séances, quite often and tried to get Robert to attend. He actually did attend one or two, but as a sceptic. However, on a visit to England, the medium Daniel Douglas Home, was at the height of his vogue and Ba wanted strongly to make his acquaintance. All the time Robert was suspicious of him, and it was mainly this suspicion that made him write a poem called *Mr Sludge the Medium* – it held the whole of the spiritualism 'business' up to derision.

The Browning's visited London quite often, but always in summertime to escape the city's winter fogs. These visits were terrible for Elizabeth, especially when her father was still alive, and on one of these occasions she met Robert's parents, who she found to be not very attractive. They sometimes visited Wimpole Street, when they knew that her father would not be in, and on one occasion nearly got it wrong when they heard his footsteps from the room above. She thought at one stage that he may come to see her but this did not happen, and she simply could not pluck up enough courage to go to him.

An illustration for Browning's poems (1879) by John Byam Shaw (1872-1919). Many of these illustrations are biographical in content and depict Robert and Elizabeth.

After the death of her father and on their return to Italy Elizabeth felt ill again, and her strength finally began to fail, she spent long hours soaking up the Italian sunshine, thinking that she again would be revived as she was before. Elizabeth still kept writing, and this was the period when she wrote her verse novel *Aurora Leigh* (1857). It was a great success, especially in England, and there was serious talk at the time of making her Poet Laureate – she scoffed at the idea. In 1859 Elizabeth was in better health. This was the time of the Italian revolution. Soon after, however, she fell ill and was again confined to bed – except for short periods. She easily became faint and on occasions had real difficulty in breathing. Robert, in a panic surrounded her with doctors, but all to no avail. Ba died on 29 June 1861.

of obscurity and illness, to writing the very best of poetry, that will always be a comfort to people. She had an overwhelming love for Robert Browning, that inspired her to want to live, and tremendous love for her father which she longed to express, but never had the opportunity. Her very last words uttered, in this life were, 'Dear Papa'.

Sonnets from the Portuguese
Elizabeth Barrett Browning (1850)

How do I love thee? Let me count
the ways.
I love thee to the depth and
breadth and height
My soul can reach, when feeling
out of sight
For the ends of Being and ideal
Grace.
I love thee to the level of every day's
Most quiet need, by sun and
candle-light.
I love thee freely, as men strive for
Right;
I love thee purely, as they turn
from praise.
I love thee with a passion put to
use
In my old griefs, and with my
childhood's faith.
I love thee with a love I seemed to
lose
With my lost saints, – I love thee
with the breath,
Smiles, tears, of all my life! –And, if
God choose,
I shall but love thee better after
death.

*An illustration for Browning's poems (1879)
by John Byam Shaw (1872-1919).*

Elizabeth Barrett Browning was a great example of an amazing woman, rising up against all odds. From years

Home Thoughts, From Abroad
Robert Browning 1812-1889

Oh to be in England
Now that April's there,
And whoever wakes in England
Sees, some morning, unaware,
That the lowest boughs and the
brushwood sheaf
Round the elm-tree bole are in tiny
leaf,
While the chaffinch sings on the
orchard bough
In England-now!

And after April, when May follows,
And the whitethroat builds, and all
the swallows-
Hark! Where my blossomed pear-
tree in the hedge
Leans to the field and scatters on
the clover
Blossoms and dewdrops-at the bent
spray's edge-
That's the wise thrush; he sings
each song twice over,
Lest you should think he never
could recapture
The first fine careless rapture!
And though the fields look rough
with hoary dew,
All will be gay when noontide
wakes anew
The buttercups, the little children's
dower,
Far brighter than this gaudy
melon-flower!

Kelloe Church still keeps the little eighteenth-century font that Elizabeth Barrett was baptised in on 10 February 1808. The church is mainly thirteenth-fourteenth century, the low tower and the south doorway are both original. In the sanctuary is a Norman cross, which was unearthed as six separate pieces during restoration work in the nineteenth-century. There are a number of holes in the cross, possibly for holding holy relics. The top part is a wheel cross, and scenes are carved down the stem. At the bottom of the cross are two medieval grave-covers, which where discovered at the same time as the cross. On the south side, near a modern window, portraying the parable of the Good Samaritan is a marble monument with these words:

To
Commemorate the Birth
in this parish of
Elizabeth Barrett Browning,
who was born in Coxhoe Hall,
March 6th 1806,
and died at Florence, June 29th
1861.
A great Poetess, A noble woman,
A devoted wife.
Erected by public subscription,
1897.

Lord William George Armstrong

1810-1900

William George Armstrong was born in Pleasant Road, Shieldfield, Newcastle upon Tyne, in 1810. His father was a corn-merchant, as well as an alderman and later a Mayor of the same city. His mother was the daughter of William Potter of Walbottle Hall, Northumberland. William attended Auckland Grammar School in 1826, where he remained for almost nine years. It was there that he found he had a passion for mechanics. Any spare time he had, he spent at a factory owned by Mr Ramshaw of Bishop Auckland and it was here that William first met his wife, Margaret Ramshaw, whom he married in 1835.

On leaving school, William was contracted to a solicitor at Newcastle, Mr Armorer Donkin, where he began to study law, the basis of which he studied in the presence of his brother-in-law, Mr Watson – later to be known as Baron Watson. Like everything else in his life, he studied law to a high standard, so much so that when he returned to Newcastle from London in 1845, he was taken on as a full partner, the practice being

called Messrs Donkin, Stable and Armstrong. However, it was not to be law that fired passion in William but science and engineering. William Armstrong studied electricity at length; he studied hydro-electricity and hydraulics.

Whilst still working at Carliol Square, in 1842, William constructed a hydro-electric generator This machine represented the most effective method of generating electricity of its time. Indeed, it remained a valuable concept for the next 50 years. After sending the generator to America, where it was reported that it charged a battery containing 33 ft^2 of coated surface, upwards of 60 times a minute, large orders for the generator were placed.

Portrait William George Armstrong.

In 1846, William shifted his interests from hydro-electricity to hydraulics. It was whilst on a fishing trip 10 years earlier that he was first inspired by power, which, could easily and effectively be generated from water. Whilst fishing, he watched the mountain streams cascade to sea level; this was his inspiration for the development. As solicitor and promoter of the Whittle Dene Water Company, William was able to appeal to the wealthy business men of Newcastle to back his development of the hydraulic crane. Thus, William invented the first water powered hydraulic crane, by using the water pressure from the reservoir of the Whittle Dene Water Company, to drive it. The water hydraulics was perfectly silent and could lift heavy loads using water pressure instead of oil.

In 1847 William gave up his legal practice to open Newcastle Cranage Company at Elswick, later known as 'Armstrong's Factory'. It was at the Elswick works that the famous 'Armstrong gun' would be created, a far different venture to hydraulics, and hydro-electricity!

Armstrong's Elswick Works and Shipyard on the banks of the River Tyne.

The Elswick works were situated on the banks of the Tyne, near to Newcastle, and fronted the river for about a mile. The Carlisle to Newcastle railway ran directly into the works, in order to transport any finished goods to their destinations. The works soon expanded, occupying 40 acres and employing approximately 400 men. In one of the workshops there was a huge and powerful steam hammer and also a set of shears capable of lifting up to 100 ton in weight. All kinds of hydraulic machinery were manufactured at the factoryincluding lifting cranes and hoists for docks and warehouses. The company erected a 100 ton crane at Barrow Docks, an 80 ton crane for Woolwich and Newcastle, along with hydraulic machines for railway stations in London, and nearly every other railway station in England, Ireland and Scotland that had to handle goods, as well as manufacturing steam engines and boilers for pumps and wrought iron bridge works.

Out of Elswick came the railway bridge over the river Ouse at Hull, with two opening spans of 100 feet each; the swing bridge over the river Tyne weighing 15,000 tons, as well as all sizes of field and naval guns, not only for England but also for every other country in the world. Gun carriages of every description, every type of shot and shell, along with armour plates and guns for warships – all meeting stringent government tests – came out of Elswick. Elswick was capable of turning out the largest of castings for ships and engines and cylinders, with the ordnance department alone, capable of turning out 60 to 80 tons of finished arms a week. Elswick was one of the few factories capable of manufacturing and supplying arms.

In 1854, an Armstrong crane was being used on the quayside at Newcastle. The crane was capable of lifting extremely heavy weights using water pressure, it had remarkable precision and ease of movement, great rapidity of action and at all times, was completely silent. Based on the success of this crane, others were ordered for Liverpool Docks, and Grimsby 'New Dock'. The hydraulic principle used in the cranes was also tried and applied to the opening and closing of dock entrances for shipping. The column of water needed to achieve this was 200 feet in elevation; at Liverpool and Newcastle the pipes were supplied by the local reservoirs, but at Grimsby a tower was built, with the tank on top in which water was pumped by means of a steam engine. Later, an alternative to the tower was the accumulator, which gave pressure of load instead of elevation. This method was adopted successfully for the London Great Western Railroad Company, where it was used for the loading and unloading of trucks. All of this was done with hydraulic pressure supplied by a steam engine with connected accumulators. The system was further modified by a small clack valve added to the cylinder, to control any extreme water movements in the pipes, after which the system was a complete success and all of this because Armstrong had a leisurely day out fishing.

During the time of the Crimean War (1854), Armstrong studied, at a distance, the procedures for moving troops as well as the transportation of heavy artillery. Observing the hard work concerned in getting two 18 lb guns into place, he remarked to his engineers that the army needed lighter and more powerful guns, with a greater range. Armstrong turned the matter over in his head, until finding what he thought to be a solution. Most things that inspired and motivated William were simple, like the stream flowing to the river. This time his inspiration was an arrow in flight, the way it rotated, and how its flight was straight and true. William Armstrong approached the Secretary of Defence and within a month was working on a new type of gun. He believed that the entire theory of gunnery and the making of shells had to be completely re-thought and that this line of thought would have to be made by one clear mind so that there would be no conflict of ideas. Subsequently, in 1855, guns were tried at Allenheads on the Northumberland moors and on the seashore and their defects were noted.

In 1856 a 3 lb Armstrong gun was presented to the Government but it was the second gun presented that impressed and was eventually adopted by the Ministry of Defence —a 5 lb gun. The trials undertaken by Armstrong's guns, along with the guns themselves, were so superior to any other system in the world, that they were adopted as the field gun of the services. The Armstrong gun was fully endorsed by the Adjutant General of Artillery and indeed the whole Ministry of Defence. Through his hard work and unselfish dedication, William Armstrong had the world at his feet; he could have had riches beyond belief, but instead, gave his country the complete patent without reward, or any consideration whatsoever. This was William

Armstrong the man; the most patriotic man of his day and this was a fine example of putting his country before his family and himself, even though at the time Armstrong was still not a rich man. All of England applauded him and in time he would be made a Peer of the Realm (1887). However, it was not only England but also the rest of the world that remarked on Armstrong's genius and patriotism.

From 1858-63 Armstrong was contracted to be Chief Engineer of Rifled Ordnance. His role was to organise the production of guns and other arms from Elswick with secrecy being paramount. He was paid a salary of £2,000. In 1856, the Government under Lord Derby, entered into a contract with Armstrong, stipulating that his company supply all machinery for the sole use of the government. This agreement continued until 1863, when it was mutually dissolved between both sides.

It was about this time (1854) that Joseph Whitworth produced the Whitworth rifle, which in many ways was comparable to the Armstrong Gun. Sir Joseph Whitworth was a celebrated mechanic and when the Whitworth Rifle proved to be unsatisfactory, Armstrong was given the job of correcting its defects. The old grooves and bands were dispensed with and a polygonal bore, with a twist towards the muzzle, was added to the rifle. The height of the trajectory was made smaller to 8½ feet. By this method it was made possible to maintain a steady accurate flight of over 2,000 yards. On completion of the modifications, the Whitworth and Armstrong guns were proved far superior to any other guns in the world.

In 1863 Sir William Armstrong, on completion of his contract with the government, decided to spend more time pursing other interests. He built Cragside, which, stands on a hillside one mile to the east of Rothbury, Northumberland. The house is set in a picturesque spot and is a credit to this area of Northumbria. The sides of the hill are steep and there are pleasant walks in the vicinity of the house. At the rear is a boulder called 'Sea Stone' there is also two artificial lakes as well as large gardens laid out in an Italian fashion. In the orchard, dwarf fruit trees grow in large pots. A stream which runs close by the house supplies all of the power by way of generating electricity, the water also supplies the lakes, gardens and is used for all of the domestic purposes.

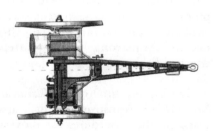

Top: Nineteenth-century field gun and carriage (sectional elevation).
Bottom: Field gun carriage (plan).

The Cragside development is an example of the sheer genius of Armstrong. The building of the house commenced in 1863 and was designed by Norman Shaw R.A. It has a high tower with a dome called Gilnockie Tower, the style is part sixteenth-century and part gothic. The roof is covered by red tiles, which give the appearance of being homely and warm, especially when the sun catches it. The interior is even more impressive, carved into the stone over the fireplace in the dining room is 'East or West Hame's best'. There is a splendid chimney of carved marble. Lord Armstrong owned many paintings: a Millais celebrated landscape, 'Chill October'; 'Japheth's Daughter', by Wilkie, 'Rabbit on the Wall' cheers the beholder; Linnels, 'Thunderstorm' which filled him with awe; Sir F. Leighton's 'Venetian Lady'; George Leslie's 'Cowslip Gatherer's'; O'Neill's 'Death of Rafael'; David Cox's 'Lancaster Sands'; and John Phillips' 'Flower Girl'. Other contributions to the house were made by celebrated artists of the day, among them, Turner, Clarkson Stanfield, Copley Fielding, and Rosa Bonheur.

These were the years when Armstrong had time to reflect on many things appertaining to the country. He was concerned by the rate the country was using coal. He attacked the use of coal for domestic purposes. At the time, it amounted to one ton of coal per head of the entire population, so that upwards of 29 million tons of coal was expended alone in England for this purpose. Armstrong believed that this could be vastly reduced by the proper use of stoves and grates without any loss of heat. He also believed that by being more competitive, by using better machinery, the nations' coal mines could stay more competitive in world markets thus guaranteeing the country prosperity. He made projections which, in later years came true. For instance, he prophesied that every home would be powered by electricity and have clean running water at their disposal.

Top: A portrait of Sir Joseph Whitworth, Bart., DCL, FSA, in old age.
Bottom: The coat of arms of Sir Joseph Whitworth.

William Armstrong greatly believed that no matter how far we go in pursuit of knowledge, there

161

would always be an immense question mark on what lay beyond. As well as being president of the British Association for the Advancement of Science, he had been three times president of the Institute of Civil Engineers. Armstrong always shared his successes with his country and also as far as possible with Newcastle.

Benton Bridge.

In 1873 whilst holding the post of High Sheriff of Northumberland, Armstrong began to delegate a lot of his business responsibilities, spending more time with his wife at Cragside. At this time, Elswick covered some 70 acres of land and employed approximately 12,000 men. Armstrong took a great deal of comfort in the fact that he was creating work for people, thus allowing them to live in relative comfort. As he was taking a step back from the day-to-day running of the Works, Armstrong's interests turned towards politics and in 1886 he hoped to represent his local people in Parliament. Unfortunately, although his politics were Liberal, he did not fully agree with Gladstone's 'Home Rule Bill' for Ireland and the Newcastle people voted two Gladstone supporters of the Bill to Parliament, rather than him – John Morley, and James Craig.

In 1887 Armstrong decided to take advantage of being a peer and claimed his seat in the House of Lords, as Baron Armstrong of Cragside. At the time he felt in his heart that he had a lot to offer the people of the country as well as his county, and he took the seat for this reason not for the money connected to the role. The same year he was chosen to second the address to the Queen's speech, and he did this very well, showing himself as the great man he was.

Some of the many gifts received by the city of Newcastle and the surrounding areas from Lord Armstrong are: The Jardin d' Acclimation, on the Western slopes of Newcastle; a lecture hall for the Literary Society, an operating theatre together with gifts of thousands of pounds to a children's hospital; 75% of a bridge across Benton Valley which cost £20,000; to the Natural History Museum he donated £10,000; a Mechanics Institute, study centre for Elswick Workers; a Banqueting Hall for the city of his birth—all of this along with, Armstrong Park and Jesmond Dene Park. In 1883, Jesmond Dene was incorporated with Armstrong Park; the council purchasing the adjacent Heaton Park. It is said that no other park in England excels it. Armstrong was immensely rich and gladly gave donations for anything that he deemed worthy, saying about his parks, 'I have enabled the people to breath the air of heaven, amid the hum and strife of earth'.

Jesmond Dene.

Prince Albert and Princess Alexandra, who visited Newcastle and Cragside in 1884.

One of the best views in Jesmond Dene can be seen from one of Lord Armstrong's seats, here an old tower and a rustic bridge are the main attractions with the tower once being used as a windmill. The Jesmond Banqueting Hall, a gift from Armstrong, still stands on the south bank of the Dene. Concerts, lectures and public entertainment of all kinds were held there. In 1884, the Prince and Princess of Wales, Prince Albert and Princess Alexander, invited by Lord Armstrong, visited Newcastle to hand over the Park and the Banqueting Hall to the people. They stayed at Cragside for three nights.

Lord Armstrong died 27 December 1900 aged 90. His great nephew, William Watson Armstrong inherited his fortune and in his uncles memory he generously donated £100,000 of his inheritance towards the building of the Royal Victoria Infirmary hospital, which was opened in 1906 by Edward II. Lord William Armstrong has been greatly honoured but he deserved it all. His great brain was forever active and his perseverance has been evident in everything he achieved; his wealth was well deserved. Newcastle had many great men, but none more loved than William George Armstrong of Cragside.

Sir Joseph Wilson Swan

1828-1914

Joseph Swan was born in Sunderland, 31 October 1828. His father, John, and his mother, Isabella, both of Scottish descent, married in 1820. Isabella was the daughter of George Cameron, a member of the Cameron clan whose forbears had settled at Esh, County Durham. George Cameron, Joseph's grandfather, was a stonemason and master builder. He built the Old Exchange, now a Seaman's Institute, which still stands in High Street, Sunderland. He was killed when a wall fell on him in a great storm in 1814.

John and Isabella first lived at Low Street, Sunderland. Their house backed onto the River Wear where Isabella could hear the regular beatings and floggings of the sailors on the men o'war from the river. After the birth of their daughter, Elizabeth, in 1821, the family moved to Pallion Hall, a large house with a garden sloping to the Wear, two miles upstream from Sunderland. It was at the Hall that a further two sons were born, John and Joseph.

John Swan was not an astute businessman. He was too easygoing and generous, always ready to help others. He was forever looking for new ideas but lost money every time. Although his family inherited neither money nor goods from him, what they did inherit was generosity, gentleness, integrity, enterprise, good brains, and finally, good constitutions. Despite his poor business dealings, and the need to move his family, now four boys (John, Joseph, George, Alfred) and four girls (Elizabeth, Mary, Jane and Emma) to a smaller house in Olive street, Sunderland, in 1837, happiness was abound in the Swan household.

Close by their new home, was a blacksmiths owned by the Allison's, where father and son carried out their work. There was also a carpenter's shop nearby, where Joseph learned to use the plane, mallet, and chisel. He was an inquisitive boy, learning quickly how horses were shod, cows milked, how grass and hay were cut and stacked and how the wheat harvest was gathered. Joseph knew all about birds, their nests and eggs and spent his days roaming the flowery banks near the sea.

One of his uncles, Robert Cameron, was a rope-maker and it was in his yard that young Joseph broadened his knowledge of this craft. It was here too that Joseph learned all about boilers and steam engines; how gas was produced and how corn was milled. After a period switching from one interest to another, Joseph joined a school, run by three elderly sisters, the Misses Herries, where he stayed for about two years. Here he learned to read and spell and to knit, darn and stitch. This was also the time that he acquainted himself with an electrical machine owned by Mr John Ridley, a friend of the family (who later invented a reaping machine used in Australia).

In 1838, Joseph's older brother, John had been sent to a school for boys, run by Dr Wood at Hendon Lodge. When Joseph joined the school the brothers were inseparable, calling each other Castor and Pollux, like the twin stars. Joseph studied at the school for two years, after which it moved to Hylton Castle. The brothers left school together, John aged 14, Joseph not yet 13. What they learned at school did not amount to much. Joseph certainly learned more out of school than in. One book that Joseph did remember with pleasure from his school days though was Ewing's *Elements of Elocution* which contained a selection of prose and verse from which Joseph acquired his love of poetry. The other book to inspire him, was the brief *Rudimentary Chemistry* by Hugo Reid. Having a druggist as a relative meant he had access to any of the raw material he needed to make things, such as gunpowder!

By 1841, the Swan family fortunes were in a downturn, mainly due to their father's generosity and concern for his workers' well-being. Joseph went to live with Captain Kirtley, his great uncle, in Elswick, Newcastle who had taken a fatherly interest in him some years before. In the autumn of 1842 he returned to Sunderland where he was articled as an apprentice druggist with the firm of Hudson and Osbaldiston for six years. Before his apprenticeship was

completed though, both partners died and Joseph became free. This opened the way for him to join John Mawson in his pharmaceutical business in Newcastle in 1846.

At about this time, Joseph became a member of Sunderland Athenaeum, with its good library. Here he studied the scientific books and journals of the day, including: *The Edinburgh and Dublin Philosophical Magazine, The Electrical Magazine, Repertory of Patent Inventions*, as well as Star's incandescent electric lamp. The lamp itself had been patented in England in 1845. It consisted of a short carbon pencil operating in a vacuum above a column of mercury. Several were exhibited in London but they were not a commercial success as the glass quickly blackened. It was however an incandescent light and represented the beginning of the development of electric light, with which Swan was to become most famously connected.

Joseph Swan was 18 in 1846 when he moved to Newcastle. His friend and future brother-in-law, John Mawson, had started his chemist-druggist business on The Side, off Dean Street. When they moved to Mosley Street, in the same year, the business had become Mawson & Swan.

John Mawson was well thought of wherever he went. When still a young man he had stood surety for a friend who defaulted and became liable for payment which he was unable to discharge. He became bankrupt, but later he paid all of the creditors, which did much for his reputation. He eventually became

Sheriff of Newcastle. Joseph in his turn became an asset to the business. He was especially useful when chemical manufacturers needed technical data, and in return, Mawson allowed Joseph to explore his scientific ideas.

Swan often worked late into the night at their photographic studio (this addition to the business occurred in 1856) in Mosley Street, assisted by the apprentice, Thomas Barclay. He was intent on producing permanent photographic prints which would not fade. At the end of 1858, Swan began to experiment with the carbon process. He formed a relief picture whose surface contour perfectly corresponded to the light and shades of silver print. His first attempt to carry out the idea consisted of coating a plate of glass with a mixture of lamp-black and a solution of gum arabic and bichromate of potash. Swan exposed the plate when dry in a camera, with the uncoated surface of the glass turned towards the light, passing through a negative lens. The plate was then washed with water to remove from, the back of the sensitive coating, those portions of the film which the light had not rendered insoluble. The experiment, though right in principle, was not a success because of insufficient exposure and it was not perfected for another six years, when it was eventually achieved by separating the film and paper completely during the initial stages. Swan patented his carbon process in 1864. The half-tone process for making typographical blocks is still in use today to illustrate books, magazines and newspapers. Patents covering this process, the 'Carbon Process' were registered in July 1865.

Between 1855 and 1856 Swan contracted a serious infection of the lungs due to the chemicals he had been working with, and was sent to Rothsay on the Isle of Bute, where the west coast air healed his lungs. It was also here that he became acquainted with a young lady from Liverpool. Fanny White was a teacher, vivacious and with a lively sense of humour. In 1861 she became engaged to Joseph and in 1862 they were married at Camberwell chapel, Newcastle. In 1863 a son, Cameron, was born and the following year, a daughter, Mary Edmonds. The family moved to Leazes Terrace, Newcastle, where in April 1866 a second son, Joseph Henry, was born. Joseph and Fanny made a trip to the continent in July 1867, where Joseph followed up his interest in the carbon process. They visited Germany, Switzerland and France. At the end of the year they were blessed by the birth of twins.

Not long after this happy event, tragedy struck the business and then the family. A large amount of nitro-glycerine had been found in a stable in Newcastle. John Mawson, as High Sheriff, had the job of disposing of the explosive. It was decided to bury it on the Town Moor but before it could be disposed of it exploded killing all present, except for Mawson, who was fatally injured. Everyone was full of grief, none more than Joseph Swan, who was also left with the full responsibility of the business. Joseph made the widowed Elizabeth Mawson a partner, giving her the wage that John would have earned. Unfortunately, there was more grief for Joseph when shortly after this, his wife passed away, with the twins joining their mother in death soon after.

Brilliant inventor, Sir Joseph Wilson Swan.

Joseph Swan devoted the next few years after the death of John Mawson in 1867 and that of his wife and children in 1868, to organising his business, focusing mainly on photography. This led him to another discovery, bromide paper and printing or printing by artificial light, which Swan patented in 1879. It is still in universal use today.

For a while Swan stayed on at Leazes Terrace, with his wife's two sisters, Maria and Hannah, who looked after the remaining children. However, the stress of recent times was telling on Joseph's, health and spirits. He suffered from intense weariness and feared he was not fulfilling his duty. In June 1869 he went to the Lake District for a well-deserved rest with his friends, John Hancock, the Northumbrian naturalist and a pupil of Thomas Bewick. His intimate knowledge of birds and every form of wild life was impressive and rambles with him in the Lakes gave Swan tremendous pleasure, who was himself an ardent naturalist. The beauty of natural forms, colours and sounds filled him with pleasure, even rapture and he still pursued his love of poetry, his favourite poets being Shakespeare and Tennyson.

That summer, Swan moved his family from Newcastle to Low Fell, Gateshead, noting in his diary of 1869, that 'we live too long in smoke and anxieties, which robs the body of its natural nourishment'. It was with mixed feelings that he left the old house in Newcastle which held so many sad and happy memories. The new house, called *Underhill,* had a garden overlooking the Ravensworth countryside and the valleys of the Tyne. Several other members of the family lived in Low Fell, which was then a little village set among green fields.

All this time the business of Mawson & Swan was progressing satisfactorily. A stationery and book-selling business had been acquired, formally run by Marston of Grey Street but in fact managed by Thomas Morgan, a very able Irishman. From time to time photographs appeared on show at the shop; there was as yet no art gallery in Newcastle.

At about this time Swan began to think of re-marrying Hannah White, a sister-in-law who had kept house after his wife's death. It was, however, against the law to marry one's sister-in-law in 1871 although the matter was being debated in Parliament. When the Bill, which would have legalised the marriage, failed, Joseph and Hannah decided to marry in Switzerland. They left England on 9 September and the marriage took place at the Reformed Church, Neufchatel, on 3 October 1871. They returned via Paris, where the recent siege of the Paris Commune during the Franco-Prussian war was much in evidence in the city. The newly-weds were present during the trial of Louis Rossel, an idealist leader of the Communards. Rossel, with two other Communard leaders, was sentenced to death and shot in the presence of 3,000 soldiers on 28 November 1871.

Swan's second marriage was very happy. Hannah took immense interest in her husband's business and scientific pursuits. Between the years 1873 and 1880 five children were born: Hilda, Isabel, Kenneth, Percival and Dorothy. They were raised with Swan's three other children as one big happy family.

In August 1876, Hannah Swan and the family went on holiday to Moss Hill, a farmhouse near Carlisle. Summer holidays were important to the Swans. Sometimes they went to Dunbar, in Scotland, sometimes to Whitby (where Swan met the American poet James Russell Lowell). One year the family rented part of Bamburgh Castle, overlooking Holy Island and the Farne islands. The Christmas holidays were usually spent at home. Although, in 1900 the family went to Caux in Switzerland, where Joseph Swan enjoyed lugeing (tobogganing) as well as the relatively gentler sport of curling.

Swan resumed his investigations into incandescent light a few years after he married Hannah. The work of both Thomas Alva Edison, the American inventor and that of Swan was independent, although each knew what the other was researching. The principle of generating electricity was being considered on a large scale after 1849 although the benefits were not seen until 1862 with the Dungeness Lighthouse. The first commercial electric lighting plant was installed in the lighthouse consisting of a magneto-electro machine of a primitive type and a Serrin arc light. After this there was immense activity in electrical engineering and by 1877 street lighting, lighthouses, and large buildings could be fitted, economically with lighting.

Dynamo-electric machines of various types were designed more efficiently after 1877. But the invention of a mercury vacuum pump by Herman Sprengel in 1865 had made Swan rethink the manufacture of his incandescent lamp. One problem he encountered was the rapid wearing out and breaking of the carbon. The other was the obscuring of the lamp-bulb by black smoke. In 1878 Swan solved this problem by passing a strong current through the filament in order to render it brilliantly incandescent, whilst the process of exhaustion was continued at high temperature. It was found possible to obtain a vacuum. It was further found that the carbon, because of being exhausted and sealed, did not waste away. This procedure in 1878 proved invaluable and solved the problem of lighting by incandescent lamp.

Above: Retail chemist advertising for Swan & Mawson.

Left: Swan incandescent lamp, produced at Benwell, Newcastle upon Tyne 1881.

Below: Swan in his laboratory at Holland Park London.

At a meeting in Newcastle of the Chemical Society on 18 December 1878, Swan was able to show an incandescent carbon lamp which consisted simply of a glass bulb pierced by two platinum wires, supporting between them a thin, straight carbon conductor one twenty-fifth of an inch in diameter. On 17 January 1879, his lecture with the bulb was repeated. The *Sunderland Echo* of 18 January reported that the bulb worked. News quickly spread around Tyneside that Swan had solved the problem of the incandescent lamp by means of a

vacuum. Swan delivered his lecture and exhibited his lamp again on 3 February to 700 people at the Literary and Philosophical Society of Newcastle with Lord William Armstrong presiding. A further lecture was given in front of 500 people at the Town Hall Gateshead on 12 March 1879. The lamps were not patented, however, until 1880.

Meanwhile, Edison, the, now-famous young American, was making similar experiments in his well-equipped laboratory at Menlo Park, New Jersey, where he employed 100 people. In October 1878 an announcement was made from America that caused a terrific slump in English gas shares—Edison had solved the incandescent problem. The American press was now making daily claims that he had done this by using carbonised paper. Swan had already tried this method without success and wrote to Edison informing him so. But Edison had applied for a British patent, even though he was aware that his lamp did not work perfectly. Swan was urged to register his lamp, but because he had already exhibited the lamp working on two occasions, he did not rush to do so. Consequently on November 10 1879, Edison registered his in broad terms as 'A carbon filament within a glass receiver from which air had been exhausted.' This patent was to have important consequences for the business of both Edison and Swan.

Early in 1880 Edison discontinued the use of carbon paper, adopting carbonised strips of bamboo. More than a year after Swan had invented and adopted parchmentised thread as a filament material, Edison was still using bamboo.

In 1881 litigation began between Edison and Swan with regard to the incandescent lamp. The evidence was laid before judicial consideration. Swan had already exhibited his lamp before the date of Edison's British patent. In fact though Swan was accepted as the inventor of the incandescent lamp, the Edison patent with its broad fundamental claims was valuable to their subsequent partnership. Later, in August (1882), the merger of their companies gave Swan and Edison a valuable monopoly. (The Edison & Swan United Electric Light Company Limited).

Earlier, in November 1880, Joseph Swan formed his own small company in Newcastle called The Swan Electric light Company Ltd. He also opened a factory at Benwell near Newcastle and another factory specifically for the manufacture of filaments and glass bulbs at Birkenhead near Liverpool. It was here that the glass-blowing was done. Since no glass-blowers could be found in England to carry out this task apart from Fred Topham of Birkenhead it was decided to engage German glass blowers to work under his supervision.

The first residence, apart from Swan's own, to be lit by incandescent lighting was his friend Lord Armstrong's great house at Cragside, near Rothbury. Swan personally supervised the installation in December 1880. The lighting was powered by the first hydroelectric generating plant in the country. The motive power was supplied from the waterfall in the Cragside grounds. The success of this project started a chain of lighting events starting with Alnwick Castle, the Northumberland home of Sir William Spottiswood, president of the Royal Society. Shipping came next—all the giant liners required lighting.

After many mining explosions in the north of England, Swan was approached to see if he could help. In 1886 Swan produced a miners' lamp with a firedamp indicator. Swan adapted another electric lamp designed for underground conditions which revolutionised mine work. The miners were amazed at the clarity of the lamps.

Meanwhile, early in 1883, the Swan family had moved south to a new home, a house called Lauriston in Bromley, then a small Kentish town in rural surroundings. Lauriston stood on the extreme northwest fringe of the town, near to the old coaching road, which ran through Lewisham to London. It was a newly-built, good-sized house with three acres of grounds where all kinds of trees grew. The gardens were re-designed by John Hancock in a simple, natural way. In hard winters the tennis court was turned into a skating rink, the sheet ice being gradually sprayed and formed as they do in Switzerland. By this method a good surface was possible and the Swan children loved it. An arc light was rigged up and Swan, with his beard and fur coat, must have looked like Father Christmas as he served coffee and soup to the skaters.

Cragside, Northumberland, the seat of Lord Armstrong and where Swan exhibited his incandescent lamp for the first time.

Honours began to shower on Joseph Swan. In October 1901, Durham University conferred on him the honorary degree of MA; in 1902 the Royal Photographic Society awarded him the Progress Medal for the invention of the autotype process. The medal of the Society of the Chemical Industry was given to him in 1903 for conspicuous service in applied chemistry. In December 1904, the Royal Society awarded him with the Hughes Medal for his invention of the incandescent lamp and other electrical inventions. The President, Sir William Huggins, when presenting the medal at the Royal Society also mentioned his innovations in dry-plate photography, which increased the possibility of experimental investigation. Finally, a knighthood was conferred on him in November 1904.

By now, the Swans were well established in London. Swan was a director of the Edison & Swan Electric Light Company as well as the Notting Hill Electric Lighting Company. Nonetheless, during his later years in London, Swan had financial worries. He had stood as guarantor to a bank for a friend from his younger days. Unfortunately the amount Swan had to pay back due to his friends' bad debt far outweighed the initial amount after exorbitant bank interest. The debt was eventually met, but not without pain. It affected Swan's personal fortune and taxed his strength and well-being. He was no longer up to the strain of life in London .The time had come to move again.

In the autumn of 1908, the Swan family moved away from London to a house called Overhill in Warlingham, a village on the North Downs in Surrey. The fine country air and an undisturbed life made a marked improvement to Joseph Swan's health and he was able to continue his experiments. During the summer of 1909 he was able to travel back to Newcastle to attend to important business. As he headed north to 'God's Country' as he called it, he noted in his diary, 'When we are abreast of the Cleveland Hills, past Thirsk wild roses were in abundance. Durham! Glorious in the mellow light of a far sunset, we go right on, without a moment's haste to drink the beauty of it. The most precious things are the most neglected! Ravensworth! Low Fell! The Tyne with its new bridge, which must not be crossed till after to-morrow when the King has proved that it is safe for his subjects. The Old Castle and the new! A very good journey'.

Swan had been naturally endowed with a good constitution and a virile physique. He had led a life of moderation calculated to prolong his life. Not a rigid tee-totaller, he seldom drank wine or spirits. He was a non-smoker, except on occasions to be sociable in company. Later in life symptoms of heart trouble affected him but with the help of Miss Gosling, a trained nurse and Dr Etches, his doctor who attended him at Warlingham, he was able to attend his son's wedding in London on his 85th birthday in June 1913.

The following year, on 26 May Joseph Swan's health suffered a marked change. This particular May had been rather cold. Doctor, Sir Thomas Barlow, was called and pronounced him to be very ill but in no immediate danger. The same night, however, Swan's heart failed and in the early hours of 27 May 1914, Joseph Swan passed peacefully away. He was buried in Warlingham churchyard. Carved on his tomb are some lines from Tennyson's *The Day Dream* which were often on his lips:

> ....*were it not a pleasant thing*
> *To fall asleep with all one's friends;*
> *To Sleep thro' terms of mighty wars,*
> *And wake on science grown to more,*
> *On secrets of the brain, the stars,*
> *As wild as aught of fairy lore.*

Sir Charles Algernon Parsons

1854–1931

Although born in London, Charles Algernon Parsons is fundamentally a 'northern folk'. Parsons embarked and completed his life's work in and around Tyneside, inventing the turbine engine and testing it successfully on the famous ship *Turbinia*. Not so long ago, any Geordie, asked whom he would want his son apprenticed to would undoubtedly have replied 'Charles Parsons', so esteemed was he in the North East of England.

Charles Parsons was born 13 June 1854, at 13, Connaught Place, Hyde Park, London the youngest of six children to the Earl of Rosse, President of the Royal Society. It was from this London address in 1854 that the Earl of Rosse sent a letter to Sir John Burgoyne, who was Chief of the Engineering Department for the British army, saying it was his dream to build an iron steamer, that could run at the enemy ships sinking them with one blow above the cut water. Three-in-one plate would be used, and the funnel would not appear above the deck. A 300 horse power engine would be required.

It would take Charles Parsons 30 years to start to realise his father's dream, first of all solving the propulsion method of such ships, and in the process finding other discoveries.

The family home was Birr Castle, Co. Offaly, Ireland. There Charles and his five brothers enjoyed advantages that other people would envy. The months of May and June were always spent in London, July with their grandmother in Brighton, returning to Ireland in the autumn. A fire had destroyed the central part of Birr Castle in 1835. However, after restoration the castle still retained its thick walls, and a forge and workshop were constructed in the old moat. A furnace was also added to melt brass. Another addition was an engine house with machinery for polishing specula for telescopes. There were also lathes for wood and ironwork. Every kind of repair was possible. According to Sir Robert Ball (man of science, scholar and humorist) Birr Castle was, a noble place surrounded by a moat, situated in a park through which flowed two rivers, that there unite, about the Lake which was made by Lord Rosse, The waters of the lake operated a water wheel to drain the low lying lands. The telescope was supported by two parallel walls, situated between Birr Castle and the Lake, the tube of the Newtonian, sixty feet long and more than six feet across carried at its lower end the mirror and at the top the eyepiece.

The workshop was where Charles and his father spent all their spare time when Charles was a boy. Many projects were conceived and problems solved here, but mostly the brothers had an out door life, rowing, fishing and shooting. Lessons began at 7.30am, followed by breakfast at 8.00am, then more lessons from 9.00am until noon. They were out of doors until lunch at 2pm, with lessons again from 5.00pm until 6.30pm. During these days in Ireland there was much unrest; murders, and robberies were not uncommon. Charles's father often went to his observatory with pistols in his belt. All shrubs were cut down to deprive intruders of cover but the family was always left alone.

During his spare time, Charles could be seen in the workshop making all kinds of machines. In 1866 the Parsons brothers kept a 20 ton yacht at Ryde, Cowes, and sometimes at Southampton. The yacht wintered at Lymington or Dublin. They later bought *Themia,* an iron yacht of 150 tons. The brothers crossed the English Channel in her, they also visited Cherbourg, via Land's End, prior to visiting Ireland. After *Themia* they purchased *Titania,* which was 188 tons and also iron, but very fast. *Titania* had belonged to Robert Stephenson. They cruised in her from Dublin to Stornoway, Cape Wrath, and Wick, then to the east coast of England. They also cruised to Belgium and Holland and Amsterdam and the Zuider Zee where they visited the workshops of the diamond cutters. In 1867 they visited Cologne, Basle and Geneva. However, after the death of Lord Rosse in October 1867, family holidays came to an end. The brothers remained at the family home a year after their father's death then took a house in Dublin, spending summer holidays of 1868 and 1869 at Birr Castle.

In 1868 Charles and his brother Clere began their studies at Trinity College, Dublin, where their father had been Chancellor. Charles did very well, winning prizes for mathematics and German. He proceeded to St. Johns College, Cambridge where he gained a distinction in mathematics and rowed for his college. On graduating from Cambridge in 1877, Charles Parsons went to Elswick, Newcastle upon Tyne on a three year apprenticeship at the famous Armstrong Whitworth Works. This was the beginning of his long association with the north of England.

During Charles's boyhood Ivan Lupus a naval officer, invented the torpedo. In 1870 the Whitehead torpedo carried 18 lbs of dynamite and was purchased by the Admiralty for £15,000. In 1872 the famous Peter Brotherhood engine for driving torpedoes appeared. All of this development impressed Parsons immensely. From 1877 to 1884 Parson's research in this area kept him fully occupied. He built an experimental compound engine with four cylinders revolving at half speed on the crankshaft. He applied it to drive a Siemans dynamo at 7,000 revolutions a minute. At 10 horsepower, for a time it supplied the arclight at Elswick jetty. The engine was put to work in a millwright shop at an ordinance works. Later an Erith firm used the engine and it was so satisfactory for their needs they made more, with good results.

By now Charles Parsons had finished his apprenticeship at Armstrong's Works. The following letter was sent from the Works and endorsed by William Armstrong himself:

Elswick Works,
Newcastle Upon Tyne,
June 3rd 1881

The Hon. C. A. Parsons,

Dear Sir,
In reply to your request for a recommendation from our firm to assist you in your search for a partnership in an Engineering establishment, pray make use of this letter in which we have pleasure of bearing testimony to your high theoretical knowledge, your constructive abilities, and your promising business qualifications. With this letter we hand you your indentures, which you will observe Sir William Armstrong has kindly certified. We are Sir

Yours faithfully
W. G. Armstrong & Co.

At this time Charles's thoughts were constantly on turbines, rockets and torpedoes but it was also on marriage. He met his future wife, Katherine Bethell, in 1882. The marriage took place on 10 January 1883, in the Church of All Saints in Bramham, Yorkshire. Their first home was in lodgings in Leeds. Parsons was so absorbed in the design of torpedoes that during his honeymoon he took his bride and also a mechanic to the local engine trials every morning.

They arrived daily at 7am in bitter cold and frosty weather. It was during these cold mornings that Katherine caught rheumatic fever. By the spring she had fully recovered and they resumed their honeymoon, this time in warmer environments. In five months they visited America, New Mexico and California. In Chicago, as if Katherine hadn't suffered enough, she was attacked by one of a herd of cattle and was pinned between its wide horns! Shortly after this they returned happily home.

In 1883 Charles joined Clarke, Chapman and Company of Gateshead as a junior partner and for a while studied electric lighting and steam turbines instead of torpedoes. He soon discovered that with a suitable dynamo, the turbine would power the electric lighting of ships.

Charles and Katherine started to turn their attention to a suitable home. Initially they decided on a house in Corbridge on Tyne. This meant that Charles had to leave for Gateshead at 7.30am returning at 8pm; this proved impossible and within a year they made their home at Elvaston Hall, Ryton on Tyne, County Durham. Rachel Mary Parsons was born on 25 January 1885, followed by a son, Algernon George born on 19 October of the following year – both at Elvaston Hall. The young family stayed happily there for 10 years. From the home workshop, with his daughter Rachel by his side, Charles produced all kinds of toys. There was the 'spider', a small spirit fuelled three wheeled engine which travelled around the garden chased by the dogs, a steam pram for carrying the children, and even a small flying machine, also fuelled by spirit and was actually photographed in full flight.

While his family life offered peace and tranquillity, his career was forging ahead. In 1884 his first steam turbine was running successfully at Gateshead. The Chilean battleship *Blanco Encalada* arrived at Elswick in 1885 for new boilers and armaments. This was the first warship to be fitted with a Parsons turbine and dynamos-set for electric lighting. By the time Charles Parsons was 30 years of age he was well on his way to a successful engineering career. In May 1887 Parsons was making 4 Kilowatt 'sets', for the Suez Canal and he was also completing similar contracts for the Italian, Spanish and Chilean navies. His turbines were rapidly being improved and the relationship of the velocity of the steam to the velocity of the blades received careful attention to improve the efficiency. During 1884-1885 two small portable turbine sets were completed at Gateshead.

In January 1886 there was a severe frost and the swan pond near Sheriff Hill was frozen hard. The Chief Constable of Gateshead, Mr Elliott, suggested that if the pond could be illuminated, skaters could be attracted and charged a small fee for admission, thus raising some cash for the local hospital. Clarke and Parsons gladly loaned a portable turbine in order to generate the lighting. R.N. Redmane in the *Newcastle Evening Chronicle* of 22 July 1931 described the occasion, 'Elliott carted the

Turbine up to the ground, where it was set up. Lamps were hung round the pond, and the Turbine was got to work. Mr Joseph Swan supplied the lamps. It was a great success from Elliott's point of view, because the place was so crowded, that few people could really skate. But every one paid to get in, to say that they had actually skated by electric light. As far as I can remember the frost lasted three days and the Royal Infirmary benefited by £100'.

In 1887 Parsons became known as the 'Designer of Plant for the Generation of Electricity'. In that particular year, 10 of his turbo generators, from 15 Kilowatts to 32 Kilowatts each, supplied most of the lighting for the Newcastle Exhibition by means of incandescent lamps, the turbo generator being made at Clarke, Chapman and Company. This was reported to be the most efficient exhibition of incandescent lighting at the time.

These were exciting days for Charles Parsons. He established the suitability of his turbo-alternator for town electricity supply, as well as building machines for Newcastle District Electric Lighting Company. It was mainly due to this wonderful period that Charles Parsons won the freedom of the City of Newcastle upon Tyne in 1914.

In 1889 the Partnership of Clarke, Chapman and Company was dissolved. Prior to this, in 1889, Parson founded the firm C. A. Parsons and Company at Heaton, Newcastle upon Tyne. The Heaton Works primarily manufactured steam turbines for use on land, as well as high-speed electrical machinery suitable for coupling straight to turbines. There was also a blacksmith's shop, testing rooms and offices. At the time the total staff was 48. This was a sharp contrast to the works in 1931 when C. A. Parsons and Company Limited of Heaton covered 20 acres and employed 2,000 people.

The Hon. Sir Charles Parsons O.M., K.C.B., M.A. DSc., F.R.S.

During 1895, Westing House Machinery Company acquired the American rights for installation of Parsons turbines on land in America. In 1901 Messrs Brown and Boveri, acquired the American rights to manufacture Parsons Turbine in the United States of America.

By the 1920s, the Parsons name was certainly well known. However, not always for positive reasons. At one of the land stations in Shanghai, in November 1923, there was a terrible accident with a 20,000 kilowatt turbo alternator. At the time it was running unloaded at moderate speed. The turbine rotor shaft forging burst and some lives were lost. There had been a concealed defect in the interior of the forging. The shaft had been made in 1921 from a cold ingot of medium carbon steel of unknown history. An independent company, who accepted responsibility for the defect, had manufactured it. News of the disaster came when Parsons was attending a dinner in London of the British Electrical and Allied Manufacturers Association. Parsons was dining with fellow directors and had to sit right through dinner knowing about the accident. They convened a Board meeting at midnight that very evening and decided to cable Shanghai accepting responsibility as follows:

Deepest regrets at serious accident and loss of life. Sending immediately two chief experts to investigate. Keep all parts for evidence. Will replace turbine and recondition the whole of your plant, entirely at our cost.

Another setback was an explosion aboard *King George V,* on 29 September 1927, when two ship's firemen lost their lives. This greatly distressed Parsons. The cause, after some time, was traced to scale in the water. Later it was decided only to use distilled water in these high-pressure water boilers. The ship, after rectification, resumed service with satisfactory results.

On parting company with Clarke, Chapman and Company along with the £20,000 he had initially invested

Charles found that leaving with the patents for his turbines was a little more difficult. For some years there was arbitration and litigation, all stemming from an agreement on individual patents taken out when a board of directors resigned his directorship, these became the property of the company. When Charles tried to regain these, he found that he would have to pay a very large sum, namely, the present day value of the patent. It did not seem quite right that he would have to pay Chapman and Clarke an inflated amount of cash just to work his own patents so Parsons decided to fight the action, which had been endorsed by the arbitrators. Another point raised at the time was that the patents would be virtually useless without Parsons himself. Litigation continued for years until it was decided that Clarke, Chapman and Company carry on with Parsons' patents without Parsons; in effect develop them on their own. Parsons carried on with his turbines using a different design from the original. As for Clarke and Chapman, they never made any money out of the patent and later, Parsons was able to regain the patents for a very moderate sum.

In 1894 a new Company was formed, the Parsons Maritime Steam Turbine Company at Wallsend, Newcastle. It had a registered capital of £500,000 divided into 5,000 shares, each of £100 with a first issue of £240,000. The original company, C. A. Parsons & Company, transferred to this company all its powers under the Parsons patents. It took over the right to any future extension or improvements. The prospectus

added: 'it is proposed forthwith to acquire the advantages of a site on the Tyne for manufacturing turbines and the equipment of Torpedo Boats, Destroyers, and vessels generally. The technical management of the undertaking will remain with Mr Parsons as Managing Director'.

Charles Parsons began to research the possibility of turbines being used in ocean going shipping, which included warships. He summarised the advantages of marine propulsion:

1. Increased speed.
2. Increased carrying power of vessel.
3. Increased economies in steam consumption.
4. Increased facilities for navigation of shallow waters.
5. Reduced initial costs.
6. Reduced weight of machinery.
7. Reduced cost of attendance on machinery.
8. Diminished cost of upkeep of machinery.
9. Largely reduced vibration.
10. Reduced size and weight of screw propellers and shafting.

Parsons had to prove these claims and in 1897 decided to construct an experimental vessel 100 feet in length, to be propelled by a turbine of 1,000 hp—the *Turbinia*.

The *Turbinia* had 31 trials at full speed. Single, two bladed, single four bladed, multiple treble propellers, with every modification fitted. The best results were obtained with treble propellers, 22 inches in diameter which at 1,780 revolutions gave *Turbinia* 19¾ knots. It was an advance but it could do better; more experiments were needed. Gerald Stoney, who took part in early trials with the *Turbinia*, said its reverse gear was imperfect. On one occasion they tried to turn about in the Tyne, they reached the side of the river but owing to the current could not go further round, and collided with a cargo steamer, the *North Tyne*. The *Turbinia's*, sharp bow made an 18 inch hole in the side of the ship. Parsons and the crew did well with boat hooks, but the collision could not be avoided. The *North Tyne* put into dock for a new plate.

The Turbinia

On another occasion when Lady Parsons and Miss Rachel were on board, the skipper sighted one of Armstrong's 23 knot vessels off the Tyne. They closed the *Turbinia's* hatches and accelerating to 28 knots, overtook the vessel, leaving her far astern. She responded with a friendly blast from her whistle. One of the officers from Armstrong's boat said that all they saw when the *Turbinia,* went past was a big wave, with a black bow emerging and a flame of fire shooting out from the middle. The bow wave of the *Turbinia,* swept the deck and all on board were drenched, including Miss Rachel, who stepped down into the forward stokehold to dry off with her brother.

There was a great deal of French interest in the *Turbinia,* and in 1900 the boat was an important part of the Paris Marine Exhibition. Arrangements were made to have speed runs on a wide part of the river Seine. *Turbinia* was taken there the day before the trial. The French Minister of Marine was there and small steamers from Rouen formed a lane, through which *Turbinia* sped, and the crowds cheered loudly. Later she proceeded to Le Havre. In the distance the Newhaven-Dieppe steamer was travelling towards England. *Turbinia* easily caught up with her and circled round her, finally breaking off to make for Grimsby then the Tyne. The Paris trip took three weeks. The *Turbinia's* success prompted Parsons to look towards expansion. Two further vessels *Cobra* and *Viper* were constructed both of which would unfortunately end in disaster. On 3 August 1901, *HMS Viper*, fitted with Parsons turbines, floundered on Renouquet Island, near Alderney, and was a total wreck. On 18 September 1901, *HMS Cobra*, fitted out exactly the same as her sister ship, broke in two off the Outer Dowsing Shoal, on the Lincolnshire coast. She was being navigated from the Tyne to Portsmouth.

There were many enquiries regarding the two ships and in December 1905 Parsons gave a lecture at Armstrong College, Newcastle. Although the *Viper* and *Cobra,* were lost through no fault of the turbines, he said it was apparent that the whole system was in danger of collapsing. This directly led to the building of the first turbine propelled merchant vessel, the *King Edward,* in the spring of 1901.

After the *Turbinia* and its sister ships it became well known that Tyneside could provide propulsion for war vessels. Nearly every navy, in the world adopted Parsons's turbines. The speed required by Navies averaged 25 knots. The Royal Navy required even faster ships than this which was not achievable without Parsons's turbines. In 1906 the first turbine driven capital ship *HMS Dreadnought* was built. That year Cunard got *Lusitania* and *Mauretania,* fitted with 70,000 hp turbines. The Royal Navy ordered battle ships like *Dreadnought, Invincible, Inflexible* and *Indomitable* in 1908 and 1909, all with speeds of 26 knots. In World War II, *HMS Hood* built by John Brown and Company and propelled by turbines of 150,000 hp, reached speeds of 32 knots.

Lusitania the ill-fated Cunard liner, sunk 7 May, 1915.

However, it was inevitable that some of Parsons's turbine fitted ships would come under attack and they did. The best known of these vessels are probably the Cunard liner *Lusitania,* torpedoed without warning by a German submarine on 7 May 1915 with the loss of 1,198 lives, and *HMS Hood,* sunk on 24 May 1941 by the German pocket battleship *Bismarck.*

The Mauretania on official trials in the autumn of 1907.

Although turbines were his passion, Parsons also found time to develop other interests. In 1906, two trumpet shaped objects appeared at the Queens Hall, London. These were for increasing the volume and richness of tone, mainly of stringed instruments, and they were on trial at the hall. Charles Parsons had earlier taken out patents in various sound recorders which improved over the years from the initial gramophone recorders. In one of the earlier types of Auxetophone, the gramophone needle was fixed into a socket formed integrally with the valve cover. The needle ran in the groove on the face of the 'record' disc. Parsons used the Edison counter-weight lever and sapphire stylus for picking up and transmitting sound waves. Auxetophone gramaphone concerts were given in towns throughout the country as well as in Australia and New Zealand. By 1909 the fame of the auxetophone had increased. Musicians, and especially Sir Henry Wood, the prominent conductor, received it very well.

Parsons was also bent upon digging miles below the earth's surface, where he believed unknown treasures may be awaiting discovery. One reason for this interest in extreme mining was that it might yield oil and coal that could not have been accessed from moderate depth mines. Parsons consulted Mr John Bell Simpson, the eminent authority of the times on mining in the north of England. Shafts were sunk in stages each about half a mile in depth. It was estimated that at the time it would cost £5 million to bore to a depth of 12 miles. Simpson observed that, 'beneath our feet are unexplored coalfields' and went on to say that 'it would be most interesting geological investigation of National and Commercial importance; if workable seams at moderate depths could be proved it would add another 200 years to the Great Northern coalfields'.

Parsons visited the Geothermal Power Plant of Larderrello, in Italy which was operated by the steam springs of Tuscany on the extreme northern border of the Maremma marshlands. Prince Ginori-Conti in July 1924, during the world power conference at Wembley, explained that these natural jets known as 'saffoni' emit only steam, thereby differing from ordinary geysers that release steam and water. An engine successfully ran for 15 years from this steam. At a meeting of the Royal Society, at the time, Charles proposed that the earth's natural heat should be utilised by drilling a well of sufficient depth to reach high temperatures. The Prince said that Parsons' idea had been implemented in their system in his country and was very effective.

Parsons was also greatly interested in astronomy and products related to the science, such as lenses for searchlights and other astronomical equipment. In 1882 Dr Schott joined forces with Ernst Abbe (glass experts and manufacturers; especially optical) in Jena in Prussia. They also became associated with Carl Zeiss (1816-1888) who, since 1846, had made scientific instruments in a factory at Jena. They came together to form a company. Schott and Abbe began experimenting on the improvements of lenses to obtain sharper definition, equal central and marginal magnification and absence of colour fringes, together with a maximum intensity of transmitted light. Their activities at Jena during the World War were amazing. They employed more than 10,000 people. Their findings caused Parsons much anxiety as he saw England dropping behind more experienced countries in the manufacture of optical glass. It had been estimated that prior to 1914 Jena produced about 60% of the Worlds optical glass, Paris 30% and Birmingham the remainder. In 1917-1918, Wood Brothers Glass Company of Barnsley had been asked to supply optical glass for the War Office and the Admiralty and the Ministry for Munitions.

After 1920 the Wood Brothers Glass Company business was imperilled and it looked certain to collapse. Parson intervened acquired the shares, paid off all of the creditors, and allowed funds for cash flow, so that the company could continue. Charles knew he would have no financial gain whatsoever, but he was determined to save the company, as he knew the industry was necessary for the scientific and industrial welfare of his country. By 30 June 1929, the capital contributed by him for the project was £57,000. Later England perfected the art of optical glass manufacture and due to his perseverance, when all seemed lost, this industry was able to hold its own. Because of his father's interest in astronomy and his own interest in lenses, Parsons was able to foresee this problem, and with his financial strength was able to avert a very serious catastrophe for England.

Parsons never had one day of poverty in his life. He was always a very active man; when he could he cycled to work. He rarely consulted a doctor but for others he would insist on the best specialists possible and any aids to make life tolerable. Most of his time was spent at his works office than anywhere else. He was slightly deaf and at times seemed deep in thought, but any visitors received a warm, even overwhelming, welcome.

Parsons always considered the future not the past. On 6 November 1902 he received, from Sir Michael Foster, the secretary of the Royal Society, the Rumford medal for his invention of the turbine and its extension into navigation. On 5 March 1910, when he was living at Holeyn Hall, Wylam on Tyne, he was appointed Sheriff of the County of Northumberland. On 10 June 1911, he was appointed a Knight Commander of the Bath, just prior to the Coronation and on 13 September 1915, he was made

chairman of the Tyne & Wear Board of Management under the Ministry of Munitions.

Parsons was a keen fisherman. He enjoyed trout fishing either in lochs or rivers, always remembering that his best catch was at Lord Armstrong's home. They were catching one after the other, forgetting that it was the first day of September when a water bailiff approached them telling them he was confiscating the fish and their rods as they were fishing illegally (after 1 September it is illegal to catch fish in the UK until the following year). Lord Armstrong intervened and the bailiff let them go. Meanwhile, Lady Armstrong was waiting to cook the trout that never arrived.

Like everyone else Charles Parsons had downturns in life. When he heard about the *Cobra* disaster he locked himself in his office and stayed there all day long and 1918 brought him sorrow beyond belief when he was informed about the death of his son, Algernon, killed in action on 26 April, in France. Algernon had been at the Front with the British Expeditionary Force in France from 13 November 1914 until his death. His army career is too vast and illustrious to list in a small work such as this. His body is buried at Lijssenthoek Military Cemetery in Belgium, Plot 28, Row C, Grave 4. Charles daughter, Rachel, was a godsend to Charles over this period. She had been educated at Roedean and at Newnham College Cambridge, where she studied mechanical science, entering the Heaton works when her brother went to do his duty in France and competently filled the role of director. From 1922-1925 she served as a member of London County Council and she had the distinction of being one of the three woman members of the Institute of Naval Architects.

Parsons was a sincere man, always having an air of refinement about him. He greeted friends warmly and with a smile although his handshake was curiously limp. A good conversationalist, he was also a good listener. Parsons loved the sea, being ever in the engine room or on the bridge. On cruises, he visited Canada, South America and the West Indies.

In January 1931 he and Lady Parsons travelled to the West Indies on board the *Duchess of Richmond* and then on to Venezuela going by car to Caracas where he fell ill. It was thought that the climate did not agree with him. He returned to the ship and spent the following day in his bunk thinking that he had a customary chill. There was apparently some problem with his circulation, but it was thought that it would improve with rest. Sadly, in Kingston Harbour on 11 February 1931, as the sun was setting, Charles Parsons slipped silently away.

Sir Edwin Alliott Verdon Roe
1877-1958

During World War II, Belfast Airport was an RAF Coastal Command Station. From here regular air patrols across the Atlantic were made. Sometimes the patrols did escort work, at other times anti-submarine work. A reliable plane was needed for these patrols, which were mainly low-flying, as there tended to be very low cloud. It was not unusual for planes just to disappear as low cloud dropped quickly over the vast Atlantic.

Early planes were not very reliable and aircrews lost their confidence in the aircraft. Then suddenly new aircraft appeared; the prototype of these aircraft having first flown in 1935. The new machines were powered by two 350 horse powered engines having a range of 800 miles, a top speed of 188 mph at 7,000 feet, a cruising speed of 158 mph, at 6,000 feet and a ceiling of 19,000 feet. They carried a crew of three, were easy to fly and completely reliable. The aeroplanes renewed the confidence in the aircrews. The aircraft was the Avro Anson and served the RAF for the rest of the war and for a long time after.

The *Lancaster, Shackleton* and later the *Vulcan V Bomber* all came from the Avro company and all played their own part in the war, especially the *Lancaster* which was a brilliant bomber.

One of the original engineers of this amazing company survived being swallowed up by Avro Anson. This was Edwin Alliott Verdon Roe. He was born in Manchester one of a family of seven. His father was a doctor. Edwin attended St. Paul's school, Manchester, where he excelled in athletics. He wasn't very bright at school and left as soon as he could to help his father support the rest of his family. His father did not push the possibility of extra education as he thought that Edwin was not an academic high-flyer. He did however allow him to go to British Columbia to learn civil engineering.

Edwin Alliott Verdon Roe.

After a period helping to survey for a railway which was still in its early stages, Edwin returned to start a five year apprenticeship at the old Lancashire and Yorkshire Railway, after that he worked as a fitter at Portsmouth dockyard. He also studied marine engineering at King's College, London, where he sat an examination for the Royal Navy. He subsequently passed the engineering part but failed badly in mathematics. In the event of this, in 1899 he joined the African Royal Mail Company as fifth engineer. It was at this time he became interested in flight.

During the voyage his attention was drawn to the elegant flight of an albatross off the coast of Africa. The bird actually kept up with the ship without any effort. He felt sure this was down to the shape of the bird and in his spare time made models of planes as near as possible to the albatross. He then launched them from the side of the ship, expecting them to take flight and glide like the bird. The rest of the crew was rather amused. Initially the models did nothing and fell into the sea, but as Edwin shaped his model more like the bird he had been observing, it started to take flight and glide, staying in the sky for a long time, even rising with the thermal currents. This continued to inspire him and when the ship docked he decided to quit his job and investigate powered flight.

Doctor Verdon Roe was not very impressed by his son's decision but was assured that he would work to keep himself, with a job in the motor industry. Edwin read all he could with regard to flight and then wrote to Wilbur Wright, the American who was the first man ever to fly a powered aeroplane. In 1906 he wrote a letter to the *The Times* observing that although Wright had flown 20 miles in America, no one seemed interested at all in flight in England. He further remarked that there was no reason why a powered flight could not take place in this country by the summer. The engineering editor replied that any attempt at flight was doomed to failure and very dangerous to human life.

Not long after this, in 1906, an advertisement appeared in the press for a secretary for The Aero Club. Although the Club was mainly concerned with ballooning, Edwin applied, and despite the fact that he did not have the qualifications as such, he got the job and hoped that he might meet others with similar interests in flying. His first introduction to powered flight in fact was by way of a model. The *Daily Mail* offered a prize of £250 for anyone who could build a model of no less than two pounds that could sustain flight, propelled over a distance of at least 100 feet. Edwin built three models in his brother's stables at Putney, the largest having a wingspan of eight feet and weighing five pounds. He propelled the machine by means of twisted elastic.

The actual competition was held at Alexander Palace and Edwin should have won a total of £250 according to the classification. However, he only received £75 from the organisers who said that his entries did not justify all the prize money. If Edwin was disappointed he didn't show it but instead knuckled down and used the small amount he did receive to build a full size aircraft.

His first actual aeroplane was a monstrosity, a bi-plane with no fuselage or tail. The elevator was in front of the propeller, and behind the wings. The pilot or aviator sat in the front of the engine. The whole thing ran on four wheels. The aeroplane was built at premises where his brother, a doctor, had his daily surgery. This aircraft, called the *Roe*, was 23 feet long with a wingspan of 30 feet. It was powered by a nine horse power motorcycle engine. The aircraft was completed in September 1907, when he also decided to compete for a prize of £2,500 offered for the first powered flight of a full size aeroplane. The competition was to be held at Brooklands motorcycle track at Weybridge. One condition was that the flight had to take place by the end of the year.

Unfortunately when Edwin had completed the aircraft, he found that the engine wasn't big enough to lift the machine off the ground. He was loaned a 20 horse power French Antoinette engine but alas the engine arrived too late for the competition and his chance was lost. He did however try his plane out. He drove it round and round the track towed by a car. The wheels, having no springs, were jumping and juddering on the field and then he was momentarily airborne. This happened a number of times with Edwin able to land each time. He devised a system to let go of the tow-rope, after which the plane glided to a halt, most times crashing, sometimes putting himself in danger. More often than not he had to repair his plane.

The Brooklands track manager, where he undertook his early flight trials, eventually ordered Edwin off the track and he found he had nowhere to go. He finally found a field on part of a swamp land. He spent the very last of his money on posts for a shed. He had to live in the shed and had just five shillings a week to feed himself with. Unfortunately, the manager of the field forbade him to sleep on the premises so he left the shed to return later to sleep in a packing case. It was about this time that he managed to fit the Antoinette engine but found it too powerful for the propeller which snapped at full power, until he strengthened it.

On 8 June 1908, Edwin brought out his aircraft as normal early one morning, checked out everything then started his machine and brought it to full power. He used the elevator and the front wheels came off the ground. The aircraft was completely on its back wheels when, without warning, it was airborne. The aeroplane was in flight. This was the moment he had been dreaming of ever since observing the albatross in flight off the African coast. He gently eased his machine down. The plane had flown a hundred yards and although there had been no-one to observe it, his aircraft had been the first British aeroplane to fly.

After this great breakthrough, the manager of the field caused Edwin much distress by hiring out his plane-shed at ten shillings a day. Edwin had to remove his machine and make sure it was out of sight. Unfortunately, the men carrying the plane dropped it and it was found to be beyond repair. Edwin had still not experienced the worst. He was eventually told to remove his shed completely, or sell it to the manager for £15—having cost him £60 in the first place. Unfortunately he had no alternative but to let his shed go. He was now back where he had started. Returning the Antoinette engine to France, all he had left in the world was his 9hp engine. But Edwin was not beaten. He returned to Putney where he built an aircraft around his own engine. This one was rather different from the first. It had a fuselage and tail and the propeller and engine were at the front. He made it a tri-plane, with three flat planes on the rear tail and three wings at the front. The framework was made of wood, including the wings, held tight with piano wire and covered with muslin backed cotton-oiled paper, for which he had paid two pence a yard. The under-carriage was two bicycle wheels on forks and there was a bicycle wheel at the back. To act as a shock-absorber for himself and the petrol tank he used elastic straps.

Edwin Alliott Verdon Roe's Tri Plane.

Edwin called his plane the *Bull's Eye Avro* and with him on board it still only weighed 400 pounds but he worried whether the 9hp engine would ever be able to lift it off the ground. He decided to test the plane at Lea Marshes, north east of London, where there was about half a mile square of open, if rather muddy, ground. The River Lea was on one side and a railway line on the other. Two unused railway arches adorned the field in which Edwin kept his machine and where he also lived. For cooking and keeping warm he used an iron brazier. The only time he ever left his machine was to go to France where Wilbur Wright was giving exhibitions of flight, when he cycled to Southampton, taking his bicycle on the boat to St. Malo, where the display was being held.

Wilbur Wright and Verdon Roe had a long talk and Edwin was allowed to inspect Wright's plane. Soon he had to return to England. By 1909 he was ready for a trial flight. *Bull's Eye* at first only covered about 20 yards at a height of two feet, the plane then tipping over to one side on its wing, hitting the ground. After fixing the damage, he tried again and the same thing happened. He found it was caused by a gusty wind and he soon learnt to control the plane. With practice, he was soon flying 100 yards at a height of 10 feet. These flights were monitored and later accepted as being the first ever British flights by a British aircraft and a British pilot, over British land. This success spurred Edwin on.

Public opinion at the time was that Edwin was a crank and madman but in July 1909 something happened to make people think differently. M. Louis Bleriot, the French aviator, landed in Dover after flying over the Channel. From that moment people in Britain started to sit up and take interest. All of a sudden flying displays were arranged. At Blackpool, for instance, £150 was offered to any British citizen who could fly a plane over 100 yards. On paper this seemed easy for Edwin but again fate was to intervene. He took his aircraft to Blackpool and the very day of the show it rained as if it had never rained before. The oilpaper covering most of the plane got soaked and it could only manage 50 yards. He had endured the expense of taking the plane there and back for nothing.

There was further harassment back at the field when the local council considered his trials a nuisance and barred him from flying when cattle were grazing in the vicinity. They eventually barred him completely. Edwin just could not win. To further hinder him, his cash situation was desperate. He owed his father £300 and his brother £150, although there was no family pressure on him to repay these debts. Indeed, his family carried on backing him, recognising his enthusiasm.

Eventually Edwin managed to build, with his brother's help, a small aeroplane factory in Manchester and actually sold a tri-plane on the first day of 1910. He then found the perfect place to practice flying, back at Brooklands in Surrey. A new manager had taken over who was very interested in flight and had constructed a strip for taking off and landing within Brooklands. To cap it all he even supplied hangars! Things seemed to happen all of a sudden for Edwin, and he pushed on, again with his brother's financial help, to build a bi-plane.

Realising that the 9hp engine was not suitable, Edwin bought two 35hp engines, fitting them on to two more planes. Initially there were difficulties but eventually, after adjustments, one of the aircraft took off and climbed steadily. It was when he tried to level off that Edwin found that he had a problem. The only way round this, he thought, was to cut the engine speed and allow the plane to stall and drop to the ground. In the process, he injured himself and the plane was in a bit of a mess too. He thought deeply about the problem and decided that the weight was too far back. When he adjusted the tail accordingly, *Roe IV* worked perfectly.

Competitions seemed to be bad luck for Edwin. There was another competition at Blackpool in 1910 and again he entered. This time, leaving nothing to chance, he entered two machines both having to be dismantled and sent by train. The packing boxes were in the carriage next to the engine, covered with tarpaulin. Both planes were destroyed completely on the journey, the railway company denying responsibility as the planes had travelled at the owner's risk. The planes had been worth £1,500. He would still not be beaten however and within four days built another aeroplane at his Manchester factory, this time ordering an engine from the makers to be delivered straight to Blackpool. He spent all night assembling the engine. The plane was ready two hours before the show and he had time for only one short test-flight. His troubles were still not over—both his tyres burst, leaving him with just the rims to take off with. The plane played up. It had not been tested properly and he narrowly missed crashing into the crowd, but his skill prevented this. For all his efforts Edwin was awarded a consolation prize of £75.

In August 1910 after marrying his fiancé Mildred Kirk at Holy Trinity church Blackpool, he sailed on the ship *Cymric* from Liverpool to America, to demonstrate the aeroplane he had sold to Harvard University. Up to that point it had never flown. Edwin also took with him the machine that had got him out of trouble at Blackpool. As it happened, in America he had trouble with both machines and actually fell more than 60 feet after stalling. This was reputed to have been the worst accident in his life. He was rushed to Hospital with blood flowing from a head wound but after three days he was out again, busy with his aircraft. One plane was produced from the two he had taken to America and Harvard bought this one.

In 1911, the War Office decided to have a competition to find a warplane to meet their specifications. Nine months were allowed for the build. It was to be crewed by two people, and be able to stay in flight for four-and-a-half-hours with a full load. Speed in still air should be 55mph, and it should have a rate of climb of 200 feet per minute for 1,000 feet. It should also be able to maintain a height of 4,500 feet for one hour. The plane must arrive in packing cases by railway, and be easily assembled.

Edwin Alliott Verdon Roe's Works.

The competition, which took place on 22 July 1911, was open to the whole world, first prize being £4,000 and second prize £2,000. A class was also reserved for British designers with a first prize of £1,500. For the competition, Edwin launched a revolutionary plane, containing an enclosed cockpit, the pilot having vision through windows of celluloid. To gain access the pilot had to go through a trap door in the roof. On 15 June it was flown by Commander Oliver Schwann who purchased it for the Navy. Edwin decided that this would be his entry for the competition. He was also keen to use a British engine so discarded his French Gnome engine in favour of a British 60hp engine. A Lieutenant Parke piloted his plane. At the test it did all that was required except for one thing – it did not climb as stipulated. This was because the propeller could not take the full power of the engine, which had to be throttled back. Consequently the plane took nine minutes to do the climb instead of five minutes. As a result the full prize money was awarded to Colonel Cody, an American who had lived in Britain for some years, for his own construction with an American engine. Edwin's machine performed impeccably but he got nothing. The government of the day gave little encouragement to their own air pioneers.

Nothing knocked Edwin off his stride in his search for a good reliable aircraft. In 1912 he sold 12 standard Avro bi-planes and his business began to prosper. On 1 January 1913, a firm called A. V. Roe & Company Limited was formed with £30,000 capital. The money took no time being raised. However, for some reason, shortly after, things got a little quiet, and there was some concern about the future of the company. Strangely, it was the German navy who shook the company into life again when they ordered a seaplane. This was new for Edwin and it made the War Office sit up and take notice. The First World War was only one year away and here was Germany purchasing an experimental seaplane.

By 1912, Edwin had completed his fourth bi-plane, which had its own cockpit for the pilot and decided he would change the way he numbered his planes, calling this particular one *Avro 504*, making a tremendous difference to his business. The 504 was perfect and continued in production for 18 years. During World War I, more than 1,000 were built, initially as reconnaissance planes, then as bombers. In 1914 three *Avros* made a raid on a German zeppelin shed at Friedrichshafen, on Lake Constance. The planes flew 100 miles with four 20 lb bombs on each plane. The *Avro* only had an 80 hp engine with top speed of 80 mph. The planes released all of the bombs

except for one, damaging the zeppelin and blowing up a gas works. The main job of the *Avro* plane was as a trainer, due to its reliability and hundreds of Royal Flying Corps pilots were trained on them. Prince Albert, the future King George VI, earned his wings in an *Avro 504*.

Avro 504.

After the war the aviation industry slumped and Edwin again found it hard going. He manufactured planes for the times, producing inexpensive light aircraft, the most popular being the *Avro Avian*, an 80hp engine with a maximum speed of 100mph which only cost £700. In 1928 the Australian Bert Hinkler, making the most of this wonderful plane, completed a solo flight from London to Australia in just 15 days.

Avro Lancaster Bomber production.

Edwin Alliott Verdon Roe pioneered aviation as much as anyone but in 1928 he relinquished control of his company when he was bought out by the Armstrong Whitworth

Company. He must have given a considerable sigh of relief because of the trials and tribulations he had suffered simply to keep his country abreast in the development of aviation. He had risked his health, money and indeed his very existence to establish the British as leaders in the field of flight. There is no doubt that planes such as the *Lancaster*, *Vulcan* and the *Avro Anson 500* series all played their parts in keeping this country free from domination and persecution, thanks to this remarkable man.

Edwin Alliott Verdon Roe was knighted in the New Years Honours list of 1929. He died aged 81 on 4 January 1958.

Top: Avro 621 Tutor
Middle: Avro Anson
Bottom: Avro Lancaster.

Index

Franco-Prussian War 169